MONEY, MEMORY
AND ASSET PRICES

Pascal BLANQUÉ

MONEY, MEMORY AND ASSET PRICES

ECONOMICA

49, rue Héricart, 75015 Paris

For Claude and Annie,
Delphine and the kids,
Guilhem, Alaric, Bertrand

For Homo memor (economicus)

INTRODUCTION

This book provides an overall theory of interest, the business cycle and memory (Part 1) and offers an analysis of stock market phenomena and their dynamics (Part 2).

By placing time at the very heart of the global dynamics of the real and financial spheres, as well as their crises, the first part of the book provides keys to interpret the contemporary economic and financial regime and its imbalances.

Everything economic is, always and everywhere, reducible to a time differential. The various relative and absolute states of the equilibrium, as well as the economic dynamics, are based on the value granted to time and, in particular, on memory and forgetfulness. The cycle unfolds from this value that governs preferences and substitutions between goods, services and financial assets; steers the monetary dynamics of liquidity; ultimately determines prices and activity. This is because there is a close analogy between money and time-matter. Like a chunk of wax changes when warmed up, money is "informed" by memory and forgetfulness, and interest as a phenomenon boils down to this information.

Economic policy action is pertinent and efficient when it takes into account the dimensions of time-matter, whatever its objective may be. Action will be able to draw on memory or forgetfulness effects or, on the contrary, will strive to modify them just like one may seek to divert a river. Economic policy action operates on the very near term only in appearance. Its purpose always consists in getting some old stone to move, in dealing with a thicker temporal dimension, in calling to mind a memory or forgetting something.

For every cycle encompasses, like its DNA, an indelible memory trace.

The second part of the book gives an understanding of the Stock Market, a major research issue since the original work by Louis Bachelier at the start of the 20th century, certain fundamental intuitions of which seem to be contradicted when subjected to examination, and up until the theory of fractals.

The book shows that there is a space-time reference frame which is unique to the stock market universe, is of a psychological nature and which structures a financial imagination. Within this reference frame, time is not governed by clocks and the phenomena of memory, memory lapses (forgetfulness), continuum and rupture determine the fundamental energy of the Stock Market and the speed of asset prices. One moves around within the said space-time in the same way as one remembers or forgets.

Stock market dynamics set three elements in motion. The stock market value is a function of events, facts and variables which are memorised and which contain a coefficient of memory lapse. Preferences lead, at any given time, to an arbitrage between the Stock Market and everything else – assets, goods and everything outside the Stock Market. Finally, because the Stock Market reflects the world in a much wider sense than that of its constituent companies, there is a global risk premium.

The resources of the financial industry, which are often dedicated solely to monitoring the immediate moment in time and are only focussed on the direct components of the Stock Market, are not sufficiently oriented towards an understanding of the true issues at stake.

PART 1

THEORY OF INTEREST,
THE BUSINESS CYCLE
AND MEMORY

This first part of the book focuses on the implementation of economic policy as an extension, i.e. the logical culmination, so to say, of the previously established foundations of economics, just like a triptych can hardly be distinguished from its third part.

Simply in order to be efficient, and even more simply pertinent, economic policy action needs to take time into consideration. Taking the powerful effects of memory and forgetfulness, not to mention duration, into account in terms of designing it as well as setting its objectives and defining its deployment is a prerequisite if it can hope to leave a trace.

Such action fits in and unfolds within the framework of a referential or a regime whose temporal, static and dynamic dimension is deeply structured by memory. While there is definitely an absolute determination of the equilibrium, the equilibrium that unfolds in action is merely relative, in other words relative to what from the past is fain to, or manages to, make itself present. Movement and therefore the cycle are determined by the value granted to time, which governs the deformations of the referential, temporal contractions or dilations, trade-offs and preferences within the real and financial spheres. The global theory seeks to shed light on the action of economic policy – the final subject of this book. The characteristic feature of what is global consists in aiming at the unitary and simple point of gathering and transcending specific or simply general situations and interpretations. The economic and financial cycle is primary the product of the dynamics of value granted to time that also happens to be the monetary dynamics of liquidity. Interest as a phenomenon and determinant of the cycle, remains enmeshed within such a referential of a relative equilibrium over-determined by alterations and deformations of time-matter, which has to be seen in the same way as we look at a chunk of cold wax. In other words, the way in which it is warmed up and the process via which it is modified are the very subject of a theory of action (in the field of economic policy). Most economic policy issues and problems can be reworded to some extent by drawing on this prism.

CHAPTER 1

TIME-MATTER

§ 1.   In the financial and economic regime ushered in with the new century, there are no general economic facts, only global ones. The global nature of variables reflects the noticeably high level of real and financial integration reached by economies and financial markets. Accordingly, we will exclusively deal with global theory in this book. The powerful interaction of factors and variables in the open economy of globalization leads us to think differently, i.e. in accordance with this global reality, about the entire range of economic phenomena. This period of globalization may turn out to be no more than an interlude in a longer history of opening and closing of economies. Nonetheless, for a contemporary of this new century, this horizon of globalization shapes the economic world's timeframe.

§ 2.   Most economic phenomena are marked by memory-related phenomena. Every present behavior with respect to a current variable is, in one way or another, determined by a more or less faded memory or souvenir of the past of said variable. This means that when the rationality (in the sense that one commonly understands that an economic agent is rational) of an economic action takes form, this rationality includes the influence of memory. A "rational" individual is someone who determines him/herself in accordance with powerful influences from the past. When final demand or prices are formed, once more powerful influences from the past always operate.

This also means that a correctly estimated rational expectation has to include the temporal dimension of memory; and any expectation depends on what has occurred beforehand.

Economic action has been opposed to, first, perfect rationality and, second, pure forgetfulness (expectation formed in an absolute present). In the former case, the action fails because the rational individual has from the outset anticipated the action and its impact. In the latter case, the action fails for a nearly symmetric reason because the individual does not have a good enough memory, not to circumvent the action under way but support it positively thanks to the acquisition made possible by learning.

Economic action has to postulate imperfect rationality, imperfect in the sense that decisions are formed from memorized matter and adaptive learning.

§ 3.   Economic policies and action would gain from improved knowledge of the powerful effects of heredity and memory effects at work in the business world and, also, in everyday life.

Action that comprehends such effects will seek, in the appropriate manner, to reach or change the stored elements of a given variable or a combination of variables that are the most sensitive to long-run time, stockpiled with a more or less great density of matter. At the very least, one needs to ensure these elements are known and located, either to modify them (or possibly eradicate them), or merely draw on them to trigger a series of desired effects.

In the first scenario, obviously we are not dealing with an individual able to anticipate fully the entire consequences of a decision. This kind of situation does not occur in the real world and nor does this problem – for indeed this would be a problem should such an individual exist. By contrast, a more realistic problem consists in a situation where (economic policy) action is disrupted (to the extent that it fails) by the presence, albeit unknown or barely known by the acting authority, of a specific memory in the relevant variable or combination of variables. This case represents a sort of unexpected variation in the theme of rational expectations. Knowing, or modifying, are the two purposes that can steer action with regard to this temporal dimension.

Admittedly, action conducted by central banks takes into account, to a quite large extent, developments related to the inertia of memory when analyzing expectation and credibility regimes. However, it is striking to see how most economic policy initiatives do not factor in, or fail to do sufficiently, these temporal effects in the most diverse fields, well beyond the case of inflation.

§ 4.   So-called "confidence", understood in particular as the successful outcome of an economic action, operates through the "return of confidence" and maintains a direct and robust link with what forms the memorized sediment from the past. When it is said that confidence is here, the idea is that what is being done (action) is in tune with what, in the field of the action concerned, has occurred beforehand. When it is said that confidence has made a comeback, one is asserting that this long-term and memory-matter dimension, lost for a while (or ignored), has once more been taken into account or stimulated.

Economic action, which is able to take memorized matter into account, in fact takes confidence and its determinants into consideration. Confidence is not something that comes as an additional layer to an economic action or reality. It is the very name of what creates a tight link between the economic Subject and the economic world via the thick time of memory.

The foregoing means that an economic policy action can very efficiently draw on memory effects, whether conscious or unconscious, and this is the same as playing on the regime of expectations in an adaptive world. By consequence, this also means that there are memory effects, because they might hamper, delay or prevent a justified action, which must possibly be tuned down or discarded.

§ 5.   Any economic policy action is aimed at producing effects in the world from the full knowledge of memory or time-matter effects that compose the field in which the action unfolds, or from the modification, utilization or erasure of said effects.

§ 6.   A situation of equilibrium can be characterized as a situation in which all the real and financial variables are attuned in some manner to the time-matter and memory that constitute them. This situation of equilibrium is, *de facto*, a situation of confidence.

Any situation of sub-equilibrium integrates, in at least one of its market segments, a desynchronization between current economic phenomena and the memorized determinants of aforesaid phenomena; between the economic policy action in a given field and these same memorized determinants. Therefore, by the way, the foregoing entails that an economic policy action, which misreads memory-matter, may very well, ultimately, increase sub-equilibria (imbalances) instead of reducing them. Conversely, the economic policy action can aim to "return to" the equilibrium by drawing on the taking into account of memory effects.

Actually, we may take a further small step forward. A situation of sub-equilibrium can result to a large extent from a powerful memorized effect: a situation of sub-equilibrium is not unrelated to the memorization of a certain dynamics of final demand.

A sub-equilibrium is therefore, potentially, a derangement of time-matter (memory) or the very consequence of this time-matter in one of its manifestations.

§ 7.   A fundamental pillar of any approach consists in taking time-matter into consideration in economic policy action, regardless of its forms, implementation details and fields. Nonetheless, this should not be understood as a call for hit-or-miss action, or permanent agitation. For business life is suffused with time-matter and its fluctuations, without any intervention whatever, are given by the dynamics and movement of this time-matter that is permeated by signals before mutating. In other words, economic policy action, naturally, does not have its place in the life of the business cycle as thus understood. Notwithstanding, its presence may be justified when the goal is to correct certain sub-equilibria – although the very unfolding of the cycle is the most corrective force. The point we are making here is that, unless this temporal dimension is integrated, action is disruptive when its forms and determinants are not in tune with the real thickness of time-matter with respect to a given issue.

Taking into account this time-matter in action holds only insofar as one sufficiently keeps in mind the extent to which the business cycle and the economic world are deeply shaped by this matter in movement. This relationship is a necessity to a great degree. Action can affect it only if justified by the best reasons.

Time-matter, as one of the pillars of action and knowledge of the hereditary character of economic phenomena in order to be able to act, remains a vast research undertaking. This research field is promising because there is a long list of fields and issues in which the existence, if at least apparent, of a sub-equilibrium may justify an action based on memory, sometimes to the point of going to extremes because of the aforementioned reasons. Action may simply integrate the following fundamental reality: the result and the schedule of a successful economic policy action are given by the time required to modify a memory regime (in the case where this regime is not spontaneously and immediately favorable to the goal of the action carried out). The agent carrying out aforesaid action must understand this point from the outset. The agent can then decide to introduce a modification focused on such or such memorized aspect. For instance, one may aim for forgetfulness, or an accelerated mutation of memory, e.g. by overweighting a given event by more recent data, and so forth.

§ 8.   There are numerous economic policy paths, channels and tools. Taking into consideration time-matter (memory) in monetary policy and, particularly, determining a correctly estimated equilibrium from powerful memory and duration effects leads to an impact on critical variables such as interest rates, prices and inflation, growth and the money supply.

§ 9.   The individual or collective history of an economic value (or variable) determines its trajectory insofar as this value is driven by the energy of its stored duration. Duration or memory-matter outweighs any other (pertinent) consideration specific to this value. The origin of any value (its history) defines the critical path followed by the economic Subject in terms of grasping it.

Many so-called situations of sub-equilibrium or disequilibrium are not really anything of the sort. In fact, these situations correspond to an apparent desynchronization between a real or financial variable and an (erroneous) estimation of the equilibrium. It is erroneous because it fails to take sufficiently into consideration the temporal and memorized depth that lies at the heart of valuation.

A wise economic policy respects time-matter, memory and forgetfulness. Accordingly, such an action is wise when it inserts its will to lower inflation into time, precisely because the inertia of expectations marked by the past calls for such a humble approach. By consequence, such an action is wise when it does not seek to decree a robust and swift increase in demand when, in fact, everything suggests that the memorized determinants of said demand – its history – point to the opposite direction, at least for a while. Taking into account time-matter is a school of humility and patience for economic policy action.

§ 10.   The powerful effects of memory-matter (inertia and delay) virtually doom economic policy action to a certain kind of inefficiency, when said economic policy action does not know well enough the determinants of these temporal effects. This is definitely the case except when the authorities conducting this action have included, after an in-depth study, such determinants in their action.

Economic policy action fails nearly certainly when long-term and memory dimensions are misapprehended. More broadly, paltry knowledge of the time dimension in economic phenomena results in being repeatedly disappointed, at least from the viewpoint of the efficiency of action.

Conventional policy mix action will always miss its objective when this temporal dimension is not understood. Drawing on fiscal policy to correct a sub-equilibrium, as defined by Keynes, may very easily be hindered by the inertia of demand, as such inertia is a memorized function of certain elements, whether monetary (money supply), financial (interest rates), real (prices, activity), etc. Action may have been well thought out, designed, calibrated and implemented. It can even be justified and meaningful to some extent. Nevertheless, it will fail, after gobbling up in all likelihood the monetary requirements of a stimulus package.

The inertia such an action may come up against may eventually give in as any memorized temporal reality can be eroded, erased, forgotten. One of the goals of an economic policy is to produce forgetfulness effects on certain determinants that delay it and/or are negative (whatever the pertinent field of action), and memory effects on other determinants that are likely to play a more stimulating or positive role at the time when action is taken.

§ 11. Keynesians saw in the so-called classical equilibrium a special "case" of a more general theory where the commonest situation consists in a sub-equilibrium or multiple underemployment equilibria. Compelling arguments suggest that the existence and persistence of hereditary effects (marked by the inertia and density of a quasi-matter) in the determination of economic facts and phenomena explain most sub-equilibria. In this case, the counter-cyclical action of economic policy will seek to correct the sub-equilibrium. The term "countercyclical" clearly expresses in its way the extent to which action is then desynchronized with respect to a reality of economic life. When economic policy is said to be "countercyclical", what is being said in fact is that the action of this policy ignores determinants operating in the current situation; it is also being implied that action will clash orthogonally with this reality. Using the term "countercyclical" in fact implies that the cycle as correctly understood is misconstrued, for the very essence of the cycle is found in the time-matter accumulated in memory and that is being eroded by forgetfulness. This time-matter, which obeys a specific movement, makes the cycle, is the cycle. From this viewpoint, action cannot describe itself as countercyclical. It can only be cyclical, pro-cyclical in the sense that it will draw on the movements of this matter, will support them and accelerate them. It can admittedly attack them head-on and seek to neutralize them or reverse them when they are deemed negative. Nonetheless, as we have already underlined, in all likelihood this means underestimating the fairly foreordained nature of movements of this time-matter, and this merely results in exposure to the inefficiency of such or such a measure; but also, and above all, underestimating the risk of ending (or masking, and this in a certain manner comes to the same) a macrofinancial regime, i.e. a certain unit resonance of consistencies at a given moment of economic life.

The existence and persistence of hereditary effects probably explain most sub-equilibria. And this very fact likely opens paths to economic policy action, as long as it has reasonable knowledge of this time dimension, also as long as it does not clash excessively with this dimension (limits of effectively counter-cyclical action) or simply mask, with a superficial veil, the underlying and deep movement of more powerful determinants. In other words, economic policy action that ignores time-matter and the powerful effects of memory, forgetfulness and duration, is merely a veil covering reality. The two approaches we have just described are two ways among others economic policy can fail.

Nonetheless, while heredity and time-matter are at the heart of so-called sub-equilibrium situations, there are sound grounds to think also that in reality, situations that are somewhat described as sub-equilibria are in reality simply an aspect of the equilibrium integrating time like it should be, i.e. in its thickness and duration dimension. Under these conditions, and overstating the case in order to show its limits, economic policy action must not seek to intervene too much.

§ 12.   Time is the raw matter of economic facts and phenomena. The business cycle is predominantly explained by movements of time-matter, affected by certain levels of memory or forgetfulness density — which can be called forgetfulness or memory coefficients. Economic policy action can play on the movements of time-matter, but cannot deny their existence or circumvent them by masking them.

Macroeconomic action (economic policy action) is action affecting time. An action seeking to be efficient will be able to target the most (economically) negative time effects by striving to curtail the damage or impacts they cause, but also, far more positively or far more ambitiously, by gradually bending them, just like you bend an iron bar because the high density of past temporal matter demands bending. This does not require only injecting money, in whatever manner, but working on the framework that determines this regime of past elements. How can an economic policy action ensure that what in the past runs counter to its objectives is forgotten? Is it right to seek forgetfulness to substitute one memory for another? Is it simply possible, given the fierce autonomy of economic facts and phenomena due to the fact they delve into the dense matter of what has been?

Macroeconomic action tries to modify the relationship binding the Subject (whether individual, i.e. *homo economicus*, or collective, for instance an institution or a society) and time.

§ 13.　Insofar as the present and, to a certain degree, future behavior of economic variables is given by what comes from the past into the present and future, drawing up an efficient economic policy action is no easy task. Memory effects have to be factored in, they have to be reshaped, and new ones created.

A sub-equilibrium of activity, or an equilibrium of under-activity, is a situation in which the (current) sluggishness of demand is a lagged function of past income and, looking beyond income, of variables such as prices, the money supply and interest rates. Action may aim for an adaptive mutation of the deter-minants of demand, over time (forgetfulness effect, new memory). Notwithstanding, monetary or fiscal action (to consider exclu-sively the commonest channels) may not, *per se*, build or forge a new memory. A series of changes and achievements, as time passes, will lead to the new regime. Action can launch initiatives, or support such changes, but ultimately complex interweaving memory effects provide the solid ground needed to establish convictions and (new) certainties.

§ 14. What can economic policy action accomplish in an environment of economic facts and phenomena that, apparently, is soaked in immediacy, speed and instantaneity but, in reality, under the noisy layer of agitation, remains driven by the slow forces of the tectonic shifts of sticky time, duration and memory? Undoubtedly, this is an odd question for any era obsessed by what seems to steer economic life, i.e. the short term.

Apparently, the very situation described as a "sub-equilibrium" – although from a certain viewpoint it is in fact an equilibrium, even if one has to characterize it as an equilibrium of under-efficiency, under-employment, under-activity, and so forth – results from the inertia intrinsic to the past of the economic facts and phenomena, and to the past of the economic variable. This past, this history of the variable, which towers above it and determinates it (in the sense that it becomes what it is and is at any time what it has been), because it is sticky and heavy, as well as slow to adjust (i.e. to forget), imposes itself at any point in time on the pure presence of the economic fact or policy. There is thus a permanent discrepancy between the pure present (or the Subject's immediate consciousness) and what, coming from the past, superimposes itself. This discrepancy is at the origin of the sub-equilibrium (in fact what is called a sub-equilibrium). At the same time, however, it is an equilibrium because, at any time, any economic situation is determined by the (past) time-matter of all the elements-determinants of its environment.

We now consider the discrepancy between the Subject's temporal referential (and his action) and the temporal referential of the economic variables on which the Subject (whether an individual or collective one) acts and, therefore economic policy action, in other words time as immediacy and decision taking versus time as characterized to some extent by stickiness and spreading out. This discrepancy composes both the very possibility of action (support, correction) and its principal limit.

For there is a limit – which can turn into a form of impossibility – in the fact that action intervenes within the framework of an expectation of agents that in turn is determined by duration and memory while being adaptive. This means that contemporary action, and its capacity in the best-case scenario to produce an impact, changes, and signals will be able to dent the stickiness of memory only marginally, unless it actually triggers a real shock.

The foregoing means that unless there is no memory embedded in the economic variable or variables concerned – e.g. a radically new development, a shock with forgetfulness or a paradigm shift, but all these cases are rather unusual and unlikely – (economic policy) action can, in a first scenario, prove inefficient, with an inefficiency grading that is *de facto* a function of the density of time-matter (memory and therefore forgetfulness). In fact, $e_a = f(t_d, F)$ with e = efficiency; a = action; t = time; F = forgetfulness. There is a link between the impact of an (economic policy) action and this action's capacity to penetrate the temporal carapace of surrounding facts and phenomena on impact. For, and this is certainly an important point, economic facts and phenomena are constituted of dense temporal matter, i.e. duration/memory. We could draw a comparison with a bullet that has been fired at a target and penetrates it more or less well on impact, $e_a = f(m, F)$ with m = memory. This means that where time-matter is densest, the efficiency of economic policy action is nil. Or, to rephrase this idea, the efficiency of economic policy action is a decreasing function of time-memory or an increasing forgetfulness function. Accordingly, it is crucial, *ceteris paribus*, that every economic policy action should dedicate reasonable albeit significant energy to investigating the temporal dimension (memory, forgetfulness) in every field of intervention.

That is not all. This initial conclusion, which takes the shape of a curve of economic policy inefficiency as a function of time-matter (memory) shows there is definitely a real limit to economic policy action. This limit is not envisioned by rational expectations theory or, rather, we are reinterpreting this theory. A rational expectation is adaptive by nature and is characterized by a significant time-matter effect. Action will not be impeded by the fact that agents will know everything about the impact in advance, but by the fact that the impact will be (more or less significantly) curbed by what has already occurred and, proportionally, by the memory (or symmetrically the forgetfulness) effect. Action will be impeded by the fact that agents form their expectations in the same way as they remember and also forget previous developments.

As we were saying, this is not all. In fact, a second cluster of conclusions emerges in the wake of a simple observation: as soon as there is suitably dense time-matter (this even can and must lead to research studies seeking to estimate this degree of density), action may aim at gradually eroding the existing regime (change of the expectation, memory, regime), or seek to produce a shock. In fact, in a "normal" time-matter regime (i.e. sufficient presence of memory effects for most critical variables of the field of intervention), the efficiency of economic policy action is an increasing function of the choice (distortion) the macrofinancial regime may be faced with, or that can be imposed on it.

An efficient economic policy action (in the sense that change occurs) stems from a capacity to reduce memory and produce forgetfulness. When we speak of "efficiency", we are referring to the capacity to reduce the discrepancy between a situation of sub-equilibrium and the target situation the acting authority wants to achieve.

§ **15.** The foregoing suggests that in a normal time-matter regime in a given macrofinancial regime (i.e. presence of memory effects), economic policy action enjoys no more than a restricted expectation of efficiency, and even that would require great perseverance. This poor efficiency will even be able to provide the basis for another approach, which will hold that a sound economic policy action's well-understood objective consists in respecting, in other words backing up, the specific movement of this time-matter. This action will be positively pro-cyclical, diametrically opposed to an economic policy action that, because it can only deal with time-matter (memory) orthogonally to set it in motion (necessarily running counter to its tendency), will have to be counter-cyclical. The first, pro-cyclical (albeit not in a proactive sense), will consider that the cycle (in other words, the temporal determinants of the economic variables that compose the macrofinancial regime) encompasses in itself the elements of its unfolding and there is little to be gained in unsettling it. It will also consider, for instance, that recessions are a necessary moment of the cycle. As far as the other approach is concerned, the memory effect will be a form of inertia it will need to combat in most cases (although time-matter may sometimes offer a similar direction to the one economic policy action wants to head for; but the two directions are often, too systematically in all likelihood, orthogonal).

§ 16.   The usually invoked economic policy mechanisms and forms are not necessarily appropriate for the nature of issues dealt with once it is admitted that most economic problems and situations leading to an intervention/action result to a significant extent from time-matter, memory and forgetfulness effects.

In the above, we have been trying to point out that such options as conventional injections of liquidity (whatever forms monetary policy may assume) or fiscal stimulus packages operating via a finally conventional increase in deficits are in fact not necessarily able to deal with the nature of the difficulties we have identified. They can eventually manage to do so, indirectly through a series of effects produced over time but not directly.

This does not mean that there is no monetary or fiscal path for such problems. Nonetheless, if they are to be followed, one still has to show successfully how a monetary (or fiscal) policy can manage to modify the temporal structure (thickness of memory and therefore formation of expectations) of a macrofinancial regime.

§ 17.   The limits of any economic policy action with regard to the underlying and deep temporal dimensions of a macrofinancial regime entail that any such action should have a long-term horizon if a result is to be expected, i.e. a significant movement of the slow and adaptive matter that constitutes the compressed time of memory. An economic policy action that does not unfold over time does nothing more than fleetingly scratch the surface of things and misses the density of everything economic.

§ 18.   The interest rate and the dynamics of its formation are conventional phenomena tightly linked to memory, duration and forgetfulness effects. The future is anticipated in the same way as one remembers what comes from the past and as one also forgets it.

The interest rate is always formed in relation to a temporal form, in relation to a certain memorized/forgotten density of time-matter. The object of this memorization, or this forgetfulness, is the very content that determines the interest rate, a substance such as activity (or some form of activity), prices inflation (or some form of inflation). The interest rate is, at anytime, related to a chunk of time-matter, and the Subject, when he/she uses the interest rate, does so after following through a reasoning related to expectations within which the more or less dense (in other words more or less forgotten) forms of the past dominate.

This chunk, or these chunks, of time-matter are crucial elements in terms of determining the equilibrium value, or values, of the interest rate. We have therefore, on the one hand, an interest rate that encompasses time-matter and carries within itself a reference to the equilibrium (this leaves a trace in various concepts of the real interest rate, whether natural or not). On the other hand, we have a so-called "market" interest rate that can be observed, whereas the former cannot.

In such an approach, time as duration, memory and forgetfulness – i.e. what we have called time-matter – is the essential determinant of the interest rate. The interest rate is formed in the movement of this matter that consists in the condensation/dilation of the major economic (monetary, real, financial) elements. The temporal determinants become real or monetary determinants but drawing such a distinction is partly misguided since, in fact, time-matter, as a determinant of interest, encompasses real, monetary elements.

$$i_r = f(m, F)$$

Defining the status of this time-matter (for instance, the memorized function of inflation, of activity, of demand for cash) is somewhat tricky. This is because, on the one hand, this matter is a reference equilibrium (it is the anchoring point between the equilibrium value of the interest rate and the regime of expectations) and the "market" interest rate will definitely be gauged with respect to this reference value. However, on the other hand, this time-matter, due to its very inertia, leads to sub-equilibria as we saw above. These two observations can be blended in the proven existence of sub-optimal equilibria and Keynesian under-employment equilibria illustrate, in their manner, this finding.

The foregoing is important for economic policy: the imbalance in reality is not found in the actual spread that can exist between the "market" interest rate and the "equilibrium" interest rate because the disequilibrium (the sub-equilibrium or, as we have seen, in a more Keynesian sense, the sub-optimal equilibrium) stems from temporary matter (memory, forgetfulness) that was the effective substance of economic facts and phenomena. Economic policy action can operate by seeking to position the "market" interest rate (mainly via the key intervention rates at the disposal of central banks) with respect to this "equilibrium" interest rate – albeit this equilibrium is not really one.

It can be argued that economic policy action operates in harmony with the deepest fundaments of the macrofinancial regime when it ensures the market interest is as close as possible to the equilibrium rate. Notwithstanding, as said equilibrium is not necessarily one, economic policy action can consider the possibility of lowering the market interest rate under the equilibrium interest rate.

By seeking to maintain at all times, and in the "normal" regime, the market interest rate (which we will call more appropriately the "immediate interest rate" ($i_r(i)$) because in an approach that emphasizes temporal dimensions, one should draw a distinction within time-matter between its density and thickness layers), economic policy action will ensure, in all likelihood, that it does not disrupt a determined regime. This regime will undergo, literally at its pace and in an endogenous manner, its movement (cycle), its developments, even including its breaking points. By placing the immediate interest rate under the memory interest rate, however, action is triggered on time-matter, on time-density.

$$[i_r(i) = i_r(m) + m_t/d_t]$$

The notions or concepts of an immediate interest rate, of a memory interest rate, of time-matter (time-density) are necessary if we are to understand the mechanisms in play.

§ 19. An economic policy action is aimed at contracting or dilating time-matter (time-density) by lowering the value of the immediate interest rate under the threshold of the memory interest rate.

Time-matter is a past function of the broadly defined (economic) mode of (economic) variables *stricto sensu*.

§ 20. When the immediate interest rate (for which, thus, the time-matter function, or time-density tends toward zero) is equal to the memory interest rate (where the *m* variable is positive and there is therefore time-density), everything occurs, so to say, as if the immediately present situation were entirely (over-)determined by past memory effects, as if, in fact, everything were determined by the memorized adaptive inertia and, lastly, an important point in fact, as if the present (economic policy) action were neutral with regard to this reference-time equilibrium (which as we have seen is, in fact, in many cases a sub-equilibrium or a sub-optimal equilibrium). This neutrality means that economic policy action does not exert any particularly noteworthy effect, in the field of its intervention, and therefore lagged elements (of prices, of activity, of demand, and so forth) dominate in terms of steering and determining the environment. This neutrality of economic policy lets the fundamental forces of the cycle unfurl, i.e. the forces of duration and memory (and accordingly of memory). Neutrality is therefore achieved when the immediate interest rate is equal to the memory interest rate. At neutrality, "immediate" time-density, in other words the one included in the immediate interest rate, is by definition equal to the memory time-density included in the memory interest rate. In a situation of neutrality, time-matter plays fully in the present situation. There can occur a scenario, however, where this equality of time-matter in a situation of immediacy and in a situation of memory is due to such a powerful forgetfulness effect (forgetfulness rate or maximum forgetfulness coefficient) that the immediate interest rate, so to say, hoovers up the memory interest rate through a reduction of time-matter, i.e. memory. Forgetfulness is then at its maximum. There is thus at least one economic situation in which neutrality (we do not really dare to speak about an "equilibrium") is reached when forgetfulness is at its maximum.

When the immediate interest rate is lower than the memory interest rate, after a fashion we can say that time-matter, memory, undergoes erosion and, systematically, the forgetfulness rate (forgetfulness coefficient) rises. The economic policy action that drives the immediate interest rate under the level of the memory equilibrium (sub-equilibrium, sub-optimal equilibrium) rate seeks a modification in such or such field of the economic environment through an alteration or change in the macroeconomic regime.

$$i_r(i) - i_r(m) = m_t/d_t \; ;$$

with $i_r(i) < i_r(m)$.

We have: $i_r(i) - i_r(m) = m_t/d_t < 0$.

When the immediate interest rate is higher than the memory interest rate, there is so to speak over-representation of time-matter in the present economic environment. It is just as if the present situation were congealed or shaped by what comes from the past and memory. By letting the immediate interest rate rise to a higher level than the memory interest rate, the purpose of economic policy action may be to draw on such or such memorized element that, in its own specific field of intervention, serve its objectives. This may mean positively relying on a time-variable to curtail a development deemed worrisome in a given aspect of economic activity: for instance, forcing the economy to slow down or carrying out cuts. The economic policy that chooses such an action is therefore justified in doing so given its objectives. This economic policy may also find itself involuntarily in such a situation and, unless it can be ascertained that these time-effects have an overall positive impact in view of the various objectives addressed by said economic policy, there is real risk of detrimental effects. Forgetfulness is at its lowest level, memory saturates the present and, above all, the future as the latter is a powerful and direct function of the past. The past, in many regards, does not exist.

§ 21.   There is an analogy between liquidity and time, between money and memory, the dynamics of the flow and time-matter. The stock of money is a function of time-matter and of memory $[M = f(m, d_t)]$, and this means that at any given point in time, for a given stock of money, there is what we can call a temporal "footprint" of a general memory of a whole set of elements, factors and determinants of a macrofinancial environment or regime. Thus money maintains a tight link with the value and time of duration and of memory.

Setting in motion the stock of money, its velocity (whether it operates within the sphere of the real economy or the sphere of finance and markets) and the flow of its "liquidity" – or to reword the foregoing – the density or intensity of utilization of a monetary unit in such or such a sphere of economic and financial activity, this differential of money acts on time-matter and, in a way, the stock of memory.

When velocity gathers momentum, i.e. a larger volume of (real or financial transactions is carried out per monetary unit for a given stock of money, $\left[\dfrac{T}{M}\right]$ and there is a form of dilation of the real sphere (when T applies to real goods) or of the financial sphere (when T applies to financial assets). This dilation is an inflationary form of monetary erosion of value.

It is just as if the acceleration in the circulation of the monetary stock were proportional to a form of monetary erosion, of erosion of time-matter, and therefore a form of forgetfulness. In the specific case of financial bubbles (inflation in financial asset prices), experience definitely suggests that, in phases during which transactions accelerate, there are forgetfulness phenomena, in other words phenomena consisting in a contraction, or rather a dilution/dilation of time-matter. Memory fades, while duration, the thickness quality of economic time, is diluted, is weakened.

At "equilibrium", or at least when growth in the volume of transactions and in the stock of money is proportional, the value of time-matter is maintained and remains stable for $M = a(m)$. When $\dfrac{T}{M = a(m)}$ rises, *ceteris paribus*, we can see that $\dfrac{T}{M = a(d_t = m)}$ rises and there is a decline in (a), in other words the forgetfulness coefficient increases. Time-matter, understood in the sense of memory, is a negative function of $\dfrac{T}{M}$. It is just as if

$$m = f\left(\frac{T}{M}\right)$$ with dilation of forgetfulness effects (increase in forgetfulness effects) once the circulation of the stock of money accelerates.

$$m = \alpha\left(\frac{T}{M}\right) \quad \text{or} \quad d_t = \alpha\left(\frac{T}{M}\right).$$

This approach enables us to understand inflation phenomena as, primarily, phenomena consisting in the destruction/erosion/dilation of time-matter (memory), and therefore of value (as it depends on duration-time and of matter-memory), in other words as forgetfulness phenomena. Inflation admittedly always remains everywhere a monetary phenomenon. However, it is always and above all a loss of memory. The erosion of monetary value is a superior form of forgetfulness.

§ 22.   It is commonly said that it is because memory can be worked upon or taken care of that action can envision to be applied, in various forms, to time-matter. In a certain fashion, any economic policy action consists in stimulating, or on the contrary forgetting, such or such part of time-matter (for example, stimulating the memory of a given episode, moment or sequence that, currently, will be quite useful with respect to the objective pursued), or undermining the memory of a given episode that, currently, would interfere with economic policy's action equation. Economic policy is action only insofar as it produces memory or forgetfulness.

The foregoing means in particular that economic policy action needs to have the appropriate tools and channels for such objectives at its disposal. This begins by clear awareness and the conventional action tools and methods of economic policy are themselves, and first of all, subject to memory and forgetfulness effects. There is, everywhere and always, a memory (and thus a form of erosion of said memory in the form of forgetfulness) of monetary policy and fiscal policy. An economic policy action is always launched with a layer of snow (time-matter), behind or above it, as if overhanging it. And, to a greater or lesser extent, this snow melts (forgetfulness). The efficiency of an economic policy action depends on the fact that this time-matter is taken into account. It a drastic mistake to think that any action, every action, represents an absolute beginning on a clean slate – although this belief stems notably from the fact that the political time of action is apparently structured, segmented, to a very significant degree and is highly visible. Note that the themes of change, renewal, reform or even revolution are emphasized and these themes play a major role in giving the impression of paradigm shifts and hermetic sequences.

Global memory (forgetfulness) of monetary or budgetary action is one of the key determinants of future action.

$$A_{cp} = f(m_{Acp}, F)$$

When we talk about the "global" memory of action, we thereby seek to convey the idea that we are referring to something far larger and more encompassing than just remembering or forgetting such or such variable, including the most critical ones (e.g. inflation). For instance, monetary policy is memorized "globally", i.e. in a way that far exceeds the mere awareness of an inflation regime, or a real interest rate regime, etc. A more encompassing example of determinants and effects (for what has had an impact or not had one is remembered and forgotten) composes a form of time-matter, which itself integrates, like a multi-layered whole, multiple forms of time-matter for numerous variables. For instance, monetary time-matter comprises a memory (forgetfulness) function of monetary policy action (the manner, in a way, in which the action has left its stamp on pure monetary matter, money, producing more or less noteworthy traces and erasures in memory), as this memory function encompasses the memory functions that form regimes (e.g. a real interest rate regime).

$$MT_m = f(m_e, A_{mp}, m_o)$$

Monetary time-matter is a memorized set of impressions-traces left in the pure monetary matter by the economic policy action and comes with a forgetfulness function.

One has to picture pure monetary matter as a piece of pure wax. This wax-matter is, so to speak, impregnated, permeated, literally loaded with information by what can be generally called action (carried out by the economic Subject) but also by all events, including external ones, in the (economic) world.

This means that monetary variables (the money supply, for example, but the same can be said of many financial variables) can be usefully analyzed or commented upon only by drawing on a memory and forgetfulness function. The monetary function (whether on the supply or demand side) is a memory and forgetfulness function of monetary matters (facts, events, action). The pertinent money matter is a memorized matter.

CHAPTER 2

INTEREST AND EQUILIBRIUM

§ 23.   The interest rate is the expression of the memory and forgetfulness function. Allais tried to make this same point, to a rather large extent, with his psychological interest rate. There is no need, however, to single out this "psychological" dimension (i.e. memory and forgetfulness on the part of the Subject) with regard to the interest rate because it is one of its intrinsic parts.

His use of the word "psychological" was interesting since it introduces a dimension of the Subject's acting consciousness into a variable that, at least until then, was often presented in an objective manner, in the sense of a variable external to the Subject.

This memory dimension is one of the dimensions of the natural or real interest rate.

§ 24.   Nor do savings phenomena escape from the multiple dimensions of memory and forgetfulness. This means for instance that the links between interest rate and savings can be grasped completely only by integrating a memory and forgetfulness function. The reason why many economic causality relationships that should work do not is because time-matter is not taken into account.

Adjusting the market interest rate (i.e. the only one that can be moved and observed) without assessing memory and forgetfulness functions weakens the supposed relationship between the interest rate and a given economic or financial variable. We have discussed this point above.

The Gibson paradox held that interest rates and inflation rose together. As the nominal rate is a composition of the real rate and expectation (i.e. of memory and forgetfulness), we have:

$$ir_{(n)} = ir_{(r)} + m/F.$$

The reason why it can be said that in an inflationary macrofinancial regime, as the memory of inflation is vivid, the expectation is itself strong (forgetfulness for its part is weak) is because the expectation is defined from memory and forgetfulness. When, for reasons that can be related to the individual or collective Subject's action (e.g. central banks' disinflationary policies) or external events or developments (choices or facts not directly related to the Subject's action, such as a weather shock or a natural event), memory fades (i.e. the duration of observation of less threatening inflation is extended), or, in other words, when more inflationary periods are forgotten to a greater extent, one then witnesses a decline in inflation as well as the interest rate, but the relationship between the two variables weakens.

In a deflationary macrofinancial regime (Japan in the 1990s for instance), interest rates and prices drop hand in hand, as in a reverse Gibson paradox. With $ir_{(n)} = ir_{(r)} + m/F$, an expectation of further deflation takes root, i.e. a memory of deflation function does.

Generally speaking, the theoretically assumed link between two economic and financial variables is all the more effectively observed when the memory function associated with either variable (or with both, or with their interrelation, or with another variable that determines them) is all the stronger, in other words hardly impaired by forgetfulness. This is why economic visibility is very good at the core of a macrofinancial regime, i.e. when this regime is in full swing. When a regime is drawing near its end, is mutating or collapsing, in a no man's land between what subsists and what is about to eventuate, then relationships and the keys of visibility weaken. What is weakening, in fact, is memory.

The relationship between unemployment and inflation can be studied in a comparable approach. The link slackens because the relationship is not $I_{nf} = f(E_p)$ but $I_{nf} = f(E_p, m/F)$. Forgetfulness of the very relationship between the two variables plays a part in the emergence of a new memory. This can sometimes be taken quite far because, eventually, one might perhaps overestimate the existence of (natural) economic laws. There may be a law only for one specific memory and forgetfulness function defining a regime. If it is strongly memorized by all players, there is no significant link between inflation and unemployment. To rephrase the foregoing, if the fact that there may be such a link has been forgotten, can this link exist? It is tempting to answer affirmatively, but more cautious to think that such or such a link, such or such an economic law, can be effective only insofar as it is part of the memory function within the regime.

A state of equilibrium may be defined as comprising a stable and dense memory function (i.e. a low forgetfulness coefficient).

§ 25. Let us look back for a while at the relationship between inflation and unemployment. We now seek to ascertain what might (can in fact) lead to a weakening in the relationship. We start off in reality from the implicit and explicit hypothesis that there is, objectively as it were, such a relationship between the two variables. Economic theory easily explains why a decline in joblessness can trigger pay demands that, as they lead to a wage-price spiral, result in the appearance of inflation. This relationship is accepted by theory and gains credence from empirical data. It can be written, in absolute terms, as follows:

$$Inf = f(E_p) \text{ with } E_p = \text{employment.}$$

The foregoing, in a way, asserts that everywhere and always, there will be a form of direct relationship between the two variables. The relationship does not let the Subject (his memory/forgetfulness, his action) play a role and characterizes an instantaneous (a contemporary) link between the variables.

We now introduce the Subject, his consciousness (m/F, for memory/forgetfulness) and his action (in the monetary field via the interest rate, i_r for interest rate). Introducing the memory and forgetfulness function into $Inf = f(E_p)$ primarily leads to asserting that the economic Subject knows there is a relationship between inflation and unemployment. Because he has seen it operate (driven by his own action in fact) over time (admittedly in the past but above all over a lengthy period of time), he has memorized it and, thus, knows that it belongs to time-matter in line with the definition we have suggested, i.e. our metaphor of a piece of wax being reshaped as it is heated. This could be understood as meaning that the relationship between inflation and un-employment will be all the more solid and, above all, stable (durable) when the memory of this relationship is itself all the more vivid and stable. At the same time, however, one could think that since the Subject precisely is aware of this relationship, immediately anticipates all its effects, in particular the anti-inflationary action conducted by monetary authorities (the so-called rational expectations hypothesis).

We have not yet made a decisive breakthrough. We know there is a relationship between inflation and unemployment and that this relationship is memorized, as such and with respect to the effects and actions that stem from it. We wonder whether a high memory of the relationship coefficient (and therefore a low forgetfulness coefficient), i.e. (m/F) is likely, *ceteris paribus*, to strengthen the relationship, and increase its occurrence, or whether, instead, mainly because the consequences in terms of action or reaction are anticipated (in fact memorized because they have already been witnessed several times), the opposite is true.

In fact, there may be a need to draw a distinction between two elements. First, there is a tight link between the existence of an economic relationship, whatever it may be and the memory of this relationship, or, more precisely, a high and stable $\left(\dfrac{m}{F}\right)$, in other words a coefficient of erosion via limited forgetfulness. There is also an inversed relationship, however, between an economic relationship and the memorization of the effects and consequences it is likely to result in. The Subject knows that when inflation is deemed a threat (by a central bank), because the unemployment rate has plummeted and pay demands are on the rise, the Subject may well (this is only a possibility because such an action, or the lack of such an action, depends on the macrofinancial regime and the role that given institutions at such a time) anticipate (remember) that the foreseeable move by the central rate via the key intervention rate will prevent the inflationary impact from appearing. This would therefore lead to a situation in which memorization of the "complete" relationship (i.e. including the reaction function), with a high $\frac{m}{F}$, would nearly spare the central bank, at one extreme of its credibility regime, from having to act. The relationship would then disappear, in accordance with the proportionality of the memory of the complete relationship. Conversely, if said complete relationship were forgotten, this would revive the relationship.

This may mean that it is not enough for the absolute relationship to have been stored, so to say, in the memory for this absolute relationship to exist in fact. Forgetfulness of the complete relationship coefficient (including the reaction function) needs to remain low. In other words, the monetary policy consisting in raising interest rates (to combat inflation) plays on F in $\left(\frac{m}{F}\right)$. By (re-)activating rate hikes when inflation threatens, the central bank seeks to curtail the extent to which the reaction function is forgotten and, through a knock-on effect, dilutes the memory of the absolute relationship between inflation and unemployment.

To rephrase the foregoing, the central bank increases the degree to which the absolute relationship is forgotten by increasing the memory of the absolute relationship. It optimizes $(Inf, E_p, m/F)$.

§ 26.   There are situations of sub-equilibrium, or sub-optimal equilibria because, to a quite large extent, there are temporal (time-matter) inertia effects. The very existence of these inertias hampers action, which always unfolds from the use of tools and immediate (contemporary) observations, while showing the path to be followed by efficient action which, always, claims it takes into account these inertias *a minima* and, possibly, tries to play on them or reduce/increase them. There are equilibrium situations that dominate, as it were, all the immediate forms of equilibrium, because there is time-matter that transcends immediacy and moves from the past into the present, and does so at any time.

Any variable, at any point in time, integrates or encompasses a degree of density of memory of itself and of its environment (accordingly of other variables potentially). This density of time-matter must be viewed as a stock overlain/loomed over by a more immediate and more active dimension, determined at any time by the immediate data of the environment: $v = \alpha v_o + \beta v_m$, with v_m as memorized matter.

Every variable is the subject of an act of perception (projection) by the Subject (consciousness). This act is expressed by the interest rate. The interest rate itself comprises a dimension related to time-matter, which has been called the "memory interest rate". The memory interest rate is always a function of the memory of the economic and financial variable or variables (v_m). The interest rate is an act of immediate perception of a historic reality.

Even though many things seem to be determined by flows, i.e. active moments in the surface and immediacy, in all likelihood the deformation of stocks of memory provide the key for understanding economic developments as well as expectations. This is because the expectation regime is given by time-matter, a stock of memory and of the past, and its deformations.

Time is the fundamental matter of the economy.

§ 27.   Interest rate fluctuations concatenate fluctuations in time-matter. Because it is composed of an immediate interest rate and a memory interest rate, the interest rate reflects deformations and movements of time-matter and, therefore, of the memorized stock. At any time, a given number of things is more or less forgotten or more or less recalled.

Economic action strives to outweigh, to some extent, deformations of time-matter by acting via and on the interest rate. A few conclusions follow from the foregoing. First, one should bear in mind that this action results from the key intervention rate (or any central bank's benchmark rate), as the latter has an impact on the market interest rate. The impact on the market interest rate can be achieved by an action by the central bank affecting liquidity. The action can be efficient if, and only if, the change in the market interest rate, or in some liquidity variable, leads to a modification in the market interest rate (which we have called more broadly the immediate interest rate) likely to determine effectively the stock of time-matter (memory). In other words, it needs to deform the memory interest rate. Any action that, in the best-case scenario, results in a deformation of the immediate interest rate without generating a change in the memory interest rate is, at best, neutral.

Second, any action on the interest rate, via the interest rate, is disruptive and manipulative to some extent because it modifies time-matter (memory), which itself undergoes changes at any time through the operation of the economic environment forces, while producing effects that will be memorized in turn. These interactions create major uncertainty with regard to the initiative.

§ 28. A situation of general equilibrium corresponds to stability in memory and forgetfulness functions and, by consequence, to the absence of any significant deformation of memorized time-matter. This means both that such a situation is unlikely to prevail for long and that any action undertaken by the (individual and first and foremost institutional) Subject upsets such a situation of equilibrium by definition and because of its very nature.

Does this mean (or should it mean) that the objective of any economic policy action should be to safeguard, restore or reach such a situation? Not necessarily, insofar as memory or forgetfulness plays a role in creating a situation deemed detrimental (primarily because of ethical reasons). For, from a strictly economic viewpoint, there is equilibrium when forgetfulness and memory are not operating.

§ 29. The interest rate is defined by the immediate interest rate, the memory interest rate and a risk premium, which in fact is conceptually quite close to the idea of expectation.

$$IR = f\left(i_r(i), i_r(m), (r_p)\right)$$

with: $\quad i_r(m) = i_r(i) - v_{(m)}$

$$i_r(i) = i_r(m) + (r_p)$$

$$\Leftrightarrow i_r(i) = i_r(i) - v_{(m)} + (r_p)$$

$$\Leftrightarrow v_{(m)} = (r_p)$$

Risk premia are a memorized function of the economic and financial variable. Most approaches in this field have focused on inflation and activity variables (nominal demand or nominal GDP, consumer prices, or consumer price deflator in GDP). Very little research has been carried out, although nothing should stop it from being undertaken, in investigating time-matter with regard to other magnitudes, in particular in relation with the interest rate.

The aforementioned point holds for unemployment or financial asset prices. It would be interesting to study the gap between the immediate, or market, interest rate and the unemployment rate (its changes), just like the gap between said interest rate and inflation in financial asset prices. These two approaches, insofar as they look at the memory of unemployment or financial inflation, are interesting. One can build a real interest rate from the inflation memorized in financial asset prices. Drawing on this approach, one can show that the channel of asset prices can be used by the global analysis of inflation as well as by economic policy action. The approach must be at the same time all-encompassing (inflation as a complete and unitary phenomenon) and based on the taking into consideration of time-matter (memory).

In all likelihood, the incomplete estimation of the real interest rate led to underestimating the powerful stimulatory role played by asset prices in the macrofinancial regime that took shape from the 1990s onward. As we explained in our previous book "*Monetary Notebooks*", the velocity of money in the financial sphere produces financial inflation and velocity itself needs to be studied as a fully-fledged phenomenon, which includes both the velocity of money in the real sphere (in a nutshell, transactions of goods and services per monetary unit) and the velocity of money in the financial sphere (financial transactions per monetary unit). Note that one can and one should understand that financial transactions refer to a wide range of operations that can, at various points in time, come under numerous and rather unexpected guises, as well as various names: the so-called subprime crisis is a recent example thereof.

Having a global approach therefore, first of all, entails giving preference to a broad and unitary approach when studying a number of economic and financial phenomena. The foregoing includes a geographic dimension with, also, globalization and the so-called globalization of markets.

Once such an approach is adopted in the case of the real interest rate, it can be seen that the latter can have been, may, in fact be far lower than what could be expected. One example would be surges in the prices of such or such an asset class (and even more so when they affect all asset classes because the deformation of relative financial prices, i.e. between asset classes, is not neutral from the moment that one finds oneself in a situation of asset price inflation). A reduction in the real interest rate (the memory interest rate), when analyzed in this manner, creates, *de facto*, conditions leading to stimulation (as well as, potentially, an imbalance). We have:

$$i_{r(m)} = i_{r(i)} - \left(\alpha\ inf_{(r)} + \beta\ inf_{(f)} \right)$$

With respect to unemployment, the approach is somewhat thornier because this is a second variable of general activity (GDP or demand). We will look at this point more in depth below.

§ **30.** This work is a global theory, a global theoretical effort. In that respect, this work is not a general one. General theory is itself a specific case of a more global approach, just like Keynes showed that the classical theory was a specific case of a more general theory.

Our purpose, primarily, is to adopt a broader and more unitary approach with respect to several phenomena. For instance, we refer the reader to the introduction of financial assets into our approach. When Patinkin's opening statement in *Money, Interest and Prices* asserts "Money buys goods, but goods do not buy money", he forgets securities (financial assets).

In what way do the principal conclusions of the *General Theory* constitute merely a specific case of a global theory, in a conceptual and geographic sense? An initial answer can be found in the idea that policies aiming at boosting demand are inefficient when injections of liquidity (monetary policy) or ballooning fiscal deficits primarily lead to bubbles building up (for instance, Japanese bonds in the 1990s). In a financialized economy, money is also used to buy securities and liquidity, in fact, is injected into financial markets.

A second answer is found in the idea that unemployment is not exclusively due to insufficient demand for goods (Keynes) but, also, to an insufficient monetary stimulation of financial asset prices; capital is substituted for labor induced by the demands of financial profitability. Unemployment results also from the equilibrium (of imbalances) between supply and demand in the securities market and not just in the goods market. Keynes, in his *General Theory,* considered a specific case of monetary stimulation of the economy (demand for goods, injection into the goods market).

The main contemporary economic problems are related to the major role demand for money has been led for speculative purposes. The Keynesian under-employment equilibrium may be seen as a specific example of a general theory. Likewise, Friedman's recommendations answer only one specific aspect of monetary tuning. Rational expectations are merely a particular regime of a more general regime of adaptive expectations.

§ 31. When we talk of a global theory, we are referring to something that does not simply consist in a general approach that, for its part, is defined by the fact that it goes beyond specific cases, as happened with classical theory for Keynes for instance. The approach is therefore global insofar that it admits that the contemporary macrofinancial regime is defined by the worldwide framework of the economy. This approach toes the line set by fashionable talk about globalization to a lesser extent than it would seem at first sight. It does admit, however, that in this respect there is no smoke without fire. Lastly, this approach intends to show that general theory, which reduced classical theory to a specific case, itself is no more than a specific case of another theory, global theory actually.

§ 32.   "Money buys goods, but goods do not buy money". Don Patinkin's ironical opening sentence for a long time summarized the consensus in this field. Notwithstanding, apart from the fact that money can also buy securities, it is less and less ruled out that securities can, also, acquire money as it were.

In contemporary economies, money is injected into financial markets. Monetary policy analysts can barely remain indifferent to such a fact. This kind of injection is not innocent because, before it moves back into the real sphere, said liquidity follows uncertain paths. Before, possibly, stimulating final expenditure, it starts off by driving up financial asset prices. This stimulation means that an injection of liquidity by a central bank is carried out in the financial markets, and financial asset prices are the first stage of the monetary blast wave that distorts relative prices, all the way from the beginning of the chain to its end. The interest rate is the buoy that illustrates the deformation of this wave.

The question that then arises consists in ascertaining within what theory of prices does this analysis fit in and within what definition of the interest rate; and what efficiency can monetary policy claim to enjoy?

§ 33.   Keynes clearly saw the risk of a liquidity trap in an under-employment economy. But it is also conceivable that under a given level of interest rates (memory interest rate with time-matter composed of memorized/forgotten financial asset price inflation), the propensity to use each marginal monetary unit injected for speculative purposes may be infinite. This might be called the liquidity accelerator. The use of each monetary unit for trans-action purposes increases significantly, the velocity of circulation of the stock of money in the financial sphere gathers pace while it decelerates in the real sphere. There is a transfer of liquidity from the real sphere into the financial sphere.

This liquidity accelerator generates positive real effects (psychological or real wealth effects, and financial bubbles). By consequence, there is a definite interest for a central bank facing a situation of cyclical depression in seeking to stimulate demand for money for speculative purposes – with all the related risks.

Such a monetary policy is conducted by maintaining interest rates under equilibrium levels, insofar as these two concepts have been specified.

By contrast with the "Keynesian" idea that dominated for a while, fiscal stimulation of the economy, in all likelihood, is the context of a market economy (in the sense given by the growing role of financial assets in the formation of wealth and in the circulation of money), less preferable than monetary stimulation. On the one hand, this is because the markets penalize the first kind of stimulus policy while they benefit, as parasites, from the second. Next, because the (psychological or real) wealth effects achieved by a managed acceleration in the velocity of circulation of the stock of money in the financial sphere are greater – as well as immediate – than the effects of a fiscal stimulus. Keynes saw the general case in the under-employment equilibrium, and believed full employment was the classical exception. In fact, there are situations of over-employment once demand for money for speculative purposes is stimulated. This entails risks. It also means, for instance, that the full employment equilibrium becomes the rule and not the exception, when wealth effects adjust real effects. A monetary policy that embraces these objectives aims for full employment. It can only do so after buying into monetary objectives of growth in financial asset prices. Accordingly, it is up to monetary policy to manage expectations with regard to financial asset prices and steer growth in the stock of money in such a manner that expectations of a rise in asset prices for the entire economy do not outstrip growth in the economy. Financialized market economies are threatened to a greater extent by situations of over-use of certain factors than by under-employment. The classical situation remains that of the equilibrium, but most often one finds oneself above the equilibrium. Financial bubbles are the symptoms of this situation, as well as the lack of inflation in its classical sense despite full employment of the labor factor.

§ 34.   One has to see the velocity of money as a function composed of its circulation in the real sphere and of circulation in the financial sphere, where there are transfers from one sphere into the other. One also needs to see this function as global, in other words operating on a worldwide scene, and use a very broad definition of money (all monetary bases and/or aggregates, central banks' foreign exchange reserves, etc.).

What happens?

We have:

$$MV = \left(V = \frac{PT}{M} \right)$$

but with $V = (V_r, V_F)$ where $V_r = \frac{PT_r}{M}$ and $V_F = \frac{PT_F}{M}$.

The acceleration in the circulation of the stock of money in the real (financial) sphere, in other words the increase in real (financial) transactions per monetary unit, is reflected by real (financial) inflation. The issue of the stability of V must be tackled by breaking down V into two (real and financial) segments and, furthermore, by introducing the operation of expectations, i.e. of memory. $\left(T = \frac{MV}{P} \right)$, from which we deduce that transactions evolve in line with the stock of money when V is stable. At the "equilibrium", transactions and the stock of money move hand in hand. Instability is triggered by movements of V with $V = f(a, m)$ where a is any real or financial variable and m the memory of this variable, or of any combination of determinant or pertinent variables. The velocity of money is determined by the memory of demand for cash for speculative purposes (here one talks about the velocity of money in the financial sphere). This helps understand why despite an increase in the stock of money following various forms of injections of liquidity, there may be a comparatively low level of financial transactions (V is low). The neutrality of V (earlier we called it stability), i.e. a comparable or proportional change in the volume of transactions and of the stock of money, is reached when memory effects themselves are neutral. Thus, when the memory of demand for transaction purposes is still permeated by problems in financial asset markets (in the wake of a crash or some inflection point), V will be lower than neutrality, let us say < 1, and the increase in the stock of money will drive financial transactions up to a lesser extent than to be expected proportionally. Conversely, effects resulting from the memory of a rise will probably have a symmetrical effect (it cannot be ruled out that memory effects have an asymmetrical impact on financial assets according to whether one is in a bullish or bearish period). The above means, in particular, that in order to produce a stimulation effect, monetary policy needs to at least neutralize V, and this can be achieved by increasing M to a large extent, or by an action on V. By contrast, in the case of overheating, growth in transactions far outpaces growth in the stock of money.

Because V is a memory and expectation variable, and this is analogical, the simply determining the quantity of money and/or its price will not be sufficient. A monetary policy is optimal in the vicinity of the neutrality of memory effects (optimal in the sense of guaranteeing a given number of equilibrium conditions). Furthermore, and to complicate matters, V_r and V_F, which are related in the same way as a photo is to its negative, have to be analyzed as the two major magnetization poles, and with the idea that $V = f(V_r, V_F)$ is what needs to be neutralized. This neutrality of V can therefore mask strong heterogeneities between V_r and V_F, which experience shows. Therefore, quite frequently price stability in the real sphere ("classical" inflation) is paid by financial inflation and/or various forms of financial stability. An economic policy action aimed at cooling down inflation may very well end up by stimulating financial inflation. The first action undertaken to combat inflation seeks to slow down growth in the stock of money, and this has a knock-on effect on transactions because $V_R = f(a, m)$ is then characterized by a negative memorized function of the demand for cash for real transactions. V_R is <1 and transactions can actually decelerate to a greater than proportional extent than the slowdown in the stock of money. On the financial side of the global equation (because, our use of the word global also refers to everything that, in any economic phenomenon, entwines a real part and a financial part into a whole), $V_F = f(a, m)$ likely continues to be determined by a still robust, albeit declining, demand for cash for financial transaction purposes. The deceleration in the growth in the stock of money is probably passed on less than proportionally to financial transactions. This occurs, on both sides of the global equation, until the conditions of the equilibrium are reached, on both sides of the global equation (V_R, V_F) and for $V_G = f(V_R, V_F)$. There is equilibrium when there is neutrality of $V = (V_R, V_F)$, or when V_R and V_F are both at neutrality.

Taking into account, and subsequently bolstering, memory effects are therefore crucial dimensions of economic policy action. This point holds in several respects for the $PV = MT$, global equation, and its fearsome current relevance is not called into question. First of all, this is true with regard to the globalized nature of V in a financiarized economy (V_R, V_F) that is also a globalized one (V_F depends on worldwide and global variables). Secondly, although final causality relationships cannot be ruled out (financial inflation leading for instance to real inflation), the dominant relationship between the two variables consists in a play of mirrors and of transfers, a play of non-simultaneity. Lastly, and this is undoubtedly essential, V_F plays a greater role, in a macrofinancial regime that is fundamentally a wealth growth regime, than V_R, and this means that understanding and steering

V_F, for proactive purposes (stimulation for economic policy action) or reactive ones (bursting of a bubble for instance), are not insignificant issues for action.

The velocity of circulation of money in the economy and in markets, i.e. the amount of real transactions (goods and services) and financial transactions (financial assets, securities) carried out by monetary unit, is a lagged (memorized) component of various kinds of demand for cash aimed at carrying out transactions on goods and services and transactions with speculative purposes.

§ 35.   As we have seen, V_F plays a paramount role in contemporary economies, and complicates matters for central banks. V_F is a function of demand for financial transactions T_F. Alongside V_F and T_F, there is the memory/forgetfulness of what determines the functions of demand for cash. This memory (m) or this forgetfulness (F) fundamentally express a more or less great preference for the present. There is a crucial analogy between the Keynesian preference for liquidity and the memory or forgetfulness function. We are now going to seek to explain and clarify the foregoing.

The velocity of money can be broken down into two simple terms or elements. One is related to the sphere of goods and services, the other to the financial sphere of securities. The two spheres interact and mutually influence one another. To give an example, financial inflation appears (acceleration in the circulation of money for the purpose of carrying out financial transactions), resulting from a "transfer" of means of payment from the real sphere into the financial sphere, and consisting in an increase in liquidity and the multiplication of means of payment stemming from this acceleration in the amount of transactions per monetary unit. In opposition to the preference functions for real transactions (rt) (goods and services) and for financial transactions (ft) (long-term securities and financial assets; at the other extreme polarity, there is a liquidity preference function (l). All three functions $f\left(\text{Pref}_{(rt)}\right)$, $f\left(\text{Pref}_{(ft)}\right)$ and $f\left(\text{Pref}_{(l)}\right)$ are linked to memory and forgetfulness.

The preference for liquidity is fundamentally a preference for the present. The preference for the present increases in line with forgetfulness and the erosion of memory. The extreme situation where the economy is bogged down in an infinite preference for liquidity is a situation where, for a number of sequences of events or choices, memory crumbles, and forgetfulness gathers pace. The very acceleration of forgetfulness and the erasing of memory play a part in developments experienced as "paradigm shifts" or "trend reversals". A paradigm shift is primarily an acceleration in the forgetfulness function (and, therefore, a concentration of memory-space). The so-called liquidity trap is a phenomenon of extreme forgetfulness. Nothing is left from a memory of demand for cash with the purpose of carrying out transactions, whether real or financial. At the extreme point, deliberately chosen, absolute liquidity dominates proceedings. The refusal to carry out real transactions is also a refusal to carry out financial transactions on risky long-term assets. This corresponds to the usual peak of a recession, but also, to a greater extent in fact, to the triggering of deflation or of a paradigm shift.

The extreme aversion for risk that paves the way for the (infinite) preference for liquidity results from forgetfulness that is itself infinite, but also, potentially, from the way in which (selective) memory focuses to an extreme degree on a period or an event. Because of their negative consequences (from the viewpoint of demand for cash for real or financial long-term transactions), this period or event will lead to the same type of effect as extreme forgetfulness. In the extreme, forgetfulness performs the same function as absolutely selective memory. And while forgetfulness, in a normal situation, occurs via a reasonably linear erosion of memory, non-linearity and acceleration appear in what is consequently seen to be a paradigm shift in so-called crisis phases.

In a normal situation, the most often, the metaphor of communicating vessels applies, i.e. a form of trade-off between real and financial preferences. However, before moving on to this arbitraging function, one should try to understand how trade-offs operate within both spheres, as determined by memory and forgetfulness effects. In the real sphere, the changeover from a normal situation of demand for goods and services to one of inflation in prices of goods and services occurs, as an acceleration, via a memory effect that recalls only past impressions of robust demand for real transactions. At the extreme end of the spectrum in the real sphere, there is only one (selective) memory effect left and it relates to factors leading to a rise in demand. The same point holds in the financial sphere. Once again, at the extreme ends, the selective memory function joins up with a form of forgetfulness (of longer or more selective memory). Periods of euphoria are based on this mechanism.

Between the two spheres, liquidity arbitraging and transfers are sparked and determined by a kind of struggle between memory and forgetfulness functions. The outcome is decided when a (real, financial) preference function ends up by outweighing the other, i.e. when the memory of either dominates the other one.

§ 36. Forgetfulness is never a void function, an absolute sort of way of tuning out of the world and its past. Forgetfulness always overlaps with a selective memory function in which only homogenous phenomena (periods of rises or declines) or significantly specific influential events (with an extent of asymmetry, with negative shocks outweighing positive shocks) subsist.

§ 37. Because situations of economic depression are extreme situations of the forgetfulness function, economic policy action must try to revive memory, either by rekindling an erased memory link with a more favorable demand for real or financial transactions function, or, and this is not exclusive, by establishing the conditions allowing a new memory node to be created from the beginning of a positive trajectory (since memory effects feed on themselves and are, to a certain extent, self-fulfilling). The very economic policy action, via the monetary channel (rate cuts for instance) or the fiscal channel (various stimulus packages), can trigger memory effects simply by activating them because their activation, given the way the players perceive them, sets in motion memory effects related to cause-and-effect sequences that, in the past, may have positively acted as driving forces. When a central bank lowers its interest rates, initially effects due to the reviving of the memory of comparable past periods operate, even before the automatically real effects, which cannot in fact be dissociated, in terms of their efficiency or their inefficiency, from the more or less satisfactory way in which these memory effects are stimulated.

§ **38.** All major economic functions are determined by memory and forgetfulness effects. Savings, investment and consumption cannot be comprehended, as a dynamics, without taking into account a certain memory and forgetfulness coefficient. As this coefficient is not stable, its very instability is at the heart of the dynamics of the cycle.

At equilibrium, all economic functions can be characterized by a memory and forgetfulness function. Its coefficient is either absolutely stable or neutral (= 1), i.e. does not exert any specific effect on the general equation. The equilibrium can therefore be defined as a situation of neutrality of memory and forgetfulness effects, or, in a somewhat different and more dynamic approach, as a situation of iso-distortion by memory and forgetfulness effects, i.e. constant rates of memory erosion (forgetfulness rates) or of rates of memory building. The absolute equilibrium is therefore a static (and in all likely unrealistic) situation in which time is absent. The restricted relative equilibrium is a dynamic (slightly more realistic) situation but one in which the Subject's temporary referential (memory, forgetfulness) is so to say congealed, fixed, in which there is no form of dilatation or of contraction of the temporal referential. Real life, it will be said, is even more plus definitely realistic, made of situations where the equilibrium is merely a landmark in the recurrent fluctuations of the time referential, consisting in dilatations and contractions driven by memory and forgetfulness. We will call this state a relative equilibrium.

The description of states of absolute equilibrium and of relative equilibrium (whether restricted or not) is not the same according to whether it occurs in a closed (theoretical), open, classical or global framework. Our studies are in keeping with the global dimension, marked by the significant opening of markets of goods, services and capital and the globalization of the economy's major variables, as well as of their determinants. We will come back to this global dimension later on.

The changeover from a static situation to a dynamic one (from the absolute or restricted relative equilibrium to the relative equilibrium) depends on the modification of memory and forgetfulness coefficients. At the equilibrium, it is claimed, savings is equal to investment. This equality is certainly debatable but above all it is acceptable only insofar as the memory and forgetfulness functions are effectively neutral (absolute equilibrium) or constant in their effects (restricted relative equilibrium). $I = S$ is therefore, in many respects, an exception, a specific case of the equilibrium, in comparison with a more general (and more global in the meaning we give this word) equality where:

$$\left(a_{m/F}\right)I = \left(b_{m/F}\right)S.$$

$\left(a_{m/F}\right)$ and $\left(b_{m/F}\right)$ are equal together to 1 only in the situation of absolute equilibrium. They can also take constant values $\left(a_{m/F} = \text{Cte}\right)$ to define a restricted relative equilibrium. However, the most frequent situations and, above all, the ones the most in line with what observation and experience teach us, are, by far, the ones in which (*a*) and (*b*) fluctuate widely like unstable, non-linear coefficients (dilatation/contraction of time referentials). Reality is made of numerous relative equilibria (which can, from a certain viewpoint, be deemed sub-equilibria). Economic and financial functions are characterized by the total, or restricted, relativity of the temporal referential that determines them.

The changeover from the restricted relative equilibrium to the relative equilibrium mainly results from the operation of memory and forgetfulness coefficients that, through the relationship that binds them with the reality of facts and events, deform them-selves, dilate or contract. The situation at the outset is a situation of (relative) stability in the sense that memory and forgetfulness coefficients are constant. The internal time referential (Maurice Allais calls it psychological time) is stable, or constant. Beginning from this configuration of equilibrium, the main development can be an erosion of memory (increase in forgetfulness) or a densification of memory (decline in forgetfulness) with, in both cases, possible concentration points (sudden remembrance of a sub-period or of a remote event; erasure of the distant past, over-representation of the most recent past in the forgetfulness phase).

The increase in forgetfulness reflects an invasion of the temporal referential by the present, or the nearest past. Periods of euphoria or, conversely, of gloom, stem from such forgetfulness. In both cases, so to say, the close past is densified, extended and projected. Initially, forgetfulness and memory phenomena tend to bolster contemporary economic environments. The pro-cyclicality of memory and forgetfulness plays a role in the very fact that there is a cycle and in the persistence of cyclical dimensions specific to economic and financial phenomena. With respect to a situation of restricted relative equilibrium characterized by a positive and bullish trend, forgetfulness will, at first, boost and accentuate tendencies. The same point holds for a situation of restricted relative equilibrium in a negative environment. In extreme situations, forgetfulness is total and the only thing that remains is an infinite preference for the present and the immediate. This can feed either upside euphoria (in activity and in prices of goods and services; as well as in various financial asset prices) or infinite risk aversion. The situation of restricted relative equilibrium shifts toward a new and unstable situation of relative equilibrium.

Because a restricted relative equilibrium is always already characterized by an environment and market bias, in either direction, the shift in the equilibrium at first, often, consists in an extension. This state of affairs prevails until forgetfulness, as its domination peters out, ends up as it were by calling up memory, via the return of a more cautious memory in the case of euphoria, more upbeat in the case of depression. The point we are driving at is that forgetfulness and memory erosion phenomena, which bolster and amplify trends and cycles, end up, after the completion of a process that sees the near past invade the internal temporal referential, and subsequently infinite immediacy overrun the present (which boils down, to an extent, to the same as all that is left in the memory of the past — which shrinks however — facts and events of a similar nature and trending in the same direction), by producing and gathering the conditions, often when a sudden event happens (breakdown in euphoria, upturn in gloom), or a trend reversal takes shape. Then memory recalls what will result in the trend reversal, whether the souvenir of worrisome events in a period of euphoria, or grounds for hope when there is a loss of reference p points and depression rules. Reviving and rebuilding memory, by modifying the temporal referential, leads to a new situation.

§ 39. Any situation of restricted relative equilibrium is a situation of sub-optimal equilibrium, of disequilibrium in a fashion. Such a statement is undeniable once memory and forgetfulness coefficients are not neutral. Furthermore, in reality, these coefficients can be neutral. An economic policy action could try, among many possible objectives, to stabilize these temporal coefficients, and act on them. In the first case, the sub-optimal equilibrium is stabilized; in the second case, the action strives to modify the trajectory followed to extend forgetfulness and/or help memory be recalled (counter-cyclical action). Economic policy action seeks to be counter-cyclical in situations where forgetfulness and memory phenomena are, at least in the near term, pro-cyclical. Memory and forgetfulness are pro-cyclical in the near term, counter-cyclical in the medium term.

§ 40. Appetite for risk and risk aversion, two oft-mentioned phenomena at the heart of developments affecting the economy and markets, are related to forgetfulness and memory. What is called appetite for risk corresponds to an increase in the forget-fulness rate (or, if memory remains a force, it will now contain only events leading to risk taking), to a dilatation of the temporal referential and a preference for the present and the immediate. A rise in risk-taking, which leads risk premia to drop and contract, is a period during which the memory (of risk) fades. Frequently, these periods correspond to a phase of monetary expansionism, easy credit and interest rates deemed, at least subsequently, artificially low.

There is a link between risk taking, the erosion of memory (increase in the forgetfulness rate) and the "artificially" low level of interest rates. There is an analogy between monetary erosion and the erosion of memory, therefore forgetfulness. In these periods of euphoria and outlandish appetite for risk, there is admittedly abundance of means of payment, which, from a strictly quantitative (quantitativist) viewpoint, is often invoked to explain this process. However, such an explanation is insufficient. Memory is eroded, in the sense in which, helter-skelter, the most solid sequences of events are lost although they should set off alarm bells, along with the most striking past events that should also lead to prudence, but also simple activity or inflation series. Thus, the rate at which inflation is forgotten increases (this was one of the driving forces of the dotcom bubble in the 1990s), i.e. actual and expected inflation is no longer characterized by a long-term and relatively inert memory but instead by an extrapolation of immediate trends. The real interest rate dilates.

In fact, is there on the one hand a natural, as it were, real interest rate and, on the other hand, a purely psychological interest rate? This distinction, which was drawn by Maurice Allais, is highly stimulating because it clearly acknowledges the existence of an internal (psychological) temporal referential. Nonetheless, to use once again the example of inflation, the expectation of inflation that is part of the (natural) real interest rate is definitely of a same nature as the psychological perception of inflation. We are trying to say that there may be a natural reference, as it were, of the (real) interest rate, around which the psychological interest rate as defined by Allais would fluctuate (absolute equilibrium and restricted relative equilibrium or not as we have defined it), but above all there are relative (in the strong sense of the word) equilibria oscillating around situations of a restricted relative equilibrium. Against this backdrop, the interest rate is first and foremost determined by the internal temporal referential.

In a period of appetite for risk, the increase in the forgetfulness rate leads to a drastic drop in the memory interest rate. This reduction is said to be "artificial" because of the very fact that it results from the forgetting of crucial elements that determine the interest rate regime. The decline in the memory interest rate is to be assessed in comparison with the behavior of the interest rate we have called immediate, and with the behavior of a "natural" interest rate. The latter can be drawn upon as the reference of the absolute equilibrium regime, such as we have defined it, but that will be discarded here from our approach. Our approach seeks a reference point for the relative equilibria, which is anchored in a concept of interest rates that encompasses the market rate and the memory rate. Said concept can itself be of use for a more absolute approach with regard to the interest rate and the equilibrium.

§ 41. In a relative equilibrium regime, whether or restricted or not, the spread between the memory interest rate and the immediate interest rate is undoubtedly the most fertile indicator. It is definitely when the memory interest rate slips significantly under the immediate interest rate that the conditions that have been called the exaggeration of the cycle (euphoria) are met. Analyzing this spread can help find the path to be followed by an economic policy action that, while it cannot easily act on the memory interest rate, will at least be able to try and play on the gap with the market interest rate.

This spread plays a role in the unfolding of the cycle from one relative equilibrium to another.

If the objective, and this is different, consists in anchoring an absolute equilibrium regime, the interest rate understood as a function of the immediate rate and of the memory rate, will have to be analyzed from the viewpoint of a concept of the real interest rate.

A first approach, which draws a distinction between the immediate interest rate and the memory interest rate, will endeavor to estimate the interest rate by estimating the forgetfulness rate. We will have:

$$i_{r(F)} = r(F), \text{ and } i_r = \left(i_{r(F)}, i_{r(i)}\right) + r_p$$

The spread between the two interest rates plays a key role. Another approach will consist in writing:

$$ir = i_{r(i)} - \left(x_{F/m}\right) + r_p$$

where the second term is forgetfulness (memory) of the variable pertinent to the estimation of interest rate.

There is an equilibrium interest rate for an equilibrium regime and for a general equation, or for an income equation. A restricted relative equilibrium is defined by an equilibrium interest rate (where memory and forgetfulness coefficients are temporarily neutralized), for a sub-optimal equilibrium, which leads to a new equilibrium (situations of relative equilibria) via the operation of the interest rate and, to a larger extent, via forgetfulness and memory of all variables.

§ 42.   Forgetting is one thing, recalling a memory is something else. In what type of amplitude and of symmetry can these two phenomena play? Apparently, reflection has until now especially focused on forgetfulness and the erosion of memory. After all, this is hardly surprising, as erosion reflects a linear function of the passing of time. Such continuity, however, does not match what observation or experience may suggest, since it overlooks discontinuous temporal referentials stirred by dilatations and contractions.

Forgetting something is as important as recalling a memory, in terms of understanding economic and financial events. The memory recall rate is the name we give to what comes back from the past, under one guise or another, whether concentrated or diluted, complete or partial. Its counterpart is the forgetfulness rate $(R_r)/(F_r)$. The memory recall rate does not measure the persistence of the past, i.e. its resistance to being erased (this is yet another way of measuring forgetfulness), but, literally, the return, the earlier occupation of the temporal referential by one or several past sequences. This return can be spontaneous, or triggered, or supported. Potentially, it represents one of the guidelines of economic policy action. An economic policy action is always aimed at bringing back something desirable from the past, directly or indirectly. The success of such an action involves at least setting in motion memory effects that, step by step, are going to ensure the efficient completion of the action. The "recall rate" (R_r) plays this role. Economic policy action can in fact entirely consist in reviving one or several slices of the past. Undoubtedly, this is an aspect of economic policy action that has not been sufficiently explored and utilized.

What is forthcoming is expected just like what has occurred is forgotten. The analogy brought to light by Allais between forgetfulness, expectation and interest deserves to be completed by the phenomenon of memory recall (R_r). One expects just like one recalls a memory. Forgetfulness, memory recall, expectation and interest are the four pillars of an economy of memory.

In the economic and financial dynamics that deploys from the (absolute or restricted relative) equilibrium, memory (and, to a larger extent, time) constitutes a stock of energy, a battery that gradually runs down. Forgetfulness, i.e. the erosion of the stock of time and of memory is, justifiably, seen as a driving force of the economy and of finance. In fact, it is as if energy were contained in the "initial" stock of memory and if the dynamics resulted from the combustion of this memory under the form of forgetfulness. Forgetfulness is the combustion of a fuel. This fuel, however, boasts the property of partly rebuilding itself, through the process of memory recall, which propels its own dynamics in the same way as forgetfulness propels its own. Forgetfulness and memory recall, in a certain manner, clash, repel one another and seek to neutralize one another like the two opposite poles of an energy.

The interest rate we have called "the memory rate" is therefore determined, in its fluctuations, by the tension between forgetfulness and memory recall. The temporal referential thus experiences extensive movements and dilatations. The increase in forgetfulness during an upward phase does not prevent, far from it in fact, memory recall that, often, occurs when the extreme limit of forgetfulness has been reached. Helping memory recall can also be a task of economic policy action, through statements or action as such.

Starting off from an initial situation of restricted relative equilibrium, the increase in the memory recall rate tends to exert an opposite force to the one expressing itself at the point of relative equilibrium, and running counter to the one exerted by forgetfulness. That being said, it is perfectly possible to assume that memory recall musters the past, one of its sequences, in order to intensify an initial situation of restricted relative equilibrium. While forgetfulness is in a certain degree a linear erosion process (which can admittedly undergo an acceleration), memory recall operates via shocks, discontinuities and flashes.

When it is said that there is a restricted relative equilibrium for which temporal coefficients are stable and constant, it is therefore claimed that the forgetfulness rate and the memory recall rate are then neutralized, stable and constant. Such a situation of restricted relative equilibrium makes it possible to define an equilibrium interest rate from a memory interest rate combining a constant value of forgetfulness and of memory.

$$ir_{(F/m)} = f\left(R_r, F_r\right)$$

and at the same time,

$$IR = f\left(ir_{(i)}, ir_{(F/m)}, r_p\right)$$

§ 43. The second interesting gateway leads from the absolute equilibrium to what we have called the relative equilibrium. At the absolute equilibrium, there is equivalence between investment and savings functions for instance. This equivalence is possible, just like the very idea of an absolute equilibrium, only because time is excluded from it as it were. The equivalence, the equivalences obtained at the absolute equilibrium postulate an absolute neutrality of the time of forgetfulness and of memory and, therefore, of the forgetfulness or memory recall coefficients with a unitary value.

The appearance of time displaces these coefficients by starting to create, through its accumulation, a stock of temporal energy (of memory), and afterward of forgetfulness, as only what, initially, belongs to a stock of memory can be forgotten. This would seem to suggest that the first sequence after the absolute equilibrium is a period of initial accumulation of time-value, of what will become memory-matter. This initial matrix sequence is pure in the sense that memory erosion (forgetfulness) or reconstitution (memory recall) do not operate yet. At the end of this initial phase, energy has been loaded, i.e. a track record and memory have been built. In very absolute, and accordingly fundamentally unrealistic, vision of the equilibrium, the following sequence witnesses the first appearances of erosion and of memory recall.

As we have already pointed out, forgetfulness phenomena, once they are triggered, result in an extension and intensification of the short-term trend. One therefore exits from the absolute equilibrium of equivalence via the extension of the trend that will have dominated the initial phase of pure accumulation of memory. The latter can be guided in one direction or another. Whatever this direction, in all likelihood, it will be accentuated by the erosion of memory-time, the real matter. This phenomenon will unfold until it ends up, by its own forces, by setting in motion the forces of its reversal and of its cancelation. We therefore have, beginning from the starting point of the absolute equilibrium, a phase of pure accumulation of memory-time (initial phase), followed by a phase of accentuation (phase of forgetfulness and extension) in which, essentially, one moves into a situation of relative equilibrium (of disequilibrium in the sense where the absolute equilibrium of equivalence of the major economic functions cannot be maintained; of sub-optimal equilibrium we could also say). Savings suddenly exceeds investment, or *vice versa*. In a third phase, following an accentuation at both extremes of the main trends in the economy and markets, extremes reached by a sharp increase in the forgetfulness rate (for a memory that keeps only the pure elements of a trend and projects them *ad infinitum*), the conditions of a reversal are progressively met, as the rise in the memory recall rate (discontinued return of events or sequences temporarily erased from memory beforehand) ultimately sparks the reversal.

Above, we have described in a crude and simplified manner, the fundamental sequences according to which the equilibrium shifts. We are seeking to make the point that the shift itself cannot occur without time playing a role, and, more precisely, if a stock of time is not built up within an internal referential (memory), and if there is no memory erosion/recall either.

There is an analogy between the (monetary) constitution of the stock that savings represents, and the constitution of the stock of memory. There is an analogy between the two phenomena of accumulation of time and of "money". We have a deep analogy between monetary accumulation (savings) and temporal accumulation (memory). Moreover, there is also an analogy between the processes via which the former erodes (from savings into investment) as well as the latter (from memory into forgetfulness). There is also a learning mechanism at play in the changeover from one equilibrium to another, from one disequilibrium to another, once reality retains only relative, restricted or, the most often, complete equilibria.

§ 44.   There is unemployment only for a relative equilibrium, i.e. for and with a memorized or forgotten form of time. At the absolute equilibrium, from which time is driven out, there are pure equivalences of the major economic functions. Reality is not the absolute equilibrium but an infinity of relative equilibria. The concept of unemployment can be studied in this context and starting from this observation.

Unemployment corresponds, as a worrisome phenomenon (i.e. when it exceeds residual unemployment), to a high memory and/or forgetfulness coefficient associated to one of the economic functions. This high coefficient establishes the relative equilibrium at such a level that it includes a significant under-employment component. The Keynesian approach of the unemployment equilibrium, which is in fact what we call the relative equilibrium, is clarified once time is integrated by memory and forgetfulness (Keynes had understood the role of expectations, which, to a quite large extent, are memory and forgetfulness facts).

Let us take the simple equivalence between investment and savings, which could actually be discussed. We have $I = S$ at the absolute equilibrium, but we also have $\alpha I = \beta S$ at the relative equilibrium where α and β are memory and forgetfulness coefficients $\alpha_{m/F} I = \beta_{m/F} S$. We can then make the hypothesis that the investment function is determined, on the one hand, by the remembering and forgetting of a pertinent function or variable (directed demand, for instance) and, on the other hand, by the past of the investment function itself. A high level of α, for example after a period of depression (during a period of depression), will help bring about a sub-optimal equilibrium where equivalence is achieved at such a level that it entails unemployment.

Unemployment reaches its values which we call residual when the memory function is pure and homogenous (i.e. only a past of positive order remains for the decisive variables of activity and of employment). This is a situation where forgetfulness has fulfilled its work of chasing out from the past everything radically "different"; when the forgetfulness function is maximal, i.e. when there is an infinite preference for the (positive) present, as there is a negative alternative (situation of infinite hoarding and of liquidity trap). Subsequently, memory and forgetfulness coefficients are distorted, and this distortion is precisely the definition and the dynamics of what is called the cycle.

The cycle's *fatum* (fatal) dimension is related to the deployment of the memory and forgetfulness dynamics, which are characterized by significant inertia.

Underemployment, in its cyclical dimension (cyclical in the preceding meaning of the cycle), can result from vivid negative memorization of activity (as broadly defined). Its erasure itself can only be progressive (forgetfulness rate), and this accounts for the quite usual extension of cyclical phases, whether bullish or bearish. Underemployment, in its extreme or more moderate forms, is therefore of the following type: unemp = $f(r_m, r_F)$. Economic policy action, by consequence, will seek to reduce before inversing the rate of memorization of activity (which includes the memory of unemployment itself, which results in the variable retroacting on itself), and/or accelerating the forgetfulness rate.

A situation of underemployment is characterized by the existence of a stock, matter that can be imagined nearly physically, a stock of memory, a stock of negative past for activity. Action must reduce this stock. In a way, every resource can be useful and utilized to chip away at this block of memory. The key feature of the internal temporal referential (psychological referential for the economic Subject's consciousness) entails that the efficiency of any action must be assessed according to its capacity to distort the referential. The efficiency of the most conventional and the most technical tools and actions ultimately depends on this point. As well as the interest rate. As long as the interest rate we have called the "immediate rate", i.e. the market interest rate, has not been driven into the vicinity of, and probably even lower, the interest rate integrating the negative memory of activity (a somewhat different concept from the psychological interest rate as defined by Allais), there will not be any efficient action on the stock of negative memory of activity that maintains a level of underemployment, for a situation of equivalence between savings and investment.

The interest rate integrating memory and forgetfulness is the interest rate that the action on the immediate interest rate must seek to modify, as this interest rate of the memory of universes of relative equilibrium (reality) has to be itself compared with the interest rate we will call the natural rate, the reference of the absolute equilibrium.

We will now try to fine-tune the concept of an interest rate for the relative equilibrium. We have mentioned the idea of an interest rate integrating memory and forgetfulness as the benchmark interest rate. We therefore start off from the immediate interest rate that we then subject to a modification by the memory and forgetfulness rate. One approach could simply consist in working on the form of the real interest rate, by establishing the similarity or the difference between the immediate interest rate and the past average rate (by more or less equiweighting the various sub-periods) of a decisive economic or financial variable. One can also seek to estimate the forgetfulness rate more directly. The concept of a forgetfulness interest rate is then distinct from a form of the real interest rate. The interest rate is the forgetfulness rate itself, i.e. the memory rate as well. One can envisage defining such an interest rate by the past average rate of a key activity variable (thus, the memory interest rate would be equal, for instance, to the past moving rate of GDP growth, plus or minus a risk premium). In this case, we have:

$$ir_{(F/m)} = f\left(Y_{F/m}\right), \quad \text{with } Y = \text{income.}$$

However, one can also seek to compare the memory interest rate with the erosion function of this past average of the key activity variable. The memory interest rate is then, for instance, the rate of change in the equiweighted ten-year average of demand. We have:

$$ir_{(F/m)} = \left(\Delta Y_{F/m}\right)$$

We would like to draw attention once again, by the way, to the possibility of an approach drawing on the form of the real interest rate. We then have for the memory interest rate:

$$ir_{(F/m)} = \left(ir_{(im)} - Y_{F/m}\right)$$

Lastly, a somewhat radical approach may lead to the defining the memory interest rate as a past function (more or less adjusted or weighted past average) of the nominal interest rate itself. We have:

$$i_r(F/m) = i_{n_{F/m}}$$

An ultimate variant could consist in drawing exclusively on the rate of change in $i_{n_{F/m}}$, or $i_r(F/m) = \left(\Delta\, i_{n_{F/m}}\right)$.

§ 45. We therefore have, at this stage, the immediate interest rate, a market variable that can be observed at any moment and expressed in nominal terms. We still have, within the relative equilibrium regime as we have defined it (it is reality), the immediate interest rate, which fluctuates around a relative reference point, i.e. relative to time, and therefore within a temporal referential that undergoes deformations. This reference point is a composition of the relative real interest rate, relative because always relative to the economic regime and referential, and of the memory interest rate that here expresses the memory and forgetfulness function as previously described. The two concepts $i_{r(r)}$ and $i_{r(m/F)}$ are interconnected and compose the immediate interest rate. We have:

$$i_{r(n)} = i_{r(r)} + m/F,$$

and we can write this in the following manner:

$$i_r(n) = i_r(r) + i_r\left(m/F\right),$$

hence ;
$$i_r(r) = i_r(n) - i_r\left(m/F\right) ;$$

like
$$i_r(n) \cong i_r(i),$$

we have :
$$\left[i_{r(r)}\right]_{\mathrm{rel}} = i_r(i) - i_r(m/F).$$

We can see in such an approach of the relative equilibrium regime that the spread found between the immediate interest rate and the memory interest rate, and their relative changes with regard to one another more generally speaking, play the role of a driving force in the changes and distortions in the relative real interest rate. However, these distortions make the cycle. When the immediate interest rate is lowered well under the memory interest rate, the relative interest drops until it possibly moves into negative territory. It is then an economic policy action (cut in the key interest rate) or a market phenomenon, and the two often remain linked. This action, or this movement, results in, from a given significant decline in the immediate interest rate, an "attack", as it were, on the stock of memory. A negative relative real interest rate means that the memory rate (the stock of memory, therefore) is higher than the market interest rate. This can be interpreted, as is most often the case, as meaning that the market rate is low, very low, and has been reduced. This is correct and such an interpretation via the immediate market interest rate underscores the stimulating character of the real rate. However, if we consider the other term that makes up the real rate in the way we have outlined, a low or negative relative real interest rate, also, entails a quite substantial stock of memory, which is being eroded (forgetfulness rate). This erosion is the purpose of the decline in immediate interest rate aimed at by the economic policy action. In the transmission link that ranges from the decline in the real interest rate to the stimulation of the economy, there is definitely the idea that any trough in activity consists in the accumulation of a negative stock of memory that must be reduced (increase in the forgetfulness rate or recall of the positive memory fact). This is what the reduction in the real rate expresses.

When the relative real interest rate is negative and increases, or $ir_{(r)} = ir_{(i)} - ir_{(m/F)}$, we can have, as we have just seen, a movement initiated by the cut (economic policy action) in the immediate interest rate in a situation where the memory interest rate encompasses a negative memory with respect to activity. This is the case of a stimulus package in a rather troubled situation with respect to activity. On could also imagine the case of a stimulus package that activity, as it is quite robust, does not justify, but which is nonetheless implemented: the memory interest rate is rather high, the immediate interest rate has been lowered, and accordingly there is a decline in the real rate. In this scenario, the situation may prevail where, although the immediate interest rate does not fall $\left(i_r(i) = cte\right)$, the real interest rate drops and therefore activity is stimulated, and we could characterize it as a sort of self-stimulation. This situation is interesting since it enables us to understand why cyclical trends are self-fulfilling. The fact that positive memory effects are built up, until only positive effects are kept (purity of memory), leads to, *ceteris paribus*, a decline in the relative real interest rate. This situation can be analyzed in the case of a negative effect that is quite persistent since, then, the memory interest rate defined, as we have done, from activity drops: all other things being equal and without any movement in the immediate interest rate, the relative real interest rate rises. This also has a self-validating consequence, i.e. it boosts economic and financial activity to a slightly greater extent and extends the cyclical trend until it reaches its inflexion point.

When the relative real interest rate is positive and rising, this can result from an economic policy action consisting in steering, with or without backing from the market, an increase in the immediate interest rate. By increasing above the memory interest rate, the market interest rate, in the most usual interpretation, exerts negative pressure on activity. This is the conventional configuration of a situation of overheating once the memory rate is high: by raising, at the end of a positive cyclical trend, the immediate rate above the memory rate, a central bank steers cyclical reversal. Nonetheless, such a configuration is finally one case among many others. First of all, the increase in the relative real interest rate does not signal a determination to cool down activity: a positive and rising real interest rate also points to a memory (stock) that, *ceteris paribus* (i.e. without any change in the immediate interest rate), automatically tighten screws on activity. In other words, the erasure of positive memory effects, all other being equal, drives the real interest rate upward. A positive real interest rate therefore either reflects an economic policy action that raises the immediate interest rate, or reflects the fading of positive memories of activity (decline in the memory interest rate) – or to reword the foregoing – the decline in the rate at which positive phases are forgotten or the increase in the rate at which negative phases are remembered.

We can sum up the situations of $i_{r_{(r)}}$ from those of $i_r(i)$ and of $i_r(m/F)$. The relative real interest rate can find itself in the territory of positive or negative values (in fact neutral or positive; neutral or negative). These positive or negative values can be reached by $i_r(im)$ or $i_r(m/F)$ by making the hypothesis, which is admittedly impoverishing, albeit useful in terms of sketching out a simplified vision of situations, that when the immediate interest rate or the memory interest rate changes, the other variable does not change. The movement in the real rate is thus obtained by the movement in one of the two forms of interest rates. We end up with four situations:

$i_{r_{(r)}}$	(+)	(−)
$i_r(im)$	↗	↘
$ir\,(m/F)$	↘	↗

The four situations can match four moments in the unfolding of the cycle. In the downward leg of the cycle, initially the accumulation of negative memory, through the rise in the memory interest rate, leads to a decline in the relative real interest rate. Subsequently, the immediate interest rate decreases, once the depression or the low cyclical level is established, as this decline can be triggered by the central bank. In the trough of the cycle, the real interest rate moves into negative territory because memory effects (or, at least, the memory of activity) outweigh at a given moment the level of the immediate interest rate. At the starting point of the trough of the cycle, the real rate is probably positive; in fact it will become increasingly positive as the memorized value of activity weakens (memory interest rate), for an unchanged immediate market rate. Then the immediate interest rate can begin to decline, as economic policy action lowers the immediate rate below the level of the memory rate. At that point in the cycle, there is both erosion of the memorized value of problems (forgetfulness rate) and memory recalls (expectation) better days. This dilatation of positive memory (or the increased extent to which negative memory is forgotten) drives the real interest rate into even more negative territory. These three phases structure the trough of the cycle.

At the top of the cycle, symmetrically, the real interest rate is negative to start off, in all likelihood, and will become increasingly negative as the memorized value of activity increases (memory interest rate), for an unchanged immediate market interest rate. We also see a similar self-perpetuating mechanism in the description of the trough of the cycle. Then the immediate interest rate can begin to rise, as economic policy action is aimed at lifting it above the memory rate. At that point in the cycle, the erosion of positive memory and the recalling in memory (expectations) of tougher days lead to a dilatation of negative memory (or an increase in the extent to which positive aspects are forgotten) that drives the real interest rate into even more positive zones. These three phases structure the top of the cycle.

Characterizing the memory interest rate is not a very easy task. The immediate interest rate faces only two types of situation, apart from stability which we do not consider here as a situation in its own right: i.e. a decline or a rise. For the memory interest rate, matters are slightly more complex because, as we have said earlier, the relative real interest rate can be positive via a decline in the memory interest rate (decrease in the memorized value of activity); we have $i_r(r) = i_{r(in)} - i_r(m/F)$. The relative real rate can be negative because of an increase in the memorized value of activity. These situations correspond to the phases that structure the cycle presented above. However, when one considers matters more closely, we can see other situations come into view that deserve to be introduced into our approach and studied.

$i_{r(r)}$	(+)	(−)
$ir(im)$	↗	↘
$ir\,(m/F)^1$	↘	↗
$ir\,(m/F)^2$	↗	↘

We are highlighting the case in which the relative real interest rate is negative, *ceteris paribus* (i.e. stable immediate rate), first because there is an increase in the memorized value of activity (memory interest rate driven upward since all that is left in memory consists in increases of activity, characteristic of the top of the cycle). The real rate becomes negative at the top of the cycle, and this is one of the characteristic features of the top of the cycle. This phase in which the relative real interest rate declines at the top of the cycle, precedes the three phases that structure the trough of the cycle: the real rate is positive and rising because of the contraction in the memorized value of activity; the immediate rate drops; the value of activity is recalled by memory, and the negative values of the real rate are accentuated. We therefore now have four phases, which we also find in the description of the top of the cycle.

A significant point is certainly that a real rate can be negative because of positive memory effects; conversely a real rate can be positive because of negative memory effects. The dilatation and contraction of temporal referentials are crucial phenomena.

In the above developments, the memory interest rate has been considered as the memorized value of a past of activity, or an average value. This therefore means that the past average value shows the direction of the stock of memory. However, it does not tell us whether memory, of positive or negative facts, is more or less strong, or more or less affected by forgetfulness. Likewise, this approach does not really deal with forgetfulness, i.e. the rate of change in the average value of such or such a variable. We have seen above that the paths to be followed for researching new expressions of the memory interest rate have been found.

§ 46.   We therefore have the immediate interest rate, which fluctuates around the relative real interest rate within the given economic and financial regime (and that explains why there is relativity), and is a composition of the relative real rate and of the memory interest rate. The distortions of the relative real rate make the cycle, accounting for the noteworthy significance of movements in the immediate and memory interest rates. We still have to deal with the absolute real interest rate, but we shall tackle it more in depth later. It is the reference point of the absolute economic regime, i.e. the regime that does not integrate time.

The immediate interest rate is positioned, like a planet with respect to a sun, in relation to the relative real interest rate, and the relative real rate, for its part, is positioned in relation to the absolute real interest rate. We have seen that:

$$i_{r(n)} = i_{r(r)} + i_r(m/F)$$

$$i_{r(r)R} = i_{r(im)} - i_r(m/F)$$

If the relative real interest rate is defined by the existence of a temporal referential that deforms itself or can be deformed (contraction/dilatation of time) – as this referential is internal, the Subject's consciousness, or is defined by a temporality that is, if it were, external – then, if one is effectively in such a configuration, the absolute real interest rate is defined by the lack of such a referential. This rationale can be extended and it can be argued that not only are the safety and forgetfulness functions neutralized, but they are in fact eliminated, and $i_{r(r)_A} = i_r(im)$. From the outset, the limits of such a line of thought can be seen, as it ends up by defining the absolute by the immediate. That is something worth meditating upon because, finally, this is one of the characteristics of modernity, in other words thinking of time both as an immanent and transcendent immediacy, a congealed presence that is simultaneously thought of as extended.

However, while one cannot but observe this modern characteristic, one will instead consider, in the absolute referential, that the relative real interest rate fluctuates around the absolute real rate and the latter is defined by starting from memory in the sense of duration, a radically different conception of time from that of immediacy. Here we will rather draw on a conception where time is a mode of placing in the presence of what is. We therefore have:

$$i_{r(r)_A} = \left(i_{r(r)R}\right)_{m/F} \cong f\left(i_{r(m/F)}\right)$$

We accordingly renew here with a conception of the absolute real interest rate in which time is not expelled or absent but, quite on the contrary, there is an intimate link between what is (value, the equilibrium, etc.) and time understood as duration, memory. This standpoint contrasts with the one propounded by economic modernity, for which time becomes the immediate dimension of what appears.

The foregoing therefore means that the relative real interest rate provides a reference point for the referential of the relative equilibrium regime, while this relative equilibrium regime itself is in movement, as it were, around an absolute equilibrium regime from which, apparently, time has disappeared, but which in fact results from a highly dense temporality of memory and of duration – so dense that, at a certain point of memory condensation, a form of fixed point is reached. The existence of this inertia of the fixed point determines the absolute nature of the regime. The absolute real interest rate no longer has any reference other than in duration and memory. In this respect, it pulls away from the immediate but, at the same time, it keeps a link with the Subject's temporal referential if the referential is that of an internal temporality, and with the external temporal referential if the temporality comes to the Subject. In both cases, what is absolute is what, permeated of memory and duration, takes the consistency of matter.

This approach enables us to maintain time in the definition of what is absolute, and to give the relative equilibrium regime (our reality) the possibility of anchoring itself, and basing itself, within an absolute regime in which there is a degree of continuity of reality and temporality.

§ 47. Our reality is dominated by the immediate interest rate, because it alone can be observed, but this is not the only reason. We have:

(1) $i_r(n) = i_r(im)$

(2) $i_{r(r)_R} = i_r(im) - \left(i_r(m/F)^1, i_r(m/F)^2\right)$

(3) $ir(r)_A = \left(ir(r)_R\right)_{m/F}$

We therefore have three layers or three strata of reality, matched by three concepts of interest rates: immediate, relative real, and absolute real. The last two concepts integrate the crucial role of the memory interest rate. This memory interest rate has at its disposal an extremely wide field of application because no real variable, no financial variable, can remain beyond its reach. In particular, the memory and forgetfulness functions of financial markets are found in $i_r(m/F)$, as is likely the key for understanding said markets.

§ 48. Interest is tightly linked to time, and this process relates it to duration and memory. Furthermore, there is a deep analogy between the monetary fact and the memory fact, between memory and money, given the extent to which both share the characteristics of a non-linear referential of contraction and of expansion. This analogy, which makes it possible to understand the monetary origins of the interest rate, has other fields of application, notably those consisting in financial asset prices. It is because financial asset prices, which play a specific role in contemporary market economies, are themselves determined by powerful memory and forgetfulness effects, and by money on the other hand (but the two phenomena are linked), that financial asset prices are at the heart of the equations of contemporary reality, for instance changes in inflation or the appearance of new equilibria and disequilibria. Lastly, all the variables are global. Here we have the key words of an applied theoretical approach.

§ 49. The global interest rate exerts a balancing force on all markets of goods, services and securities. This means especially that the link maintained by the interest rate with the savings and investment functions includes a relationship with the equilibrium and the disequilibrium in the securities markets. This global approach of the interest rate enables us to understand how the equilibrium reached in the goods and services market can include a disequilibrium in the securities market, and therefore how there can be underemployment equilibria related to disequilibria in the financial markets. The memory interest rate, an intrinsic part of the composition of the immediate interest rate, either relative real or absolute real, is the rate that incorporates the temporal function (memory, forgetfulness) in the goods and services markets as well as in markets of financial assets. There is a memory interest rate that establishes an equilibrium in both kinds of market, and consequently an immediate and real interest rate.

$$I_{r(m/F)} = f\left(I_{r(m/F)}\right)_{gs}, \ I_{r(m/F)_{fa}}$$

with gs = goods and services and fa = financial assets.

The interest rate is said to be global in the sense that it includes all markets and defines for these markets an equilibrium via the memory and forgetfulness function. Thus, at every moment of the cycle, there is one, and only one, memory interest rate that makes it possible to put in equivalence savings, real investment and demand for securities functions. The (nominal) immediate interest rate, the only observable variable, encompasses this phenomenon, and it is in fact possible to influence its formation.

Indeed, one of the thorniest issues is the endeavor to ascertain to what extent economic policy action, and particularly monetary policy, can and must seek to modify the "natural" memory and forgetfulness functions. For there is, as it were, an absolute sort of memory and of forgetfulness function (and an absolute rate). It would be witnessed as long as no distorting action operated. This natural memory rate is not the one we have used in our definition of the relative and absolute real interest rates, which *de facto* incorporate economic policy action as an element of the formation of the temporal referential. However, one can bear in mind, and this is undoubtedly pertinent, the existence of a natural memory interest rate that ensures an absolute equilibrium for a pure memory function, i.e. unaffected by any economic policy action.

We therefore have defined a natural memory function and therefore a forgetfulness function, which enables us to considerer the idea of a natural interest rate, or $I_{r(n_a)}$. Everything that, at any time, has not been affected by economic policy action is deemed natural. The natural rate of memory accumulation, the rate of erosion and forgetfulness, are by consequence two natural concepts because such rhythms of accumulation and erosion exist. We have positioned the two phenomena of memory and forget-fulness at the core of our approach, drawing on the simple idea that there is a fundamental analogy between the dimensions of stocks and of flows observed for most economic and financial variables and, on the other hand, the dimensions of stocks and of flows that memory (stocks) and forgetfulness (dynamics of flows) include. The fundamental dynamics witnessed in the economy and in financial markets is fuelled by rationales of stocks and of flows. With respect to these rationales, frequently, the price is the component that leads to a certain stock, at a certain price, no longer being wanted (is the price such that I may want to change my stocks?). The dynamics according to which stocks are modified, steered by prices as we have said, displays a striking analogy with the dynamics of memory erosion (forgetfulness). Actually, what may often appear to be primarily phenomena of flows, in fact corresponds to a differential of stock, to a distortion (contraction/dilatation of a referential that we also find in temporal phenomena of memory) of the stock.

If we look back at the natural memory interest rate as we have analyzed it (memorization and forgetfulness rate in an economic universe in which no institution acts voluntarily with respect to the formation of the interest rate, a somewhat unrealistic vision that will have to be corrected by re-introducing institutions, including the central bank, into the configuration while neutralizing economic policy action, i.e. by seeking to ascertain what economic policy action does not disrupt economic developments, and, for that reason, is "natural"). If therefore we want to go back to this natural memory interest rate, we have $I_r(m/F)$ and $I_r(m/F)_{na}$, thus two definitions of the memory interest rate or, rather, a memory and forgetfulness function at play in what we have called a relative equilibrium regime (i.e. our reality) that maintains a link with a reference point that is the natural memory and forgetfulness function. The complexity of aforesaid link is easy to fathom.

The foregoing means that the spread between the memory interest rate as defined within a relative equilibrium regime and the natural memory interest rate contains important information, at least about the dynamics of the cycle. If we consider that the natural function accepts "non-disrupting" economic policy action, there is at any time in the relative equilibrium regime a natural memory interest rate (defined in its strong version as what is memorized or forgotten without any economic policy action, and in its moderate version as what is memorized and forgotten in the presence of an economic policy action that does not exert any disrupting effect) and a memory interest rate that is not natural in the sense where it, for its part, is immerged in a reality where the economic policy action is neither absent nor neutral. The extent to which the memory interest rate can diverge from the natural rate (which can, in some respects, evoke a form of neutrality) is undoubtedly a significant component of the comprehension of the processes of the economic and financial dynamics. Moreover, starting from such a line of thought will make it possible to identify soundly the economic policy action approaches aimed at modifying the natural trajectory of memory and of forgetfulness and, by consequence, influencing economic and financial developments. For, and this is a crucial point, identifying a natural memory interest rate that corresponds to a form of neutrality non-disruptive of economic policy action does not entail that one must always and in any circumstance act to inflect natural trajectories. As we have already pointed out, one of the guidelines of economic policy action that has not been considered sufficiently so far is the modification (contraction/dilatation) of memory and forgetfulness functions. To do so, one needs to understand and measure the spread that can prevail at any time between the immediate rate and the memory rate, as well as between the memory rate and the natural memory rate on the other hand.

§ 50.   When the memory or forgetfulness rate significantly differs from the natural memory or forgetfulness rate, such a situation reflects the impact of economic policy action. Thus, in either direction, there can be contraction or dilatation of the temporal referential defined by memory and forgetfulness. In the case of an economic policy action implemented in a depressionary context, the objective will be to reduce, decelerate, the "negative" memory rate and symmetrically accelerate forgetfulness, in comparison with a "normal" pace of erosion of the stock of memory. Economic policy action will, always, try to play on the contraction or the dilatation of the unit of time in the temporal referential of memory and of forgetfulness. Forgetting faster what is painful, recalling on the contrary pleasant and rewarding past experiences: these are its objectives.

As a result, we can see that there is a link between the (nominal) immediate interest rate, which is at least partly determined by economic policy action (including the central bank), the memory interest rate and the natural memory rate. The action exerted on the immediate interest rate moves the cursor between the memory rate and the natural memory rate. We have:

$$I_r(im) = I_{r(r)_R} + I_r\left(m/F, m/F_{n_a}\right)$$

hence:
$$I_{r(r)_R} = I_r(im) - I_r\left(m/F, m/F_{n_a}\right)$$

We are faced once more with the various forms of interplay of hypotheses mentioned above, where moves in the relative real interest rate are achieved by moving the immediate interest rate and/or memory interest rate. In these various forms of interplay of hypotheses, the immediate interest rate and the memory interest rate would be alternatively put on hold. If we now get them to move simultaneously in relation to one another, we can see that the immediate rate exerts influence on the memory rate via the natural memory rate.

Thus, an action exerted on the immediate interest rate moves the memory and forgetfulness rate in relation to the natural memory and forgetfulness rate. A cut in the immediate rate at the top of the cycle will tend, *ceteris paribus*, to concentrate memory effects on the most recent past (decline in the long-term forgetfulness rate), as experience shows there is a propensity to store in memory only items that were felt to be positive in the upward leg of the cycle, and therefore expect exclusively an indefinite extension of such positive developments. This means that the relative real interest rate declines either via a drop in the immediate rate or via an increase in the memorized value, assuming that one, and only one, item is made to vary. However, in a more open equation, the decline in the immediate interest rate lifts the memorized value above the natural memorized value, i.e.

the one characterized by a "natural" depreciation/erosion rate for a non-disruptive economic policy action. The fall in the immediate interest rate increases the preference for the present and forgetfulness.

Likewise, the rise in the immediate interest rate at the top of the cycle drives the memorized value below the natural value (reduction in the forgetfulness rate, dilatation of memory), with therefore an increase in the memory rate. All in all, the relative interest rate rises.

The immediate interest rate exerts influence on the forgetfulness rate, on the memorized value (an increase or a decrease). We start off again from the idea that there is, as it were, a stock of memory, i.e. a memorized value that in a way has the status of matter. This memorized value undergoes a linear, or more likely a non-linear, erosion (discontinuity of time, contraction/dilatation, temporal accelerations/stretching). This erosion of the stock of memory-matter is forgetfulness. The forgetfulness rate is, in a fashion, a differential of memory, a flow, and constitutes the phenomenon of interest as defined by Allais. In this sense, the interest rate and the forgetfulness rate are one and the same and it can be considered that the interest (forgetfulness) rate is the price at which economic agents will decide to modify their stock of memory-matter. In this respect, whereas most economic and financial phenomena take the appearance of flows, and are observed, commented upon and analyzed as such, in fact what seems to be flows corresponds to the shifting of a stock of memory for a given price (the interest rate, the forgetfulness rate).

In the approach we have adopted, there is no strict analogy between the interest and forgetfulness phenomena, but rather between interest and memorized value, as this stock is affected by a depreciation (forgetfulness) or recall/revival coefficient, because it is a living stock. The interest phenomenon is an updating/depreciation of a stock of memory-matter: by consequence, forgetfulness is a possible interpretation of the interest rate. However, there is also an analogy between the interest rate and the memorized rate of increase of the value (which includes a depreciation or, on the contrary, revival phenomena), as the value potentially corresponds to a series of real and/or financial variables. This is what we have called the memory interest rate $I_r(m/F)$, with:

$$I_r(m/F) = r(V_m)$$

with r standing for the growth rate applied to V_m = stock of memory-matter. (r) corresponds to a form of historical average growth rate. (r) primarily represents what is remembered, what is literally stored in memory. (r) incorporates a certain forgetfulness or memory recall rate.

$$(r) = r_{m/F}(V)$$

By now coming back to the influence the immediate interest rate exerts on the memorized value, we can see that the reduction in the discounting rate of the future value (cut in the immediate interest rate) corresponds, all other things being equal, to an increase in the forgetfulness function or, at least, to a new discounting price given to the stock of memory value that is used as a reference for expectations in an approach where, essentially, one expects just like one remembers. We are trying to establish the link between the decline in the immediate interest rate and the price of the memorized value (what we have called the memory interest rate), with this price being estimated in relation to the natural memory rate. The reduction in the immediate interest rate, *ceteris paribus*, entails a reduction in the memory interest rate (memorized value) in relation to the natural memory interest rate, i.e. in relation to the neutral or normal rate (insofar as this term can be defined). The recollection undergoes a form of erosion (depreciation of the stock of memorized value), and this can be considered an increase in forgetfulness. Here one is playing on the "price" of the stock of memorized value. Conversely, when the immediate interest rate rises anew, there is an increase in the memorized value in relation to the natural memory rate.

Whether we are dealing with the analogy between interest and forgetfulness or, as we have suggested, with the analogy between interest and memorized value, it is obvious that explaining the erosion of this value (i.e. forgetfulness) remains a deficient approach. This is because it does not give their rightful credit to discontinuous memory retrieval/recall phenomena ("remembering"). However, the issue plays itself out there, in the temporal referential, between forgetfulness and memory recall.

§ 51.   It is true that, traditionally, there are two concepts of interest rates. One is visible (the monetary rate) and the other invisible (the natural rate). The dynamics of either in relation to the other plays an important role in the cycle's fluctuations. We have shown that this dynamics was based on the distortions of the temporal referential (either internal, i.e. the Subject's, or external when we adopt a broader definition of temporality) and moves in the visible rate (the monetary rate) could not be understood without taking into account those of the memory interest rate, which itself can be likened to the natural memory interest rate. By moving, the immediate interest rate sets in motion the "memory interest rate/natural memory interest rate" pair.

The ways in which this pair moves are to be assessed in relation with what we have called restricted relative, relative and absolute equilibrium regimes. When the memory interest rate falls below a level deemed natural, this expresses and materializes the phenomenon of forgetfulness, as this natural level has itself of a more or less stable form (hence the concepts of restricted relative, relative and absolute equilibrium). In economic tradition, when the monetary rate falls below the natural rate, this shifts, through money and credit (upward), the equilibrium between savings and investment, in favor of investment and to the detriment of savings. The opposite is true when the monetary interest rate rises. By taking into account the temporal referential of memory and of forgetfulness, and also by making a reference to tradition, it can be said that the natural memory interest rate incorporates and/or reflects both the memorized value of a "global economic function", i.e. a set of real and financial elements and variables that are part of the composition and the definition of an economic and financial regime and, for this is symmetrical, an expected future value since there is a fundamental analogy between the way one expects and the way one remembers. The natural memory interest rate is therefore, in the first instance, what comes from the past through memory, affected by a forgetfulness coefficient, as well as, thus, what is expected from what is going to happen.

The natural character of this memory interest function stems from the hypothesis of (restricted relative, relative, absolute) stability of the forgetfulness (or memory recall) coefficient. The reason why, and this is a crucial point, the instability and/or the distortions of memory and forgetfulness coefficients are what causes so-called "disequilibria, as prices (and, above all, inflation expectations) provide an important conduit between the temporal referential and the financial and real spheres. The relationships between unemployment and inflation cannot be understood without taking into account memory and forgetfulness functions for the two variables, and not just inflation. This is because there is a memorized value of unemployment that is more or less eroded, and this value permanently interacts with the memorized inflation function. Inflation expectations enable us to understand in what way, eventually, the curve of the inflation/unemployment relationship is flat and why a form of neutrality prevails. However, there is also a memorized value of activity and of unemployment that happens to be distinct from the instantaneous, immediate, value. The conventionally described effects can occur only insofar as the change in the immediate (i.e. "visible") unemployment rate has an impact on the memory unemployment rate, triggering either forgetfulness or memory recall. Let us take the example of a decline in the immediate unemployment rate that would not have any impact on the memory unemployment rate (for a high, i.e. negative, memorized value, assuming therefore a situation following a period of depression), and furthermore would not spark any memory revival or recall effect (in other words, would not dredge up the memory of a more remote period of low unemployment triggered by suddenly low values of the immediate unemployment rate). In such a configuration, inflation expectations and inflation itself would not be stimulated.

Therefore, there are declining unemployment rates (or low ones, and this is not the same thing) that are not linked with inflation in the sense where, whether increased or not by expectations, this relationship can have been described. Said relationship prevails only in proportion to the capacity of inflation rates and of immediate unemployment to modify the memorized values of activity (of unemployment) and of inflation.

We therefore have the fact that inflation, as it were, is a function of unemployment, in its immediate component of course but, above all, in its memorized component and, to an even greater extent, in the capacity of unemployment of modifying the stable memorized value (the one that plays a role in defining a restricted relative or relative equilibrium). We also have the fact that unemployment is a function of inflation in its immediate and memorized components with the same importance granted to the relative distortions of immediate and memorized variables (or their ratio).

We have:

$$Unp(im) = f\left(inf_{im}, inf_{m/F}\right)$$

$$\Leftrightarrow Unp(im) = \left(inf_{im} / inf_{m/F}\right)$$

and
$$Inf(im) = f\left(Unp_{im}, Unp_{m/F}\right)$$

$$\Leftrightarrow Inf(im) = \left(Unp_{im} / Unp_{m/F}\right)$$

Accordingly, it is clear that a real relationship between unemployment and inflation exists only insofar as instantaneous (immediate) changes in inflation and/or in unemployment are able to modify the memorized values of inflation and/or unemployment. There are therefore zones where an immediate movement in unemployment (in inflation) has no impact on (is not at all related to) immediate inflation (unemployment). Behind the apparent movement in immediate inflation and unemployment data, thus the absolute and relative operation of memorized inflation and unemployment values pulls the strings. The foregoing could be reworded by saying that an immediate movement in unemployment or in inflation will be all the more meaningful, and will in particular last all the longer, in either direction, the more it will have so to say stimulated, prodded, set in motion the memorized values likely to consolidate it. We will come back to the relationships between unemployment and inflation later. One has to keep in mind the idea that, looking beyond the cases of inflation and unemployment, the immediate data of the economy and of finance play out a game of appearances, underpinned by the relationship that the immediate data of the economy and of finance maintain with the more stable values of memory (and of forgetfulness). It therefore seems that there is a quite strong relationship heading from immediate data toward memorized values although the existence of a form of retroaction of memory toward the immediate cannot be denied.

When we now return to the concept of a natural memory interest rate, we can see that it will apply to a set, i.e. an aggregating function, for a certain number of economic and financial variables of activity and of prices. This set exceeds the definition given by economic tradition of marginal profitability of capital, or even the net productivity of capital, i.e. the investor hopes for the profitability of the investment. This hope, which is an expectation, puts the approach under the influence of the formation of expectations and of time, therefore in our viewpoint, under the crosscutting influences of memory and of forgetfulness.

The natural memory interest rate is equal to the memorized value of growth and of output, affected by a forgetfulness coefficient, as this memorized value and this forgetfulness coefficient are characterized by a degree of stability to define a restricted relative, relative or absolute equilibrium regime. In addition to the memorized value of growth and of output (affected by a forgetfulness coefficient), there is a risk premium that reflects uncertainty. This is an initial approach, undoubtedly the most macroscopic. We have:

$$I_{r_{(m/F_{n_a})}} = G \cdot p_{m/F} + Rp$$

where G = growth

p = price

and Rp = risk premium.

By following the path of the profitability of the investment hoped for by the investor, i.e. the net productivity of capital, we will seek to substitute for the macroscopic proxy $(G \cdot p_{m/F})$ an expectation (and therefore a memorized function) of profitability. If the latter is to be more complete, it must incorporate the two dimensions that the real and financial spheres represent. The point we are making is that after a first level deemed macroscopic (i.e. the growth function, $G \cdot p_{m/F}$), a second level appears, in which the broadest macroeconomic growth function is reduced to a function of expectation of real and financial profitability, before going toward more fine, in a fashion, levels, the refinement of the function of expectation of profitability (net productivity) can be carried quite far.

The natural memory interest rate will therefore, in our second approach, be defined as the memorized value of the profitability hoped for by the investor from a real and financial investment. We have:

$$I_r\left(m/F_{na}\right) = f\left(R_{inv}, F_{inv}\right)_{m/F}$$

More precisely, this expected profitability will be of a level close to a memory of the investment's profitability in the past, affected by a certain forgetfulness coefficient. It will be considered, in such an approach, that the natural memory interest rate is a composition of the average (more or less equiweighted) profitability rate of the physical investment and of the average (more or less equiweighted) profitability rate of the investment in the main financial asset classes. We have:

$$I_r\left(m/F_{n_a}\right) = f\left(i_r(R_{inv})_{m/F}, i_r(F_{inv})_{m/F}\right)$$

Thus, we are arguing that in the financial market (we are referring to all the pertinent asset classes), the immediate (monetary, instantaneous) interest rate, while pertinent in terms of steering choices, tradeoffs and decisions, must be compared with the memory interest rate specific to this market because the relative behavior of the immediate and memory interest rates is what determines the dynamics of the formation of profitability and of prices in this market. The point holds not only for the financial market but also for the market of real productive investment. As these markets themselves can be segmented and sub-divided *ad infinitum*, the natural memory interest rate covers a general tree structure of natural rates specific to each market. The point to be held in mind is that a natural memory interest rate is expressed in each market and that the confrontation of this rate with the immediate interest rate is the driving force of the dynamics.

Therefore, the price of a financial asset, for instance a share price equities in the securities, maintains a strong link with the immediate interest rate (the strong relationships existing between prices of equities and of bonds are well known). However, the price of the financial asset maintains the strongest causality or explanation link with the relative distortion of the memory and immediate interest rates. The price of the financial asset is determined by the impact of the movement in the immediate interest rate on the natural memory interest rate. The latter encompasses a stock market profitability regime (in the case of the stock market), as the natural rate is established within the framework of a given regime (ranging from the most general macrofinancial regime to the profitability regime specific to each market or segment of this market) and by expressing the equilibrium or an equilibrium. The equilibrium is not static, as its dynamics within the regime results from the coefficient of erosion of forgetfulness that is supposed to be stable in the regime. Note that a disequilibrium, a crisis, in the regime can be precisely defined as a significant change in the forms of forgetfulness and therefore as stability in the modalities of forgetfulness.

We therefore have: $Eq(p) = f\left(I_{r(im)}, I_{r(m/F)_{eq}}\right)$

The immediate interest rate, visible and general (theoretically it concerns all markets), here intersects a natural memory interest rate in every market or market segment. In the stock market, the real game is played by three parties: the market price, the immediate interest rate and the memory rate. In a growth and inflation regime, the relationship between the immediate rate and share prices is significantly negative; in a growth regime without inflation or volatility of inflation, the relationship weakens; it becomes strong and positive again in a deflation regime. Ultimately, the intensity and the nature of the relationship between the immediate interest rate and stock market prices depend on the more or less strong stimulation or activation of the memory and forgetfulness function of the expected (i.e. memorized) profitability of the asset class, in a given macro-financial regime – growth and inflation, growth without inflation, deflation – operating via the natural memory rate. Note, by the way, that the immediate interest rate is, therefore, itself at least a partial function of the natural memory interest rate, which partly determines it.

The foregoing enables us to better understand why the stock market the most often maintains a relationship with the nominal interest rate and not with the real rate (so-called nominal illusion). One of the main reasons is simply the fact that the most commonly chosen nominal real interest rate does not include any memory and forgetfulness effect and is restricted to just instantaneous inflation. Furthermore, it is known that $i_r(im) = i_r(m/F) + \alpha$, with α having the value of the risk premium whatever its definition. The memory interest rate is definitely more pertinent than a mere real instantaneous rate, first because it incorporates memory and forgetfulness, and second because it encompasses the memory, i.e. the expectation, of the profitability hoped for by the investor. The immediate interest rate is equal to the hoped for (past) profitability rate of the investment to which a risk premium is added. This premium, as we saw above, can correspond to the distortions of memory-matter (mt) and of time-density (dt), or mt/dt. We define in the financial sphere of equities

$i_r(m/F)$, i.e. the memory interest rate, by the memorized value of the profitability of equities. Its forgetfulness coefficient is unstable, and this explains why the value of the memory interest rate fluctuates around a "natural" value that defines the equilibrium within a regime (concept of natural memory interest rate).

From $i_r(im) = i_r(m/F)eq + \alpha$, we can see that the risk premium on the stock market can be understood as the spread between the immediate or monetary interest rate and the memory interest rate as memorized (forgotten) value of the hoped for profitability of a stock market investment. We can also see that when the relationship between the immediate (nominal) interest rate and share prices is strong, this means that we are in a period where the stock market is primarily steered or determined by the memory of stock market profitability as the expectation of future profitability. There is even a situation where the risk premium is zero, meaning that the immediate rate is equal to the memory interest rate.

Since $\alpha = i_r(im) - i_r(m/F)eq$, we can consider situations in which the immediate interest rate can end up under (above) the memory interest rate. In the first situation, where the monetary interest rate is lower than the memorized value of (expected) stock market profitability, α takes a negative value, with erosion of time-matter (memory) and, symmetrically, an increase in the forgetfulness rate $\left(mt/dt = \alpha \right)$. The risk premium that α represents in a fashion is in negative territory. These are moments in the stock market where only increases in memory remain (strong preference for the present, high remote forgetfulness rate).

By playing on $i_r(im)$ and $i_r(m/F)eq$, we can obtain different configurations for α. α can take a positive or a negative value. The immediate interest rate is higher than the memory interest rate on the stock market either because there is a rise in the immediate rate, or because there is a decline in the memorized value of profitability (in a "normal" situation, a positive value can be reached by α). α takes a positive value at two extreme points in the cycle: at the bottom of the cycle, only depressed stock market profitability levels remain in memory and in expectations; at the top of the cycle, the rise in the interest monetary rate leads to a cooling down and an inflection point in the cycle once the value of variable α becomes positive. We therefore have the trough of the cycle in which first a depressed value of $i_r(m/F)\,eq$ coincides with a still relatively high immediate interest rate (P_1). Subsequently, the decline in $i_r(im)$ leads to $\alpha < 0$ at a time when $i_r(m/F)\,eq$ is still depressed, even though the instantaneous price of assets starts to rise (P_2). Afterward, the rise in the instantaneous price of assets ends up by driving up $i_r(m/F)\,eq$, which at the top of the cycle rises to a higher level than $i_r(im)$ (P_3). Lastly, the hike in key intervention rates at the top of the cycle restores the positive value positive for α, via the effects resulting from the rise in the immediate rate, then those stemming from the decline in the instantaneous price of the asset, which ends up by driving down $i_r(m/F)\,eq$ (P_4). We therefore have, during the cycle, four configurations. Two of them imply a positive value for α, and two of them a negative value.

§ 52. The various concepts of what is instantaneous (immediate) set themselves apart, by drawing on a different temporal referential paced by memory and forgetfulness effects, from the concepts of what is permanent (natural, normal). This is a fundamental distinction at the very heart of economics, and we have already explored its meaningfulness in previous works. Here we would rather like to look again at the analogy found between the distinction made between the immediate interest rate and the (natural) memory interest rate, and the distinction drawn by economic tradition between instantaneous income, which it claims plays a role in determining the formation of savings, and normal, or permanent, income that it claims determines, for its part, the consumption function.

The permanent stands out from the instantaneous (the normal, the immediate) just like memory made of time-matter and time-density stands out from the pure present (pure in the sense where no lesser memory effect can exist, and this can also be described as an infinite forgetfulness rate). Permanent or normal income corresponds to the memorized value of the pertinent income for an individual and, therefore, to a form of expected value. By this very fact, the concept of permanent income is incorporated into the more general (the most macroscopic one we said above) of the natural memory interest rate, in which

$$I_r\left(m/F_{na}\right) = G \cdot p_{m/F} + R_p,$$

where G is the broadest approximation of activity and of output. There is thus a strong link between permanent income and the memory interest rate, just like between instantaneous income and the immediate interest rate.

As we have seen above when studying the issue of the interest rate, the instantaneous (the immediate) is determined by the memorized (forgotten) but, at the same time, movements in the immediate and in the instantaneous exert a ricochet influence on memorized values. This is true of all economic variables and functions. Accordingly, in principle permanent income is highly unlikely to determine the consumption function on its own. It is more probable that the consumption function is written as the composition of an instantaneous variable and of a variable memorized, a value itself related to a referential in which interact permanent (memorized) income, the memory interest rate, and, most generally speaking, $G_{m/F}$ in the sense of the broadest possible value of memorized and partly forgotten activity.

We have:
$$C_{im} = C_{m/F} + a$$
$$Y_{im} = Y_{m/F} + b$$
$$G_{im} = G_{m/F} + c$$
$$\ldots$$
$$x_{im} = y_{m/F} + z$$

We therefore write in this manner the hypothesis of the existence of a specific temporal referential containing the various dimensions of memorized (and partly forgotten) of all the components of the economic dynamics. These memorized values are linked with one another and with those of another, so-called immediate or instantaneous, referential in a relationship of reciprocal determination.

By consequence, there is no particular reason consumption should be linked to permanent income alone because, in fact, instantaneous (immediate, as we have named what is present) consumption, memorized/expected (normal, permanent, natural) consumption, immediate income and permanent income are linked. Immediate consumption, actually the easiest to gauge via surveys, polls and statistics, even before it finds itself linked to, or determined by, other variables, maintains a particular relation with itself, with the memorized value of itself, which in turn is related to other memorized values (that of income notably). (a), (b) and (c) can take nil values in the equations mentioned above, meaning that forgetfulness rates can lead to immediate values and memorized values converging. Conversely, (a), (b) and (c), insofar as they do not take a nil value, express the intensity of a preference for the present/the immediate or, on the contrary, a preference for memory (the preference for the present, which has been abundantly commented upon, has for its flipside, as it were, a preference for the remote past, as the two preferences are linked and the preference for the present results from the erasure of a memory; likewise, the preference for liquidity, which reflects the preference for the present, in a fashion symmetrically echoes a preference not for illiquidity but for a thicker time-density, a thicker time-matter, a thicker memory, inserted in a longer term dimension; the preference for liquidity $pf_{(liq)}$ is an eroded, debased function of a preference for long time, for memory $Pf_{(m/F)}$. We have, once more:

$$Pf_{(liq)} = Pf_{(m/F)} + x$$

We have, for instance, $C_{im} = C_{m/F} + a$, and this can be interpreted in the following manner: what is immediate (instantaneous, what appears, and makes itself present, observable) in the economic world is always a function of what has been memorized (and partly forgotten) (i.e. permanent, normal) and of a residual, of a spread that is a risk premium. We therefore have:

$$x_{im} = y_{m/F} + z$$

$$\Leftrightarrow z = x_{im} - y_{m/F}$$

When z is nil ($z = 0$), the immediate and memorized values converge (high forgetfulness rate, significant preference for the present/ liquidity, and in all likelihood this is one and the same thing).

CHAPTER 3

THE CYCLE

§ 53.   When it is said that time can have a more or less great value, what is being said? Insofar as time has a value, the temporal referential can deform itself in several ways, from dilating to contracting. Value then becomes what shows the deformation or deformations of temporal matter. Nothing more is being said at this stage than value increases or decreases just like time dilates or contracts. This boils down to saying that value and time are tightly linked, that there is in fact an analogy.

Saying that time can have a more or less great value may lead, as is the case of an influential current of contemporary economic thought, to consider that the greater the value time has, the greater the tendency will be to want to substitute economic goods and services incorporating little time (time-value?) for economic goods and services incorporating a larger temporal component. In fact, the most often in the expression that is given of this trade-off, the idea is found that goods produced with not much time are substituted for goods that need a lot of time to be manufactured. The manner in which the analogy between value and time is expressed is crucial because many interpretations and mis-understandings can stem from it.

This analogy between value and time is expressed in terms of the quantity of time required to make a good.

$$V = f(Q_t)$$

This quantity of time must be specified. If Q_t is defined by drawing on the number of time units, the volume of hours (worked for example), there will definitely be a tradeoff between what consumes a lot of time and what consumes less of it, in as much as time is seen to have an increasing value. In fact, in a fashion, the more or less pronounced value of time is postulated, *ex ante* and, at the same time, $V = f(Q_t)$.

However, this is not satisfactory. We can clearly see that the equivalence between the increase in the value of time and the substitution of goods that do not consume much time for those that consume a lot of it, is a sort of tautology since the rise (or the decline) in the value of time is defined by the quantity of time (or its density). We can deduce from the foregoing that the starting point is definitely the definition of value by time. However, what time? The approach via quantity $V = f(Q_t)$ does not grasp the entire idea of time-matter. The density of time is more interesting than the quantity of time. The density of time gives the idea, looking beyond quantity, of the weight of the time unit and of the heterogeneous character of the temporal referential, which can deform itself by contracting or by dilating. Temporal density is tightly related to memory. When it is said that "time has a greater value" or "time has a lower value", the idea being propounded is that dense time, i.e. the one that expresses a powerful memory (which can manifest itself), in the manufacturing of a good, is present to a greater extent. This memory can simply result from the quantitative accumulation of worked time units (we find quantity Q_t) again; it can also consist in the dense memory of this effort; it can express the lengthy educational or professional investment (which therefore produces a memory effect) that led to the production of such and such a good or service. We have:

$$V = f(m/F) \quad \text{and} \quad m/F = aQ_t$$

The proposition is no longer worded in the same way. The increase in the value of time entails an increase in density in time-matter (memory), regardless of the form or forms taken by said matter. Accordingly, the increase in the value of time, understood as meaning that it is redefined, implies the need to rephrase consequences. There is no substitution of goods that consume little time for goods that require a lot of time to be manufactured, but the opposite. And this goes as far as the need to specify (redefine, broaden) what is meant when saying "using a little (or a lot of) time", quantity (Q_t) and density m/F.

When the word "substitution" is used in this rephrasing, one is referring to something that is a "preference". Preference will head for scarcity defined by m/F, as well as the price. At the same time, goods and services with a low density of time-matter will be widely sold but it is far from certain that they are substitutable. It is definitely more reasonable and realistic to think that most goods newly created and embodying an increasingly less dense time-value (m/f) will be less and less substitutable for that reason, until at the end of the process, a reversal of the time-value regime will occur ($m/F < 1$); there is then a decrease in the value of time.

We therefore have a process that unfolds from a point where time has a high value (m/F where F grows from the unit), with erosion (F) and a changeover to $m < F$ until the value of time sinks to its trough (m/F where m grows from the unit).

Value is granted to time just like one remembers and forgets ($V = \alpha \cdot m/F$), where m and F cannot be neutral. The accumulation of time is not only quantitative (Q_t) since this accumulation is always carried out within the framework of a temporal referential of time-matter distorted by memory and forgetfulness. Q_t must be replaced by $Q_{m/F}$.

§ 54.   The dynamics of the cycle is given by m/F and money (and its quantity) exerts an influence on m/F. In other words, the more or less significant value granted to time (insofar as this wording may be possible, because value is time itself; here we are drawing on the idea that value is perceived by the economic player's consciousness) explains why there are economic fluctuations. There is a form of neutrality, a state of equilibrium in the cycle where m/F *is* stable and reaches an equilibrium value. The two major phases of the cycle are given by the two movements of deformation of m/F. In a broad outline, in all likelihood the phase during which m/F decreases then plummets is the phase of acceleration of the cycle, until the excesses of the top of the cycle. Conversely, the recessive phase is a memory phase. The very dynamics of memory recall is one of the processes of the recession. The very dynamics of the cycle (deformation of m/F) is an alteration/increase of time (or, rather, of the value granted to time). The cycle itself is the process through which gradually what does not grant a high value to time is substituted for what, on the contrary, encompasses a high time-value. The opposite movement (increase in m/F) completes the cycle.

The dynamics of growth and inflation (prices of goods and services; prices of financial assets) adopts quite faithfully the shape of the process of substitution and deformation of m/F that goes hand in hand with it. The upward leg of the growth and inflation cycle, gradually, is marked by forgetfulness; the upward period is characterized by a greater value given to time. The process of substitution of goods, services and assets is steered by the modification of preferences (at the starting point, when the value given to time is at its maximum, there is no substitution, there is a preference for the goods, services and assets that incorporate this time-value). By setting itself in motion, the process of erosion of m/F admittedly entails substitution, but even before the substitution (which disseminates contagion) there is erosion of the absolute time-value of real and financial assets. Substitution gives the dynamics of relative prices that makes the cycle because the deformations of the value given to time are those of relative prices.

Because the value of time is intimately linked to the density of time-matter present in the formation of the main functions (investment, consumption and saving), which in turn is significantly determined by expectations (memory and forgetfulness), the cycle can be described as the non-linear process of unfolding and contracting of this "value of time". This process is as much relative as absolute insofar as it moves the relative values of goods, services and financial assets. The relative price processes are at the heart of the cyclical dynamics. The deformation of the "value of time" expresses a deformation of the economic Subject's preferences in an approach based on the Subject's acting consciousness, in which there can be only value (of time) for a Subject. This deformation of preferences is also a distortion of expectations since they are fed by the value granted to time. We have:

$$\left[f\left(P_{ref}(V_t)\right) = f\left(P_{rel}, It_{exp}, C_{exp}, S_{cxp}, M_o\right)\right]_{m/F}$$

By introducing *Mo* we are seeking to indicate that money (and first as a quantity) plays a role in the process of deformation of the value of time (of preferences) and, beyond, in that of relative prices and of functions of expectations about investment, consumption and savings. The deformation of money (i.e. Q_{M_o}), through the expansion or contraction of the money supply, regardless of the definition, maintains a tight link with the cyclical process described above. It is just as if the "value of time" was a function of money, of its quantity and of its velocity. When the money supply increases and, to an even greater extent, when the rotation of the money stock accelerates, simultaneously the "value of time" erodes and declines. It is just as if the time-matter of a monetary unit, which in the process then buys a growing number of units of goods, services or assets (velocity), decreases in line with the increase in forgetfulness. This description incorporates an approach of inflation as a forgetfulness process linked to the increase in the stock and velocity of money.

We have: $$V_t = f\left(Q_{M_o}, Vel_{M_o}\right)$$

It is just as if the value that is granted to time, i.e. a preference function for a certain state of density of time-matter, was lessened by the increase in monetary units and in their circulation (the relationship is self-perpetuating in the sense where a decline in the value granted to time will facilitate the continuation of monetary expansion). Moments of inflation or, more simply, periods at the top of the economic growth cycle, correspond to an erosion of the monetary unitary value (since there are more monetary units, and money circulates more rapidly). This erosion is related to a preference for time that has changed (less value granted to time).

In this process, tradeoffs and substitutions are set in motion. The process of deformation of relative prices ensconces a process of tradeoffs and substitutions within and between goods, services and financial assets. The decrease in the value granted to time (which is related to the erosion of m/F and the rise of forgetfulness), whether accelerated/triggered or not by management of the monetary stock $\left(Q_{M_o}, Vel_{M_o}\right)$ is crystallized in a preference of the economic Subject. This preference distorts itself (toward the present) ($P_{ref}(v_t)$) and, at a given point, leads to a tradeoff between various goods, services or assets (P_{rel}), as said tradeoff expresses two ideas. First, the scarcity of value will result in a lower number of goods, services and assets (which, by consequence, are going to climb to high prices). But it also means that new goods, services and assets of lesser value (according to the definition we have given of it) will gradually be substituted for this scarcity of value, as this very substitution plays a role in the general erosion of value in this phase of the cycle, i.e. of the value granted to time.

§ 55.   The value granted to time (preference) maintains a tight link with investment, consumption and savings functions.

We have seen that the cycle could be described like a process in which there is forgetfulness, i.e. a progressive decrease in the value granted to time, and this corresponds to the upper leg of the cycle and culminates, at the top of the cycle, in various inflation and demonetization phenomena. The second leg of the cycle, the period of contraction and of recession, corresponds to an upturn/increase in the value granted to time. We can therefore see that the savings function is positively correlated with the value granted to time: savings increases when the value granted to time rises, i.e. when the value granted to (future) money itself increases to the point where it is preferred to consumption. Conversely, in the initial phase of the cycle, there is a gradual substitution of goods, services and assets encompassing a declining value granted to time, for goods, services and assets in which the density of time-value is greater. The tradeoff between consumption and savings is precisely the substitution process based on time-value; there is substitution in the real sphere between goods and services, of the nature of goods or services admittedly, but an increase in the quantity and in the circulation of the monetary stock in the sphere of goods and services (transactions per monetary unit). Here we consider consumption as a phenomenon of substitution of time-value(s) in a process of reduction of time-value.

This process is also, and this is the second aspect of the phenomenon, a substitution process in the financial sphere (of money) with an increase in its quantity and an acceleration in the velocity of circulation of the stock in the financial sphere (in money). In the first phase of the cycle, basic money (the most liquid) is gradually changed for monetary units and financial assets that incorporate increasingly remote and ever more substantial promises on the future. Initially, in a period that consists in the most normal and the healthiest growth cycle, with dissaving (and, symmetrically, the consumption and investment functions resulting from tradeoffs and substitutions), there is definitely an increase in the value granted to time in the sense where there is projection, anticipation, with respect to what results from the very growth process. The process of dilatation, of extension, of the value granted to time (preference for the future) carries on, via the indebtedness and credit cycle (promises to pay at a later date) until the point where it has run its course, so to say, where there is an infinite preference for what is yet to come. It is at this extreme point of infinite preferences for what is going to come that the paradox of the value granted to time reaches its climax because it is at this point where the value granted to time seems to have peaked (with regard to preferences), in the sense of the extension of positive expectations, that the point of inflexion is the closest. As a result of being constantly granted value by preferences, time ends up by losing any value. The paradox of time-value provides an explanation of excessive phases at the top of the cycle, of substantial dissaving, of major tradeoffs in favor of consumption and (over-)investment in the real sphere, of the rising of financial bubbles and the appearance of various expressions of demonetization. The preference for the future, one of the markers of the growth cycle, is a sign of the greater value granted to time, until this future as it were no longer has a price (inflation). Risk peaks in the vicinity of certainty.

The downward leg of the cycle is, in the other direction, a form of refocusing on the value granted to time with a growing preference for the present, saving once more and tradeoffs to the detriment of consumption and investment functions in the real sphere, preference for liquidity and basic monetary units in the financial sphere. There is a gradual substitution of goods, services or assets encompassing a higher value granted to time (the present), for goods, services or assets incorporating promises.

Accordingly, in the two major phases of the cycle, the value granted to time takes two forms: what is forthcoming and the present. Both play positively then negatively (growth followed by inflation; cooling down followed by recessions). In the two phases of the cycle, there is a process of substitution of preferences in the real sphere and in the financial sphere.

§ 56.   We need to look into this substitution process more in depth. We have seen that the value granted to time played an important role in the triggering of the cycle's sequences. The form this value – that is a preference – can take may lead both to a preference for basic money (liquidity) as well as a preference for long-term assets; it can result, in the real sphere, in a substitution of goods, services or assets incorporating a high time-value for poorer goods, services or assets, as well as the reverse. The same value granted to time, in the growth phase, leads to the lengthening of expectations and processes and, in the slowdown phase, leads to expectations and processes shrinking and to economic agents falling back on liquidity or so-called staple goods (and services). In other words, time constitutes a referential that undergoes distortions, dilates or contracts.

When the value granted to time increases, or decreases, a preference (an expectation) expresses itself. This preference must be specified because the word "time" can at the very least refer to various meanings (present, past and future). One possible approach is to consider that the preference expressed in the value granted to time signifies either a preference for the present, or a preference for the future or the past (memory). The regime of preferences in the definition of value corresponds to a temporal referential of significant distortions (present, past/future) because, finally, the value that can be granted to time shapes a deformable horizon. This is the point we have tried to make in our previous developments. At each stage of this deformation, there are substitution and tradeoff effects between (and within) goods, services and financial assets on the basis of the value (as estimated, perceived and preferred) granted to time. All of this forms a relativistic framework within which preferences and choices express themselves.

Accordingly, there would appear to be an approach of the cycle that starts off from the relativity of preferences and the value granted to time. In this relativistic theory, the growth phase would correspond to a dilatation of the temporal referential (lengthening of expectations, risk-taking and projection on what has yet to exist) with a process of substitution of what, in the real or the financial sphere, accounts for this lengthening for goods, by what (services and assets) hardly includes said lengthening. In the monetary sphere, long-term assets are substituted for immediate and short-term monetary units; in the real sphere, goods incorporating a higher density of projection on what is forthcoming are substituted for more immediate consumer or investment goods and services. The process unfolds normally, as it were, until the point where the excessive phase of this initial period of the cycle begins. The excessive phase still has a projection regime but it is combined with gradual forgetfulness and an infinite substitution of the forthcoming for what exists. This phase includes the formation of real and/or financial inflation phenomena, over-investment and/or over-consumption phenomena (over-consumption thus has to be seen as a phenomenon of infinite forgetfulness and just as infinite certainty in the forthcoming), as well as dissaving phenomena.

The second period of the cycle includes a slowdown phase corresponding to a contraction of the temporal referential (the type of temporality that gains in value draws closer to the present or to the memory of what has been, after a period of forget-fulness). It includes a process that substitutes output that carries this contraction in the real sphere or the financial sphere for output that does not incorporate it, or to a smaller extent, or no longer. In the monetary sphere, a substitution process ranging from the nearest to the remotest kicks in with a decline in the appetite for risk. In the real sphere, goods and services that incorporate a more immediate value time (preference) win out over others. The entry into the excessive phase of this period sees memory effects gradually operate like a corrective restoring force: the recession is a process based on souvenirs and memory. This phase includes such phenomena as financial crashes, deflations, under-consumption and/or excess consumption, and resaving.

§ 57.   There is therefore a relative approach of the value granted to time and, accordingly, we can build an explanation of the cycle and its phases. Can we build an absolute approach of this same value granted to time? This remains difficult because what is "granted" is granted by a Subject expressing his/her/its pre-ferences in a certain environment, and the regime of these preferences is not stable and continues to depend on the relative character of perceptions. Building an absolute approach thus supposes either, within the framework of preferences, identifying determinants of this value that are robust and stable enough to cope with the deformations specific to any regime of preferences, or emancipating ourselves from preference itself and moving on from the "value granted to time" to "time-value" itself, a more absolute approach, although ultimately it will have to insert itself and embody itself within a framework of the Subject's choices and preferences.

Having said that, what are the possible approaches? Here we are looking for a definition of time-value and/or a stable determinant of the value granted to time within the framework of a regime of preferences. One such approach, consistent with many of the preceding developments, would consist in postulating that the base of time-value is found in memory (time-matter), therefore in the past, which partly blends with the very idea of a future within the framework of expectations. Time-value would by consequence be all the higher the greater its density of memory; all the lower if forgetfulness were to increase more markedly. In this framework, the cycle could primarily be described as a progressive and non-linear process of forgetfulness, of erosion of time-value, until the appearance of the recession that would herald, on the contrary, the return of memory. Therefore, there would seem to be a framework of a stable description of the unfolding of the cycle. Time-value apparently declines in line with the ascending phase, until the most total forgetfulness to an excessive extent, as the various phenomena of cyclical inflexion and turnaround reintroduce memory.

Time-value therefore becomes a stable point in the description of the cycle. Accordingly, time-value objectively undergoes erosion before being rebuilt at the end of the downward phase of the cycle. The erosion of time-value, in other words forgetfulness, corresponds to a depreciation of the value granted to time. Therefore, here we define the decrease in the value granted to time by forgetfulness and its increase by memory. Thus, there could not be any growth phenomena or growth cycles without forgetfulness, as forgetfulness characterizes above all phenomena of disequilibria, inflation and crashes. Likewise, such phenomena as a cyclical inflexion, cyclical turning points and contractions in the real and financial sphere would thus mainly result from a recall dynamics. There would seem to be an analogy between forgetfulness and expansion, between recall/memory and contraction. Forgetfulness goes hand in hand with a growing preference for what does not yet exist, for goods, services and financial assets that incorporate a greater future value; memory stimulates a preference for what exists immediately. Appetite for risk and risk aversion naturally fit within this framework of interpretation, just like preferences for liquidity. This approach finds its place in a framework of expectations where forgetfulness and memory play the roles main. With Becker or other authors, the increase in the value granted to time triggers a process of substitution of goods incorporating less time-value for others that contain more of it. In the approach we are propounding here, we find by other paths certain comparable conclusions. From an initial point in the cycle where the value granted to time (as it has been defined above) is high, i.e. a point where memory effects are the most powerful (this corresponds in our approach to the trough of the cycle), definitely a gradual dynamics of gradual forgetfulness and projection unfolds and results in increasingly fewer goods, services or assets with a high density of time-value as the cycle progresses. This substitution process here is not a state at any given point of time in the cycle; it is the very dynamics of the cycle. The value granted to time leads to its erosion (forgetfulness), and this is the very way in which the cycle unfolds. We therefore here have a dynamic vision of time-value and substitution processes. Any reconstitution or erosion of time-matter triggers trade-offs and substitutions in an opposite direction in the real sphere and in the financial sphere that ensure a form of return to the equilibrium or at least a cyclical dynamics. We therefore have, in this approach, a situation where a high value granted to time sparks a substitution of what incorporates increasingly less time-value for what holds a lot of it; where a low value granted to time (as it has been defined above) triggers a substitution of what incorporates increasingly more time-value for what contains little of it.

What do we mean when we talk of something incorporating more or less time-value? We are not referring to, or at least not only, quantities of time (of work for instance) but to time-value. We encompass in this term a vaster field of relations with time, perception of time and expectations. Incorporating less time-value, undoubtedly means incorporating less time capital related

to research and innovation (this can correspond to an indus-
trialization phase during which the quantity of time needed for
production declines and, at the same time, the value linked to
innovation, to the initial period of research and development,
shrinks itself). A financial asset incorporating less time value is, in
the same way, a financial asset that, so to say, "sheds memory",
an asset that will increasingly give a higher price to what does not
yet exist (expectations), an asset of pure (and high) expectations
that is substituted for basic monetary units (immediate liquidity).

§ 58.   The prices dynamics moves in line with the process. In the
initial phase of the cycle, which unfolds after the acceleration of
growth until the formation of imbalances (bubbles and inflation),
we have seen that there was a progressive erosion of the value
granted to time, as well as a symmetrical increase in forgetfulness
and effects resulting from the substitution between preferences
(what exists and is immediate versus what is yet to come and does
not yet exist), between goods or assets on the basis of these
preferences. These substitutions of goods, services and assets
produce a rotation and its acceleration in the advanced upward
phase of the cycle results in imbalances and inflation. The
dynamics of substitution between goods, services and assets,
based on deformations of the value granted to time and therefore
preferences, constitute the dynamics of rotation of the stock of
money (real or financial transactions by monetary unit). As a
result, the substitution of long-term financial assets for basic
money, which occurs at the same time as the gradual increase in
forgetfulness in the growing preference for what is yet to be, goes
hand in hand with a rise in financial asset prices. What is true in
the financial sphere also holds in the real sphere. There is a
gradual substitution of goods incorporating a lower time-value for
goods with a greater density. The rotation of goods accelerates
with the unit decrease in time-value or in the value granted to
time, while the number of transactions by monetary unit
accelerates. These phenomena are part of inflation.

Forces operating in the opposite direction play in the second
phase of the cycle. The progressive increase in memory effects

and therefore in the value granted to time produces effects resulting from the substitution of goods, services or financial assets in the opposite direction with a deceleration in rotation rates and in the circulation of the stock of money in the real sphere or the financial sphere. These decelerations produce a slowdown in price increases (disinflation). Deflation can occur at the extreme ends of the development of this phase of the cycle. Deflation can by consequence be analyzed, like the simultaneous recession/ economic depression, as a steep increase in the value granted to time. Substitution effects favorable for goods, services or assets incorporating a high temporal density (present/present-past through memory effects) unfold at the same time as the velocity of substitution markedly slows down, until a virtually frozen situation where nothing seems to move any more. This form of glaciation of substitutions, preferences, circulation rates, frozen on extreme time values where present, future and past seem to align themselves (infinite preference for the present, expectations aligning themselves totally on memory, with the past filling the future), this glaciation is precisely the time of deflation.

Because the cycle is a movement of relative prices, the dynamics of the distortion of prices between and among goods, services and financial assets maintains a close link with the distortions of the value granted to time and, therefore, the trade-offs and substitutions occurring in the real sphere and in the financial sphere as preferences undergo changes. This means that unless we are to draw on the broadest definition of inflation, i.e. including the real sphere and the financial sphere, the inflationary phenomenon, as a deformation of the value granted to time and the resulting substitutions of goods and assets, cannot be completely grasped. It is just as if, from a starting point of the cycle (cyclical trough) where the value granted to time is maximal (and infinite in theory), the gradual decrease in this time-value and the increase in forgetfulness (both understood as a growing preference for what is yet to come in the regime of expectations drawn upon) corresponded to a rise in inflation understood in its broadest sense, which can take the extreme forms of hyperinflation in prices of goods and services in the real sphere, as well as financial bubbles (real estate, credit, equities, etc.), as both phenomena can coexist. Thus, there is a deep correspondence between the inflation phenomenon (more simply and to a larger extent the dynamics of relative and absolute prices) and, on the other hand, the decrease in the value granted to time and forgetfulness. Inflation is one of the manifestations of forgetfulness just like deflation is an extreme manifestation of memory.

§ 59.   This link between the value granted to time and the price dynamics includes money. There is at least a coincidence between the increase in money, the distortion in the value granted to time and the price dynamics, even as the referential of expectations and preferences distorts itself in line with time-value and resulting in trade-offs and substitutions in the real and financial spheres. The quantitative increase of money maintains a final link with inflation only because it sets in motion the deformation (decrease) in the value granted to time and, simultaneously, the distortion of expectations.

$$Inf = f\left(Q_{M_o}, V_{t(m,F)}\right)$$

Inflation is the product of a quantity of money multiplied by its velocity, as the latter is understood as a distortion of preferences in the sectors of goods, services and financial assets, i.e. as a substitution. In this sense, inflation is the product of a quantity of money and effects of substitutions between goods, between services and between financial assets resulting from the increase or the decrease of the value granted to time. This dynamics of substitution and trade-offs is accompanied by (includes in fact) an acceleration or a deceleration in the velocity of circulation of money in the financial and real spheres (as these two spheres are not hermetic but to a greater extent are interlinked and are themselves the subjects of substitutions and tradeoffs). We have:

$$Inf = Q_{M_o} \cdot V_{el}\left(= \frac{M}{FS, FRS}\right) \quad \text{where} \quad FS = \text{financial sphere}$$

$$RS = \text{real sphere}$$

$$\left(= P_{GSA} / P'_{GSA}\right) \quad \text{where} \quad GSA = \text{goods, services, assets}$$

$$P = \text{price}$$

The substitution dynamics is analyzed as the deformation of relative prices in the real and financial spheres. Inflation therefore results from a deformation of the quantity of money that modifies the value granted to time, which deforms preferences and triggers substitutions. The latter modify relative prices (the first level of definition of inflation, an unsatisfactory one but the most usual), and eventually alter the general level of prices. The dynamics of expectations results from the change in the value granted to time. So-called "inflation expectations" are a gradual alteration of the value granted to time in the definition we have made of this value, i.e. by a preference for what is yet to come.

$$Inf = f\left(Q_{M_o}, P_{GSA} / P'_{GSA}, Exp_{\text{inf}}, V_{t_{(m/F)}}\right)$$

Therefore, apparently, there is a link between the quantity of money and the value granted to time. One approach would consist in thinking that the quantity of money influences the value granted to time. An increase in the quantity of money gradually decreases the value granted to time. The link goes from the quantity of money to time-value. A second approach would prefer the idea according to which a modification in the value granted to time is what causes a rise or a decline in the quantity of money to trigger an inflation process. In this case, a distortion of the quantity of money is not necessarily linked with the inflation dynamics. This second approach would enable us to understand certain situations where the supposed link between the quantity of money and the dynamics of prices does not appear or, even better, appears in a surprising and unexpected manner. This approach enhances the quantitativist approach by adding a new item, the value granted to time and, looking beyond this time-value, a referential within which preferences are distorted and tradeoffs and substitutions are carried out. This referential of time-value forms the core grid of expectations.

In this approach, a change in the quantity of money can have an impact in the real sphere or the financial sphere, but, just as well, it may well have none. There is, on the one hand, a given quantity of money, or a stock. On the other hand, there is a certain value granted to time, which is also given. It is in the interaction of the two variables that the dynamics of the cycle of economic activity and prices operates. It is in and through the deformation of the stock of money (modification of quantities) and, simultaneously, in and through the deformation of the value granted to time, that the dynamics of the economic cycle operates. The word "simultaneously" is very ambiguous because explaining what is being played out there at the same time remains difficult. First of all, and this is not the most difficult aspect, the idea that deformation and change play a role. We move from what is given, the stock (quantity of money) or the state (value granted to time), to a differential that is a dynamic projection. Next, there is the question as to whether the deformation of the stock of money results (causality) from the distortion of the value granted to time; if the two deformations occur simultaneously this might leave open the option of interpreting such a fact as a symmetrical form of interaction (while the distortion of the quantity of money can be decided *ex ante,* that of the value granted to time cannot, even though this can represent one of the objectives of economic policy action); if, for a given stock of money, for a given quantity of money (it is therefore a fixed variable), a distortion of the value granted to time is able to trigger the dynamics of the cycle; if, conversely, for a given state of the value granted to time, a distortion of the quantity of money is able to set in motion the cyclical dynamics (the same, or another one); if, for a distortion of the value granted to time and a distortion (whether proportional or not) of the quantity of money, one obtains the same type of movement of the cycle.

§ 60.   In particular, we can look at two particularly interesting cases. These two cases highlight what could be called the principle of relativity applied to the quantitavist theory of money, or the relativistic theory of the quantity of money. At a constant quantity of money there might be effects resulting from the dynamics of the cycle, insofar as preferences and therefore time-value undergo a distortion. Virtually symmetrically, a change in the quantity of money would have an impact on prices or activity only insofar as there would be changes in the referential of time-value. This might be helpful in particular in terms of better understanding why economic policy initiatives fail, or at least are relatively inefficient. For instance, the so-called situation of a "liquidity trap", which can appear at the same time as definite cases of deflation, corresponds to a significant increase in the quantity of money (basic money of the central bank) which fails to stimulate either the real sphere or the financial sphere. At this point of the cycle, the increase in the quantity of money occurs against the backdrop of a substantial increase in the value granted to time as we have defined it (memory). The determination to use the monetary unit for what is not yet and, therefore, get this monetary unit to circulate in the real and financial spheres is noticeably weakened at this point of the cycle. Better, powerful memory effects dominate and, in a fashion, slow down transactions functions to the point where they stall because of an infinite preference for the immediate and the presence of what exists. The increase in the quantity of money can, because of its relentless aggressiveness, eventually produce a shift in preferences (time-value) but, in most cases, a quantitative stimulation of the economy will be inefficient, because the economic policy action will be unable to modify expectations.

Conversely, even though this might seem less intuitive, one could imagine that a contraction (substantial slowdown) in the stock of money could not be accompanied by a cyclical slowdown in activity and prices. Once again, we are dealing with the extreme situations, i.e. the cycle's peak (difficulty of eradicating hyper-inflation phenomena) after the cycle's trough (difficulty of eradicating deflation). In this situation of a cycle, the value granted to time is so low and forgetfulness symmetrically so strong that the decrease, during a while at least, in the stock of money does not have any impact. This type of situation could conceivably prevail, at least temporarily. Hyperinflation or financial bubble phenomena are related to this type of situation where the dynamics of the cycle is so strongly rooted that it seems useless to try and obtain, and even more so swiftly, just a marginal modification in it.

A second category of situations relates, this time, to the more fixed character of the referential of money (a virtually fixed variable). Time-value is the variable that undergoes a shift. This somewhat theoretical outline enables us to identify, in a way that is at the very least stylized, situations of inefficiency or in which developments are the opposite from what was expected. In a context of weak/weakening value granted to time (decrease in memory, forgetfulness and preference for what has yet to come, upward leg of the economic and financial cycle), there may be an impact of this time-value that melts down the stock of money which is not growing (or contracting) noticeably, an impact that accelerates the velocity of circulation of this stock, of sub-stitutions and tradeoffs (goods, services and assets). At a constant stock of money, a decrease in the value granted to time accelerates the velocity of circulation of the stock of money in the real sphere and the financial sphere (from a certain persistence of the effect resulting from time-value). Likewise, at a constant stock of money, an increase in the value granted to time (memory, downward leg of the economic and financial cycle), starting from a certain persistence, would produce an effect of deceleration in substitutions (preferences, relative prices), in activity and prices.

The various somewhat theoretical scenarios mentioned above (fixed quantity of money and variable time-value; fixed time-value and variable quantity of money) can correspond to sequences of the complete economic and financial cycle, at least to moments of said cycle. These sequences exist, to varying degrees, in the complete cycle. In some respects, these interlocking sequences give an interpretation of the cycle and of its dynamics.

The idea of setting the quantity of money and getting time-value to vary, a theoretical simulation, opens the door to interesting issues and applications. Monetary fine-tuning is one of the points of application, i.e. the non-inflationary steering (in particular, more generally, of money supply growth that does not generate any imbalances) of the quantity of money. Once it is admitted that at a given monetary stock (or at constant money supply growth), the dynamics of the cycle, and in particular that of prices, depends on the change in the value granted to time, it is possible to tackle the issue of monetary neutrality via the time-value referential. There is monetary neutrality, i.e. growth in means of payment unlikely to generate imbalances, including inflation, when, for a given growth rate of the money supply, the value granted to time remains stable (its deformation remains stable) as defined in one way or another from the forgetfulness and memory coefficients tied to the real and financial variables. We therefore have a monetary neutrality that corresponds to a series of pairs [quantity of money (growth) – value granted to time (change)], with one pair representing growth in the quantity of money for a certain state of the referential of time-value, i.e. of preferences, substitutions and tradeoffs that form the expectation function. Monetary neutrality is therefore defined in a relative manner. From a practical viewpoint, one should give a value (magnitude) to the value granted to time, in order to be able to estimate the neutral money supply growth rate. The estimation of Vt, in any event a difficult endeavor, must, start off from a real or financial variable and from a definition of forgetfulness and of the measure appropriate with this variable, enable us to renew in a more indirect manner with the idea according to which there must be a link between growth in means of payment and growth in the economy but, for instance, by looking into the memorized economic growth rate and/or its coefficient erosion.

§ 61.   The issue of unemployment and, more generally, of the imbalance in the utilization of the labor force, which results in most collective and individual traumas, finds a specific answer once one accepts to think within the framework of analyzing this labor. The analysis fits into a referential or regime determined by the value granted to time (memory, forgetfulness, duration and time-matter) that governs tradeoffs, preferences and substitutions from one sequence (period) of the cycle to another. The interest rate itself is determined by these factors. Action always plays on memory and forgetfulness effects to be efficient. The downward leg of the economic cycle is understood as an increase in the value granted to time and in memory, with a slowdown in the velocity rates of real and financial circulation of money and the substitution between savings and investment, between goods or services, between short-term assets and long-term assets. Moreover, it has been argued that at the equilibrium (absolute but, to remain closer to reality, restricted relative or relative), there is (absolute) neutrality or stability (relative equilibrium) of (absolute) time or of the (referential) memory and (relative) forgetfulness regimes.

Unemployment is an imbalance that marks a moment of the cycle. It can be seen as a recalling in memory with an increase in the memory rate, one of the determinants of the immediate rate. While the upward leg of the cycle is marked both by a growing preference for the present in the sphere of goods (consumption for instance) and by increasing forgetfulness in the anticipation of the future in the financial sphere (time, the future in this case, ends up by no longer having any value because it does not carry any risk, a paradoxical form of preference for the present where the risk-free future blends with the present), the downward leg sees the appearance of a concern taking the form of a greater value granted to the future (which shoulders risk). Paradoxically, this leads to economic agents falling back on the present in the financial sphere.

What is recalled is awareness, the memory of negative events and periods, and, more unconsciously, a form of average that attracts excesses towards it. A cyclical imbalance appears in the downward leg of the cycle because there was a cyclical imbalance in the upward leg. There is instability in the memory and forget-fulness functions. In this case, memory, more or less concentrated, ends up by exceeding the simple return to normal of what had been forgotten. In contrast with a situation of equilibrium in which employment would have the appropriate level in com-parison with demand for goods and services and an immediate interest rate that would include a stable memory of growth and price functions, unemployment corresponds to an imbalance in which the return of memory projects effective demand beyond the normal memorized level of demand (symmetry of excess after the upward leg) in such a way that the labor force is suddenly over-sized in comparison with said demand, at a time when the immediate interest rate is driven by its memory component.

The cyclical component of unemployment is accordingly a mismatch in the relationship between demand and labor force when the inertia of memory drags demand in the best-case scenario toward its past average standards from a situation of excessive overrun, and in fact more frequently and at the price of greater pain drives it under this standard.

Economic action will seek to correct these inertias of memory, by influencing the immediate interest rate from the key intervention rate until the immediate interest rate drops under the memory interest rate (which means a negative risk premium); by setting the objective of normalizing the determinants of the demand function for macro- and microeconomic policies. This normalization consists, in line with what we have argued, in ensuring that all players estimate this (future) demand by referring to a past period that is not too unfavorable since the formation of effective demand is carried out on this basis in a more or less conscious manner. As the downward leg of the cycle is analyzed as a significant upturn in the value granted to the time of memory, economic action will seek forgetfulness or a certain kind of forgetfulness. In fact, there are many options but there is a single objective, i.e. modify the memorized function of effective demand. As it governs demand for cash for real or financial transaction purposes, the circuit cannot start up again without a change in the regime of expectations and, therefore, in the memory that feeds it. Just like in the downward leg of the cycle, demand is driven down to form itself at lower levels than memorized demand; all the more vigorous action will be required to lift the latter above an average level in order to produce effects.

The cyclical part of unemployment thus corresponds, within the above described framework of the unfolding of the cycle, to a (cyclical) fluctuation of demand (when we refer to demand, in fact in a broader approach we understand any real or financial variable that determines growth) memorized around its equilibrium value in the way in which we have defined the equilibrium. This cyclical fluctuation in demand for goods and cash temporarily leads to a mismatch. Economic policy action seeks to reduce the gap between the memorized function of (average) demand that is supposed to be stable at the relative, or restricted relative, equilibrium, and actual demand that, for its part, has slipped well under this value. Economic action will be unable, primarily, to modify the memorized equilibrium value but will aim to a greater extent at ensuring a return toward the equilibrium value (by steering expectations toward this equilibrium value). Modifying the memorized equilibrium value is another objective. At this stage, in the action of a cyclical nature, the purpose is to ensure that the memory on which expectations are based and the formation of demand are close to an average value that we have called the equilibrium value (and more likely all the higher as this equilibrium value was lower in the trough of the cycle).

The non-cyclical dimension of unemployment is determined by the equilibrium value in a regime of restricted relativity or simple relativity, i.e. by the memorized reference value that is supposed to be stable in the regime (a historical average is its most unsophisticated estimation). The cyclical dimension of unemployment is given by the divergence between this relative equilibrium reference value – and one has to accept its (relative) stability in this line of thought – and actual immediate demand. The latter, steered by memory or forgetfulness, will be at a higher or lower level than said value. In the downward leg of the cycle, actual effective demand will be "pulled back" so to speak, magnetized by this memory value (the value granted to time increases) until it is dragged down into lower territories than this equilibrium value. Economic action primarily will seek to pull it toward the equilibrium, and in fact certainly will try to raise it higher. Action tools, of all kinds, will be mobilized with this objective. At the relative equilibrium, i.e. for a given state of memory effects and of forgetfulness erosion coefficients, $D_i = D_{M/F}$. In dynamic terms, we have $D_i = D_{M/F} + a$. (a) stands for the cyclical dimension of unemployment. $D_{M/F}$ stands for the non-cyclical dimension of unemployment.

At the absolute equilibrium, according to our definition of this state, i.e. neutrality of the temporal dimension and absence of time, we have a form of absolute identity $D_i = D_i$ with perfect adequacy because the individual-collective Subject, so to say, is not endowed with either memory or the ability to forget. In real life, i.e. in a regime of relative equilibria, (a) takes a value since there is virtually always a gap between D_i and $D_{M/F}$. From a cyclical (or economic environment) viewpoint, D_i will slide below $D_{M/F}$ in the downward leg of the economic cycle; one kind of action is possible; barring an extreme case (in other words deflation, i.e. infinite memory recall, infinite value granted to time), this gap is filled in the cycle, either naturally, or by economic action, or both. All of this occurs within a framework of referential or regime that remains intact and therefore stable. In an extreme situation, D_i is at pulled down by the corrective restoring force of memory to such an extent that the equilibrium value $D_{M/F}$ is shaken and dragged downward. One exits from the regime.

Insofar as one finds oneself in a regime of relative equilibrium, there is a memory effect and an equilibrium value $D_{M/F}$ which, when it is low, sets a limit of a structural order for D_i and, consequently, for employment. There is a structural dimension of unemployment because within the regime $D_{M/F}$ has taken a low value. Economic action is possible on the determinants of $D_{M/F}$ but what is at stake here is of another nature.

In an economy that has evacuated time, the issue of unemployment, in a way, does not arise. By introducing time, memory and forgetfulness, it can be seen that the equilibrium sets itself at relative levels, i.e. at levels for which $D_{M/F}$ can take low values, which Keynes would have called sub-equilibria. However, it can also be seen that a purely cyclical economic policy action can efficiently fill the gap opened between D_i and $D_{M/F}$, but not modify $D_{M/F}$ in a favorable way. Starting from the correct observation that there are sub-equilibria (equilibria of underemployment) one mainly ends up with a recommendation to act on $D_{M/F}$ (structural dimension of unemployment), although the relevance of purely cyclical action on the $D_i/D_{M/F}$ gap is not denied. However, the issues at stake are not the same.

In a regime of relative equilibrium, i.e. in reality, there are underemployment equilibria determined by the memorized relative equilibrium values of the main economic and financial variables. Cyclical economic action cannot have an effect on what has been memorized, or at least cannot have a major effect. Only action aimed at modifying what, by definition because it is memorized (time-matter and duration), is difficult to change, and/or the "passive" stock of events and simply time that goes by and little by little changes the memory of what has occurred, only these two approaches seem to be able to tackle full-on the crucial problem, i.e. the more or less significant inertia of powerful memory effects that can increase. Changing will consist, to a great extent, in forgetting.

Economic policy action is fundamentally justified in wanting to try and modify the memory of what has been and, accordingly, positively steer what is anticipated. For the real success of an economic policy action always depends, ultimately, on its capacity to get to move what is most inert and, furthermore, detrimental or unfavorable in time-matter.

§ 62. The stability of strategies found in Nash equilibria in game theory corresponds to (and, in a certain sense, presupposes) the relative equilibrium such as we have defined it, i.e. from the stability of memory and forgetfulness functions (*M/F is* unchanged). There is an analogy between this stability of the temporal referential (regime) and the stability of strategies, whatever these strategies may be, within the referential (regime). It can therefore be considered that the stable strategies, i.e. initiatives in terms of action by the Subject, by (individual and collective) Subjects, suppose a certain number of conditions with respect to the stability of the temporal regime which, as we saw, remains deeply impregnated by duration, memory and forgetfulness. Modifying players' strategies, as understood in game theory, consists in modifying memory and forgetfulness functions, and, therefore, altering the temporal referential (regime).

The foregoing shows that in economic action, a relative equilibrium (as understood here) is reached for all strategies, when the main temporal functions are stable. This relative equilibrium is obviously not tenable and in reality facts, events and phenomena will fluctuate around a sort of linchpin made of the conditions of stability of memory and forgetfulness functions, with this linchpin anchoring "cyclical" fluctuations (imbalances) and accordingly action within the regime (which we have previously called the macrofinancial regime). When movement breaks or modifies the linchpin and drags reality outside the regime (crisis), then there is a change of referential.

Under these conditions, i.e. the existence of a relative equilibrium guaranteeing simultaneously the stability of strategies and of temporal functions, how can (economic policy) action unfold from and around this linchpin? Economic policy action will be able to play in a fashion on M/F, i.e. seek to modify, deform, from a central point of relative equilibrium, the memory and forgetfulness coefficients tied to the main characteristics – and therefore real and financial variables – of the macrofinancial regime, and subsequently the strategies of the various economic and financial players will change; or, in another direction, economic policy action will consist in stabilizing M/F to gather the conditions required by a (relative) equilibrium.

Should one presuppose that M/F is stable or unstable? This is not neutral for economic policy action. There is always, for a given regime (referential), a value of M/F that contributes to a (relative) equilibrium. This value of M/F corresponds to a stability of strategies as defined by Nash. This pivotal value in the (relative) equilibrium can itself be the axis of movement and of economic policy action because, for instance, this value of M/F is associated with a macrofinancial regime that, for such or such reason, is not deemed satisfactory. The proposal might then be made to act in order to establish a new (relative) equilibrium value either in the same regime (a regime can host a set, a range, of equilibria), or, in a situation of breakdown (crisis), in a new referential. In this case, we are in a relative approach of M/F. The memory and forgetfulness coefficients that contribute to the definition of the (relative) equilibrium are doubly relative values insofar as they form with M/F a curve of relative equilibria for a given regime (referential) and they can provide the action variable, the lever, the tool, directly or more probably, indirectly, in other words through intervention variables, such as the key interest rate.

A more conventional approach will consist in defining first (in an absolute fashion, i.e. without integrating the information coming from the current regime and/or previous regimes) and subsequently setting as an objective one or several values of M/F understood as (more or less relative) equilibrium values. Economic policy action will first and foremost consist in steering M/F as the equilibrium value.

Economic policy action can consist either in modifying the stability of strategies, as defined by Nash, and therefore M/F *is* a relative and instrumental value; or in establishing a stability (even relative) of strategies (and therefore of $M//F$) as a condition for a better implementation of individual as well as collective actions and initiatives. The two apparently parallel axes can eventually cross one another, as the activism of the first approach could be frozen at a given moment in a form of a second strategy.

§ 63.   Achieving results through economic policy supposes being credible. And credibility requires respecting what Lucas and other authors define as temporal consistency. Credibility consists in maintaining credibility and is therefore a function of duration and, more crucially, a function of memory (and of forgetfulness). Here, we find again [M/F] as well as the major issue and the conditions of stability of [M/F] which, as we saw above, determine the stability of strategies as defined by Nash and, to a larger extent, the relative equilibrium or equilibria. Temporal consistency, by referring to the conditions of stability of [M/F] and therefore of the possibility of a relative equilibrium, tightly links temporal memory and forgetfulness coefficients, and action in its very foundation (its possibility) and, above all, in its credibility, i.e. its efficiency. This is an important point that we have already underscored: economic policy action, to be efficient, must at the very least take into account temporal duration, memory and forgetfulness functions found in the definition of what we have called a referential or regime, and, even more importantly, integrate these temporal functions as action lever variables (modification sought in M/F or instrumentalization of M/F), or as final or intermediary objectives of action in order to set them as the pivot of the regime and of a relative equilibrium.

By consequence, there is a link, in the conditions of formation of an equilibrium (a relative one as understood here), between the stability of the strategies of (individual or collective) Subjects and the compliance with temporal consistency, united by a dependency on [M/F]. Economic policy action must integrate this link. This means that action takes into consideration existing temporal functions (at any point in time, every economic fact, event or phenomenon can be defined by a certain time-matter of memory and a forgetfulness coefficient) in the various dimensions of its planning and its deployment. It also means that economic policy action seeks to stabilize these temporal functions, characterized for instance by significant volatility; and that action even tries, after having defined new values for them, to modify these values by setting objectives; and, lastly, that economic policy action is, as such, a learning process that produces time-matter. It is a process with its own temporal memory and forgetfulness coefficients, and the credibility of economic policy action depends on them. Economic policy action is a process that inherits temporal functions that it must at least take into account and that it can eventually harness, and, at the same time, is a process that produces its own temporal functions. Efficiency and credibility result from these two dimensions. The prerequisites of stability if economic policy action is to be efficient are accordingly found in the existing regime (referential) or the one aimed for as an objective. In both cases, this regime defines a (relative) equilibrium from temporal functions; in compliance with the temporal consistency of the action itself as it unfolds.

Economic policy, to achieve results, entails being credible and this credibility is deeply linked to the taking into account of temporal referentials, in the process followed to define said action. The credibility we are referring to here is built from a learning process and therefore a process of modification that unfolds over a given period of time. Rational expectations (in the sense where they are related to adaptive learning) fit in within this approach where economic policy action integrates and, at the same time, sets an objective memory and forgetfulness referentials. For this reason, economic policy can unfold only in a referential (or regime) governed by expectations that forge a link between the future and the past via learning processes and memory projection processes. expectations, just like to a larger extent economic policy action, cannot draw exclusively on past behaviors in the sense where they would merely replicate them. In fact, economic policy action stems from a projection and an anticipation and their regime is that of a modification of what is recalled by memory.

Economic time is this very process of modification, both inspired and informed by what is inert (the stock of time-matter made up of facts, phenomena and events) and set in motion by the mutation of behaviors (there is no perfect infinite replication of behaviors but, on the contrary, there is always change, whether resulting from "rational" learning as defined by Lucas or other various forces, including forgetfulness). Economic policy action is itself subject to a process of modification and learning from a temporal stock which is more or less satisfactorily stored in memory and made up of the own history of action.

§ 64.   By consequence, there are, at any point in time, in memory and therefore so to say in stock, three pillars that structure the temporal referential. A first storing site integrates all unrefined facts, phenomena and events. A second information storehouse shelters all individual and collective behaviors, the entire range of reaction functions other than the one characterizing economic policy action. The last site is the stock of economic policy. This is an initially inert matter that will come toward present time, which will make itself present in the sense where it can be said "I have this or that in mind". A lot is played out in the process of calling to mind, of recall (memory). The inert character of this matter can be found originally, as we have seen, in the existence of a certain number of sub-equilibria, of highly relative equilibria, of underemployment equilibria in particular, and finally of real and financial imbalances. This initial chunk of cold wax is going to be modified in a fashion, heated up, by forgetfulness as it entails that the action will never be recalled in its complete and total integrity. The chunk of wax more or less already deformed by forgetfulness therefore reaches the Subject's consciousness in the process and the Subject makes it present by recalling it in memory. Thereby the Subject, whether individual or collective, starts to produce behaviors and reactions (reaction functions) that are inspired by the stock of information that comes from past but cannot be mere replications because even as the action is recalled it is affected by a certain forgetfulness coefficient, and also because reaction functions include a degree of learning even though it is highly unlikely that this rational learning process is complete. On the contrary, everything is far from merely learned from the past, simply because the past is recalled only very imperfectly and is very partly present in memory.

Everything plays itself out in the process where the past becomes the present and where a chunk of cold wax, which is the past and inert stock of information, is brought to life and modified.

CHAPTER 4

GLOBAL THEORY

§ 65.   What do we mean exactly by global, i.e. by "global theory"? First of all, we are asserting that there cannot be any dichotomy between real and monetary or — depending on the terminology used — between the sphere of the real economy and the sphere of financial markets or the financial sphere. Accordingly, there cannot be any really global theory, or general theory as defined by Keynes, without any systematic thinking through of the fact that admittedly goods can be bought with money but the monetary fact, the financial fact, have a strong and specific existence and autonomy. The crucial and causal interweaving of the financial and the real (what is monetary and what is real) is at the very heart of the approach of our global theory.

When we refer to a global theory, we also mean a theory that unfolds within the framework of a global real economy and open global financial markets. The field of balances of payments is open; innovation circulates, while funding terms and conditions are standardized. This hypothesis is undoubtedly somewhat strong and several arguments could be marshaled to oppose it: limitations resulting from protectionist developments or temptations, the highly heterogeneous extent to which financial markets have developed, the radically different paces of the real and the financial (time and space units in these two spheres are not the same). Therefore, here, we understand by global the capacity to grasp what in the real and financial spheres spans, national and even regional borders.

Lastly, what we understand when we refer to a global theory, and to a far larger extent, is a theory that seeks to integrate, to compare systematically at least, the various dimensions of a certain number of widely debated issues or problems. Accordingly, the absolute and relative dimensions of various theoretical debates, which seem to echo the convergence between the real and the monetary, provide an example of such an approach. Embracing a "global" dimension in our approach is not restricted to a geographical and horizontal meaning (physical extension of definitions) but includes a vertical deepening and a mutation of the very definitions. In fact, a theory is not really global if it, merely, broadens the definition of the real, the definition of the monetary (or the financial). A theory is more authentically global if it embraces together and simultaneously the real and the monetary because there is no segmented and segmentable human reality. In fact, a theory is not really global if, for each issue, each resistance (problem), each point of contact, it will seek as a priority to isolate separately a dimension, an angle. Being global is an intellectual attitude that transforms thought's *modus operandi*, and does not content itself with grasping an unchanged world according to unchanged modalities.

This is not, simply, a conceptual posture that, while admittedly interesting, would not have any link with (applied) economic policy. Far from it, since a global approach because of its very nature is likely to modify the very manner in which economic reality is perceived and described and, by consequence, the way in which issues, questions and problems are tackled. Our global theory aims to integrate conceptually the real and the financial, the absolute and the relative, the open and the closed, the rational and the less rational (irrational), the linear and the less linear, memory and forgetfulness, all the conceptual pairs that, at the heart of economic thought, have via the dynamics of their opposite polarities, fed the discipline's reflection and creative energy. With our global theory, the objective consists in seeking to overcome the intimate barriers that, always, have remained in position, invisible obstacles, between the conceptual poles of these couples. All theories, every one of them, including the ones that have nevertheless aimed for "generality", have finally consecrated the original cleavage between irreducible dimensions since these cleavages very often refer to fundamental distinctions of thought (Hegel's "in itself/for itself" for instance).

§ 66.   The point here therefore, on the one hand, is to refuse the barren definition of globalization and global developments as an extension, a prolongation, an enlarging of what is already and, above all, of what is already thought. This definition is barren because it results from the persistence of thought patterns and to a significant extent stems from a quantitative enlarging of the angle of approach. We also need, on the other hand, to consider simultaneously the dimensions of the economic that have been thought about separately until now, as distinguishing dimensions has precisely been the conceptual trademark of this period of economic thought. For it is not easily admitted that the temporal repository of the Subject and of economic action is neither (totally) linear nor non-linear and that comprehension of the economic would benefit from the integration of these two dimensions. Nor is it easily admitted that the (purely) rational, the adaptive (by reference to the past, to memory) and the irrational (we would more willingly talk about the incomprehensible) coexist within a same reality rather than result from three separate kinds of reality or worlds. This cohabitation is a form of co-integration where the three dimensions blend into one another, overlap, overlie one another, replace one another and feed one another. Nor is it more easily understood or admitted that past, present and future are not separate dimensions that segment the temporal repository into airtight components but, on the contrary, are three "words", faces for something that is whole, i.e. time-matter where memory that makes itself present is, primarily, the heart of the regime of time, expectations, remembering and forgetfulness. The dilatations of the temporal repository, when they blur the frontiers between past, present and future to the point where they wipe them out, create the conditions required for new approaches, a different dynamic thought, a thought we call "global".

Such a "global" economic thought is not a thought that refuses the key concepts or paradigms that pave the way for a unitary interpretation of phenomena and the economic world. In other words, by establishing the crucial role played by memory (and, therefore, immediately, by forgetfulness since, in a genuinely global approach, the various dimensions of a reality, of a truth, are linked), in our understanding of the economic, we quite rapidly move on to connecting the past and the future (what is yet to be comes from), questioning the very meaning of what is called "present". When, likewise, we end up by drawing a distinction between many possible definitions of the interest rate (natural, real, memory, etc.) we are not seeking to segment what the interest rate actually is at the heart of the economic but, on the contrary, we are trying to show via wide prism that the unitary phenomenon of the interest rate recovers dimensions that are often isolated (and, indeed, can be isolated) and which need to be integrated into a unitary, global theory.

§ 67. Our global theory asserts that the separate, airtight and apparently exclusive categories on which the economic has been thought, need to be surpassed even while they are thought together, simultaneously. This conceptual integration leap is possible only if a unitary principle that transcends this new repository is identified. Memory, as a unitary and federative fact that also plays an integrating role in our global theory, represents one of the crucial unitary principles. This is how the cycle, the interest rate, money, the major functions of the economic (savings, consumption, investment) have been thought in this book from a global viewpoint (in the sense where what is usually separated is reunited, articulated and alternated; the real/monetary and absolute/relative pairs provide striking examples) as well as a unitary one (federative principles, such as memory) for global and unitary are two words that voice the same demand.

A unitary and global approach will seek to position itself beyond the distinction between open and closed (between open and closed economies), beyond the distinction between the economic (and its foundations) and economic policy. We are not denying that these distinctions are not legitimately sound but the reality these concepts intend to describe demand stifling such distinctions and, on the contrary, seeking unitary interpretations. Thus economic policy represents a modality of thought of the economic. The key distinction between what is (reality, fact, economic events) and what lies within the mode of not being (what is yet to be, to be done, what is anticipated), as well as the distinction that stems from the foregoing between temporality modes, all of this deserves so to say to be gathered within a unitary form beyond segmentations because the economic phenomenon cannot be understood without taking into account two dimensions, in the same movement.

The distinction between the real and monetary spheres is undoubtedly the most federative articulation point of a genuinely global theory. Once more, the point does not consist in saying (only because such an assertion is in fact legitimate) that finance has undergone a (mere) physical extension of its applications, of its policy instruments and of its fields of intervention (depth, number and sophistication of market segments). All of this is true but this is not how the financial is linked to the real. The diversification of financing (market) methods as well as the new generations of products are part of this stronger link in the modern era. However, the idea according to which there is no autonomy of the monetary fact any more than the "real" operates autonomously is not usually or easily admitted. The real and the monetary are hardly autonomous. Their interaction gives the key to a unitary (and therefore autonomous) interpretation of numerous contemporary economic phenomena.

§ 68.   When we talk about a global theory, we also refer to the totalizing and unitary effort of comprehension undertaken by the discipline (encompassing Economics and Finance). The approaches drawn upon in our other books (*Tractatus, Genealogy, Value and Time*) share this unitary interpretation of how the economic has unfolded since its origins and until the modern and contemporary era. Because it wants to be global, such a theory will be more naturally driven toward a restricted or complete form of relativity in the integration and the interpretation of things and of phenomena, with the absolute nature of certain aspects of the economic therefore taking place among the possible fields and dimensions of the spectrum of relativity, a wide enough spectrum to allow a unitary and integrated, global, approach. The point we are making here is that our global theory is a theory of relativity, whether restricted or not, and that the need to be able to take on board, without any exception, all phenomena, facts and events, dominates our approach.

§ 69.   A global theory is undoubtedly a form of the theory of relativity. It is, in the same movement, a theory of time (as absolute and external to the Subject; while relative to the Subject's representation) for a unitary repository that takes on board the most extreme dilatations just like the most powerful contractions of time or its representations, and takes on board the distortion of reference universes from an autonomous past until a single temporal field dominated by memory and where the past is, also, the future to the very extent it makes itself into the present. A global theory therefore is based on a unitary temporal repository that is both absolute and relative, specific to the Subject and, suddenly, external or exterior. This crucial discontinuity of facts and events as well as, therefore, the discontinuity of the repository of the economic are precious, precisely, in terms of being able to take on board in our analysis all the elements that an approach based on segmentation would deem autonomous.

Such a form of relativity is expressed in a very practical manner. A global theory does not believe that there is a single regime of expectations, of motivations and of temporality. A global theory by consequence does not think that an economic fact or phenomenon (unemployment, inflation, etc.) may be correctly described and understood by drawing on a single dimension at any time. And the fact, or phenomenon, itself very often includes several dimensions and this means that trying to keep them separate is useless. For instance, we could take the example of the relationship, or trade-off, between unemployment and inflation: inflation can be studied in many possible ways, e.g. actual or expected inflation, and indeed expected inflation can be studied from several starting-points (adaptive or rational expectations, surveys, and so forth). And inflation itself, in turn, can offer a "real" interpretation (inflation in prices of goods and services) or a "monetary/financial" one (inflation in prices of financial assets). A (unitary) global theory will seek to cover all possibilities not merely to be exhaustive from a methodological viewpoint but because reality is close to a repository of more or less restricted relativity in which most of the distinctions we draw do not exist, where duration dominates a spatial, and accordingly segmented, vision of time, where discontinuities mean that an economic phenomenon is permanently governed by numerous dimensions and a form of stability that is itself highly relative. What we see as questions or opportunities of trade-offs do not really exist as sources of trade-offs because they are merely the automatic reflection of the artificial distinction introduced where, on the contrary, unity rules or at least should rule.

§ 70.   A global theory establishes economic facts and economic phenomena beyond physical and historical points of reference. A genuinely global theory establishes its repository beyond the concepts of closed and open understood in the most immediately geographical sense. The closed and the open, in a geographical sense, are nothing more than specific cases of a more global theory. This is how movements in balances of payments have to be understood.

§ 71.   When we talk about a global theory, we are furthermore referring to a theory that builds its foundations in what is not *stricto sensu* included in the field of Economics (in the sense where this subject is usually understood) and delves into the multi-disciplinary origins of what is now (has become) economic. When we talk about a global theory, we are also referring to a theory that, although naturally interested in what is macro-economic, seeks to exceed macro-micro cleavages. A global theory is based on the widest grasp and comprehension of economic foundations (concepts) and economic phenomena, facts and manifestations. The manner in which economic concepts are formed, seen as inseparable from the manner in which thought is formed and developed as well as how it mutates, is the founding stone of any approach, which cannot be subservient to facts, however fascinating they may be. Thinking through economic facts consists in taking into account, taking charge of, the trajectory, the trajectories of Western thought, and how it was embodied by points of impact that we call economic facts or events. The trajectories of Western thought and the way in which Western thought has manifested itself (its appearance) are a whole. A global theory could hardly separate them.

§ 72. When we refer to a global theory, we also mean a theory that encompasses, on its own behalf, the global nature of what is (and expresses itself as such in economic thought) and of action understood as an endeavor of the Subject aimed at the world – action that lies at the heart of what is called human "reality". Refusing to separate what underpins action and what unfolds through action, safeguarding a sort of totality therefore, all of this is part of global theory's project.

These are some of the most ambitious pivots of our global theory. There are pillars that are both simpler and more immerged in economic phenomena and facts. The next few developments strive to portray the seven pillars on which global theory leans on as global theory, i.e. the crucial elements of the global nature of a global theory.

§ 73. Economic values have to be absolutely understood (in absolute terms), and the economic dynamics results from their relative movements. Whether we are dealing with prices or activity, we need to look for absolute values because of the very fact that they are global. Price (or inflation) phenomena recover numerous aspects of economic reality: goods and services, financial assets, output, consumption, etc. The extent to which this phenomenon of prices is segmented can be extremely sophisticated, an endless chopping up of reality. The cyclical dynamics of inflation understood as a global value will depend on the movement of relative prices. Likewise, activity, in a global sense, is multi-faceted: consumption, investment, net exports, stocking, saving/dissaving, etc. The relative distortion of its components feeds the movement of the economic cycle. The absolute value a balance of payments can constitute (and when its accounting treatment is completed it enhances its formally perfect accomplishment) in turn masks relative movements between items (trade balance, current- account balance, short- or long-term capital balance, balance of foreign exchange reserves, etc.).

A global theory will draw a distinction between the absolute and the relative while taking both of them in charge, on board. Inflation in prices of goods and services on its own will not be taken for inflation as a global phenomenon, relative movements will not be improperly likened to absolute movements. Consumption on its own will not be taken for activity even as the relative distortion of activity variables will provide precious information about the unfolding of the cycle. For there is an absolute value of activity, under which there is only relative interplaying (investment/consumption, consumption/saving, exports/imports, output/consumption, etc.), an endless inter-playing that is not the operation of activity but that of the dynamics of activity. Lastly, the trade balance on its own does not summarize the interplaying of the global flows and inventories of an economy, i.e. will not summarize the absolute value of trade which, actually, expresses the absolute variable.

A global theory will therefore tend toward a form of streamlining and quite advanced simplification, toward simple elements as defined by chemistry. These simple elements are absolute elements in the meaning we have defined, they may seem "macro" in the meaning Economics gives to this word. A global theory will strive to reduce the number of these elements, toward the single element. This tension, although unsatisfied (the absolute variable of activity is highly attractive but falls short), given the very essence of the research that drives this global theory. This quest for simple elements and absolute variables will go hand in hand with the highest attention paid to the movement that propels economic reality, whether it results from human or from the specific dynamics of economic activity.

§ 74. The key principle of global theory is the principle of relativity. Any relevant economic measurable variable has to be absolute; there is no possible economic movement that does not operate within the framework of, restricted or complete, relativity. It would be a mistake to see nothing more in this approach than (another) form of relativism. Far from it, the framework of relativity drawn upon for most repositories in the economic order (for instance the temporal repository, which witnesses permanent distortions, and the dilatation and contraction of time units) stems from absolute concepts of which the purity, the unity and simplicity is reasserted. While all the economic concepts deemed important blow up immediately, at the first contact with thought, into myriads of other concepts, like a rocket in fireworks, one must not discard the effort aimed at achieving simplification that is an effort to reach simplicity. Unemployment is given many names according to the way its possible origin is interpreted (frictional, natural, cyclical unemployment, etc.); the interest rate for its part is given a whole range of subtle names (real, natural, nominal, psychological, etc.). An endless list of such examples could be given. What we are trying to say is that there is a danger of getting lost in the maze of these names and in the labyrinth of the relative interplaying that underpins them, and of losing from sight the unity of an economic issue, as well as its simplicity. Unemployment is "one" as an economic variable, issue and problem. The interest rate is "one". Inflation is "one". Activity is "one". Trade is "one".

One must not let oneself be trapped by the relative interactions and the numerous facets of economic reality (need for absolute apprehension) but, in the same approach, one must not misunderstand them or forget them in the very comprehension of the absolute value of such a measurable variable. A satisfactory absolute understanding of the global phenomenon of inflation requires knowing and taking into account all its foundations, i.e. the forms and distortions of individual prices. Through this very process, absolute comprehension draws on relative dimensions and on their interplay.

§ 75. Our global theory does not accept the dichotomy between real and monetary spheres. Economic reality is unitary. The real does not beget the monetary any more than the monetary begets the real. The two dimensions of a same world mix their articulations and exchange their meaningfulness. Each dimension, whether real or monetary, in turn hosts further dimensions: producer goods, consumer goods, and all other segments leading to preferences, trade-offs and substitutions in the very dynamics of the cycle. In the dimension we have called the "financial sphere", new dimensions are also sheltered: liquidity, more or less long-term financial assets, which also lead to trade-offs, preferences and substitutions. The cycle, a global concept, stems from multiple trade-offs between preferences and value, another global concept, expresses an infinite series of trade-offs between relative values. Our global theory will maintain the integrity of the concept of value, and it will be able to do so only by acknowledging and preserving the multiplicity of relative movements that underpin the exuberant diversity of the economic.

Preferences determine relative values within both the real and monetary dimensions. A crucial preference, a sum of trade-offs and substitutions, plays an even more structuring role, and is what explains why money can buy goods and services, and why with said goods and services an economic agent can also demand cash or take up an exposure to longer-term financial assets. Undeniably, there is an initial fact of monetary nature (money) that is embodied, so to speak, in the real, before sometimes reverting to its original form. However, it is just as true that at the beginning the real good perhaps finds a monetary counterpart. Value, which is hosted by both dimensions and by the real and financial spheres, has a significant function.

From a methodological viewpoint, our global theory will see in preferences and trade-offs between the real and the financial, between goods and services, on the one hand, monetary and longer-term financial assets, on the other hand, one of the crucial sources of the dynamics of the cycle. The cycle unfolds, with this preference looming over it, and which in turn harbors multiple preferences in the real sphere or the monetary sphere *stricto sensu*. The expression of these preferences within and for a given idea of time (what we have called the value granted to time, which defines a repository of specific distortions of time and therefore preferences) drives the movement of relative values in goods, services and financial assets, as well as with one another. We have shown their periods, phases and cause-and-effect sequences.

We are driving at the following point: a global approach requires thinking about the real and the monetary/financial together. This requirement, granted, is partly accounted for by the undeniable fact that we are seeing a world of global economies and globalized markets taking shape. However, this point is more far-reaching. The fact that things are increasingly financialized is to be expected as fitting in with long-run phenomena, just like the globalization of things, words and human beings, cannot on its own win over total acceptance of this movement of integration between the real and financial spheres. The unitary, but multi-dimensional, fact of value underpins the inevitable nature of this requirement and outweighs these historical forms. It is because value, from the very outset, looks toward several worlds and thrusts out its various forms and faces that the world as perceived nowadays is what it is and we think it in the way we think it.

The foregoing means that the global nature of value, thus seen as a real and monetary Janus, irradiates all economic concepts: inflation, activity and trade. And we will not have to draw on two interpretations, based on either the real or the monetary sphere, but will have to deal with a unitary reality.

§ 76.   Our global theory will have as its third principle the broadest conception and approach of time, space and action. The temporal repository consists in discontinuities (which do not prevent continuity, a regime of exception), dilatations and contractions, is the temporal repository of memory, duration and forgetfulness.

The spatial repository, first of all, since this argument enjoys the widest consensus, is that of a total and complete world – complete according to the meaning the word "global" essentially entails. It deliberately positions itself, in its way of reasoning and in the connecting of its concepts, on the other side of physical or other borders. It happens to be that right now, at the turn of a new century, this aspect of global is to a quite large extent embodied in facts and also corresponds to a large extent to reality, or at least to what is perceived to be reality. Gauged in terms of a longer historical period than we take into account most of the time in our thinking, geographical integration (consolidation) as an aspect of global trends is finally not very frequent and is paced by cycles that are themselves very long. The 1990s echoed, nearly one century later, the first decade of the twentieth century. This means that this territorial, physical, geographical aspect of the global dimension is unlikely to subsist in a more or less remote future. This is not a good enough reason, far from it in fact, to overlook the requirement it represents, i.e. the internal need of economic reasoning to free itself from such obstacles. The spatial unit of a genuinely global theory is a unique manner of apprehending the world, a way of thinking before, well before, being the observation or the wish to see convergence integrating regions, powers and geographical units. Lastly, the repository of action will be unitary in the sense that the Subject will be the individual as much as the community (the institution; that is where the institutional dimensions are integrated into the economic); in the sense where action itself, as we have explained elsewhere, forms a totality in which the Subject, what is (Being) and the world of human reality deal the cards. This repository of action opens up huge areas for the institutional, sociological and political analysis of forms of action; and just as huge spaces for the analysis of the institutional foundations of action, as well as its ethical foundations.

The time, space and action repositories are individually unitary; all three together and with one another they form total meaningfulness for global economic theory. These principles, which we have developed to a large extent in our previous books (*Tractatus, Genealogy, Value and Time* and *Monetary Notebooks*) have important applications for our global theory. Without denying that an economic system may face varying degrees of closing (as history abundantly demonstrates), our global theory from the very outset sets itself within the framework of a postulate of opening. This is a postulate since its complete existence has neither been demonstrated, nor observed. However, this is the best way to drive the reasoning, its words and its concepts, to an extreme, to force the most devious approaches to unveil themselves. Any economic reasoning must be based on a totally open economy.

§ 77. A genuinely global theory will see merely specific cases in existing theories and yet to emerge lines of thought. There will always be a dimension integrated in a unitary repository (as we have defined the repository, for instance for time, space, action and trade) that will lead to a so-called general truth established for a more or less long period being deemed a specific point. The project of our global theory plays an integrating role in this sense. Just like Keynes dealt with classical economic theory as a specific point of a more general theory, we have shown in our previous works, that Keynesian theory itself could be seen as the last theory of Economic having become the theory of action and of economic policy. In this regard, Keynesian theory in a fashion is successful because from a distance it appears to be unifying. However, this unification is achieved only to the extent that Economics is radically (and terminally) transformed into the science of action leading to a transformation of the world. There is unification but Keynesian theory alone remains standing in this unified universe. In fact, the supposed unification occurs against the backdrop of a mutation of the discipline and a fundamental change in the meaning of what is economic. Starting from this point, we can turn things on their head and see in Keynesian theory the specific appendix of an evolution of our global theory where the discipline's fresh start entails moving to an extreme position. Because the very idea that Economics is a science of action consists in a specific interpretation of a far longer and broader history. This history, which is more ontological than strictly speaking historical, this intellectual history of the economic and how it spread its wings, is an intrinsic part of the economic itself and of its dynamics and, above all, is an intrinsic part of the project of global theory. Our global theory takes charge of, takes on board, the entire history of the unfolding of the economic within the field of Western thought. In fact, its very spreading throughout the world is one of the major developments in the history (understood as fate) of said Western thought. The global nature of economic theory consists in this approach based on opening and reunification of the fragmented conceptual field. The multi-disciplinary reunification of this field is included in the project of global theory. These principles have been set out in our previous studies. This work now leads us into the field of a more immediate application of the economic.

We have shown that the economic had undergone a specific adventure by turning itself in the modern era into a science of action, but at the price of dramatic forgetfulness. The contemporary specialization of the discipline reflects the scale of what has been forgotten in a striking manner. This path can now hardly take it any further. Its revival entails a conceptual reunification of this field (philosophy, history, economics, hard sciences, etc.) thanks to a reappraisal of what the economic has become in the modern era. The foregoing forms a global project because the global apprehension of the economic lies at the very heart of the project. While our theory is global from the very viewpoint of Economics as a discipline itself given its destination and its dynamics, it is just as global for any assertion or proposal that more or less holds the status of truth or certainty in the economic. Any affirmation, any contention, can and must be suspected of being particular in a repository that is not appropriate. We need to research under what conditions and hypotheses about a "regime", a "repository", any such affirmation becomes consistent or any such contention becomes truer. This research focused on regimes, periods, sequences and repositories is the marching order of a global theory derived from its global nature.

§ 78.   Our global theory will admit that what sometimes seems to be contradictory is often complementary. Because of the manner in which we see our global theory, we logically expect it to be a haven for concepts, forms and lines of reasoning that, since they seek to describe what is under way and literally occurring, can only cover one dimension at a given point in time while others, as they are more advanced, apparently contradict said lines of reasoning even though they merely answer them, as if they were echoing them. There is no contention that may not be propounded because it seems to be wrong or, at least, apparently contradicts an already existing corpus of proposals. Very often, a given argument that seems dubious will prove to be either a specific case of a more global theory that far from refuting it will show what specific position it held in the overall development of such a theory; or an advanced position of a questioning waiting to be set out and subsequently solved. This global aspect has its limitations but that provides room for opening.

Likewise, a genuinely global theory will pay attention to avoid freezing such or such concept in such or such repository, in the occurrence a certain definition of economic concepts that, even more than any course set for the discipline, confines it to a mission and a fate. We need to deliberately concern ourselves with far more than the conventional growth functions (consumption, investment, inventories, net exports, etc.), move beyond what is apparently accepted to be a law, look beyond trade-off functions deemed immutable and fixed (trade-off between savings and consumption, between unemployment and inflation), and let repositories balloon just like we blow up a balloon. Our global theory will start of from systematic and methodological doubt that, at least during this unique moment where every repository has its chances, will lead to the shelving of the particular ideas one may have about the world and economic matters.

We will therefore start off by putting aside everything that has been taken for granted, by forgetting about methods, in order to give what has not yet been voiced a chance to have its say. We will start off from the idea that a global theory is based on the concepts of a regime and a repository, as well as various forms of relativity that do not rule out the absolute formulation of any dimension or element whatever. We will start off from the idea that the value granted to time governs separate repositories of preferences, of trade-offs and of substitutions between goods, services and financial assets. Accordingly, this dynamics of relative value shapes the cycle's development and proves to be far more powerful than the individual or even relative developments related to the usual measurable variables such as consumption or investment. The point we are trying to make here is that unquestionably too much effort is allocated to these individual growth functions. When we step back and consider them within a global framework, we can see that in fact they do not describe, in particular, an economic reality *per se* (in fact, they all talk about a global activity function) but to a greater extent they describe relative distortions in the value granted to time in one of the sequences of the cycle and within what we have called a regime within a repository. When the concept of "consumption" is used, what in fact is described is a certain preference for time (for the value granted to time). This preference is expressed in absolute terms but by definition it is relative (it consists in consumption in comparison with another function). A theory will seek to be global in the very fact that it will primarily see in all these functions the global interplay of signs reflecting trade-offs and preferences, as well as expectations.

In particular, this means that as economic policy action can be derived from such or such function (stimulating consumption, or investment) it fundamentally remains relative, determined by the preference expressed, at a given point in time of the cycle, for a certain value granted to time. There are no absolute economic functions in the heaven of ideas but relative preference functions for a certain value granted to time. In fact, one would need to rechristen the old functions such as consumption, investment, savings and, to a larger extent, the key concepts built by Economics. For the very names of these functions are misleading with respect to the economic reality they are meant to unveil but which they, to be more accurate, mask. Consumption and consuming are two words that call up a rather physical concrete image of a quite mechanical process, and have led to a mechanistic description of appropriation processes (i.e. demand). This definitely matches one way in which reality is perceived but masks the fact that consumption is, first of all, a certain value granted to time and, therefore, a preference, a trade-off, a substitution.

In other words, there is no difference of kind between these conventional growth functions but only differences of degree in a repository of preferences. Consumption, investment, (net) exports, stocking, savings: all these functions basically say the same thing, only differences of degree distinguish them at a certain stage of the value granted to time. These economic measurable variables are relative values in the sense where they correspond to a certain state of (global) value granted to time. Our global theory grants to the value given to time the crucial role in the repository of preferences. The concept of time value is the global concept. All the usual functions are various ways of expressing relative values.

Our global theory will consequently acknowledge as an absolute value primarily the value that is (more or less significantly) granted to time, followed by different rankings of relative values. The absolute value granted to time determines the ranking of relative values. In fact, in the economic dynamics, there are only relative values, and it is the very interplaying of distortions of relative values that is the dynamics itself. This implies that a global theory will seek to characterize the various regimes of (absolute) value granted to time. These regimes are the ones that overlook economic developments and, on the other hand, provide the possibilities of economic policy action because said action will always seek, within a given regime, to play one of the processes or dimensions of the regime, or modify this process to adapt to this dimension. Our global theory is based on the absolute value granted to time, and this opens up an infinite field of relative values within which economic life moves. We will study further in this book the analysis of the cycle resulting from such principles.

§ 79.   A genuinely global theory cannot be a theory of the Subject and just his/her action in the world. A theory for which Economics can be nothing more than the scientific description of this action of projection and transformation, a theory for which the economic begins and ends with the Subject and with the Subject as an agent, cannot be global. The global dimension is the movement that locates the Subject in history which he belongs to and of which a significant part is the economic itself. Our era of the turn of the twenty-first century, which wants to be and sees itself as global, on global or globalized markets and economies, nonetheless is not authentically global in the sense where the (economic) Subject has ultimately taken up all the room in reality and in economic theory. From this viewpoint, the more we believe the world is "global" in the meaning of the word we usually understand, the less it is in fact because the global dimension of physical, regional or geographical reality, of tools, of resources (of appropriation of the world for the Subject) exist only for a single omnipotent Subject, the only player in the economic sphere. Therefore, exactly at the same time that everything seems very global, the challenge of ensuring everything really does become global is the strongest. Our world that effectively believes it is very global is in fact very particular, very mono-dimensional and mono-regime, to refer to the comments previously made about the global opening of repositories. The saturation of regimes and repositories, which are moreover not very numerous, by the absolute and absolutist form of a Subject acting infinitely, actually adds credence to the idea that the world, on the contrary, is very local, in the conceptual meaning of the world, although not only in this respect.

§ 80. Our global theory is unitary. All conceptual categories are gathered around an absolute value, the value granted to time, which determines relative values and the cycle. The keystone of our theory is therefore time, or rather the value granted to time. This wording is tricky enough to grasp to underscore the problems linked to the very definition of the regime or the temporal repository. The unitary nature of our theory stems from this starting-point, with the integration of money and the real as key concepts, of all the dimensions of individual concepts (such as inflation) and of the various usual concepts (growth functions) by the fact that only distortions and relative values matter. Our global theory asserts that the economic, in its dynamics, depends exclusively on relative values, and in its foundations, on the principle of time-value.

§ 81. Our global theory practices methodical doubt but acknowledges the existence of pure contentions in the sense that they impose themselves over all considerations relating to history and such or such specific event. The fact that an objection to a pure contention of this kind might be raised because of a relative situation or event does not nullify its main strength. When we talk about a pure contention, we do not necessarily mean that it takes a mathematical form. The pure nature of an economic contention, beyond any relativism, consists in the possibility of linking it to a principle of absolute value far more than to the scientific capacity of describing it mathematically. The existence of pure contentions defined in this manner matches the global nature of the theory. A theory that is subject to the relativism of historical conditions, of human perceptions, of the simple diversity of situations, apart from the fact that it is struggling to assert itself as a theory, cannot be global. A genuinely global theory takes on board the idea of a possible universality of certain principles.

§ 82. The idea that economic policy (economic policy action) is entirely determined by the principle of time-value is a pillar of our global theory. The need for, as well as the usefulness and the efficiency, of any economic policy action are contingent and have to be assessed according to the value granted to time. One of the powerful levers of economic policy action, which we will discuss more in depth below, is the possibility given to influence and modify the value granted to time by the interplay of memory and forgetfulness effects. An economic policy cannot ignore, with respect to its action, the initial immediate data of memory and forgetfulness (since each economic situation, i.e. every environment in which a fact eventuates, an event occurs, is characterized by a certain DNA of memory and forgetfulness). Not only is it impossible for action to ignore this state but also it can play on it because the efficiency of economic action consists in the change of the initial states of memory and forgetfulness.

Our global theory is effectively global in the sense that it does not isolate economic policy action from the rest of the economic sphere, that it does not postulate the autonomy so to say of this action. On the contrary, there is a global dimension (unity) of this action and the corpus of theory's crucial principles and economic policy action is organically linked and determined. In this respect, there is global integration of what is the economic and of what the Subject may expect to achieve within the framework of economic policy action, because the cap of the economic, given by the distortions of time (both in absolute terms and as perceived by the Subject) cannot be easily diverted without having to pay a price.

Matters change in terms of the course of the economic because there is forgetfulness. The process of erosion of powerful memory effects, a unitary principle of our global theory, triggers the course of events. It is this very process that results in many phenomena and developments in the economic sphere being hard to grasp, to understand. The "human" dimension is often mentioned as a reason why it is virtually impossible to establish truths or contentions that can be deemed to have the status of a law. In fact, it is found in the crucial fact that economic matter is time, while duration is its main element in combination with memory. Forgetfulness creates the dynamics from this static state. And it is because the major growth functions (notably) include at any point in time a temporal dimension of duration and memory (consumption, income, etc.); as is also the case for inflation, that economic policy action, with its various tools and channels (which one will therefore need to choose carefully), will seek to recall certain elements into the (collective) consciousness, by reviving memory once these elements are likely to meet the objective that has been previously determined, or wiping out other elements by creating a halo of forgetfulness. Choosing the appropriate tools is a significant issue in terms of selection but not as important as the right comprehension of the time dimension that is found, at that given moment, in such or such a datum according to what is looked for.

The two major levers of economic policy action are memory (recall) and forgetfulness, ahead of monetary policy, fiscal policy, or any other action instrument. And the resources of economic policy action cannot be restricted to the two usual monetary and fiscal weapons; all the forms of action that enable memory to be stimulated/revived and/or memory to be wiped out by forgetfulness, in an agreed and determined objective, are pertinent. This very fact means the approach has a global dimension since, in principle, no force dominates. The adequacy of the time dimension (for instance, the more or less powerful memory effects in consumption and income functions will determine methods of action) in comparison with objectives, will dictate which instruments are chosen. And some of these instruments can be related only to communication, understood in its widest meaning, because memory and forgetfulness effects are as sensitive to what is said (and how it is said) as to the most strictly financial channels. In fact, is there really any difference with respect to the policies conducted by the most farsighted central banks? The somewhat magical function they seem to exercise includes memory, duration and forgetfulness, in their initial analysis, in the objectives pursued, in their methods of action, which are global since they are based finally as much on a sentence as on a key intervention interest rate. Their theory is thus global in the sense where, on the one hand, there is a unitary principle of time-dimension (time-matter) that integrates memory in static terms and forgetfulness in dynamic terms; while, on the other hand, the methods of economic policy action are global in their forms because they target memory and forgetfulness. By consequence, the overall package combines the unitary principle of memory and forgetfulness with the widest range of methods of action, and embodies the key guideline of economic action.

§ 83.   Our global theory pays close attention to various aspects of the issue of confidence. It sees in confidence a key determinant of the comprehension of certain economic and financial phenomena provided confidence is understood from the temporal dimension of the economic, and of memory in particular. Confidence is one of the dimensions of the temporal repository and of time-matter. It is due to its choice to replace confidence within the influence spectrum of the unitary principle of memory that the theory asserts itself as global. The confidence the various players in the economic and financial spheres place in one another indeed governs many characteristics, biases and imbalances of human systems. The relationship with the Other, and more generally speaking the place and the role of the Other in the economic are absolutely essential and we have dedicated many developments to them in previous works. Here we are not interested in the Other and Otherness as foundations of the economic, as this is not the purpose of the theory presented in this book, since its purpose is action. To a greater extent, we are interested in the relationship that is already operating and is literally inserted in existing economic and financial life. One way of relating to the Other, some relationships, are seen to be more or less based on confidence, more or less deficient, and accordingly the intensity of the confidence/mistrust pair shows a high correlation to a given number of virtuous circles (confidence) or vicious ones (mistrust), resulting from causalities where each one dominates more conventional components of economic analysis: institutions, operation of the market, etc. Confidence and mistrust dominate in the sense where, at comparable parameters, they prove decisive from the viewpoint of operation and efficiency. They also dominate in the sense where they determine the characteristics of a social, economic or financial model, or, at least its specific features.

Having said that, our global theory will link confidence and mistrust to a unitary dimension that dominates them and from a territory that is located beyond what is strictly human, i.e. psychology – in other words, the temporal repository, memory (and forgetfulness). Our global theory primarily sees in confidence (mistrust) the manifestations of alterations, distortions, dilatations and contractions of time-matter within an economic and financial regime, which is itself defined by a time repository. Our theory therefore sees in confidence (mistrust), in a nutshell, memory (forgetfulness). People are wary, are mistrustful, just like they forget. People trust others just like they remember. The fundamental analogy of the confidence/mistrust and memory/ forgetfulness pairs is at the heart of our theory, and its global dimension results from the affirmation of the importance of confidence (mistrust) and, simultaneously, its transcending in a more unitary dimension for our theory. A genuinely global theory cannot but seek to integrate the phenomena of confidence and mistrust. We do so by seeking to escape from the shackles of a psychological bias that is tempting in the respect.

Just as we anticipate in the same way as we remember, likewise therefore interest is deeply linked to memory and forgetfulness, confidence and mistrust are also bound by a deep relationship. Interest expresses a certain relationship to what is yet to be (and, therefore, with what has already occurred) and this relationship displays, includes, what is called confidence or mistrust.

Confidence and mistrust are part of the economy "in action" insofar as they express action quite directly. In this respect, our global theory, which is interested in action, cannot ignore them and, on the contrary, must integrate them into the causality channels of action as thought by our global theory. Acting thus means acting in such a way that the parameters of confidence or mistrust may be ultimately changed, or acting to use such or such a state of confidence or mistrust. Because, by integrating confidence and mistrust under the roof, *in fine,* of time (via duration, memory and forgetfulness), our theory asserts that there cannot be any immediate interpretation of confidence and mistrust. This is due to the fact that, although involved in action and acts, they carry within them (above all confidence) a temporal density that stretches back far farther than just the present moment. Confidence and mistrust include coefficients of inertia of value and their increase or erosion operates over time. When I say, "I am confident", I am apparently voicing an immediacy in action that takes effect; nevertheless, I am expressing, in a temporal regime, a given memory of facts, gestures and events, which I am moving into the present by speaking. Memory can lead to confidence just like mistrust, and the same holds for forgetfulness, as well as remembering (recalling). The point we are making is that the underlying matter of confidence and of mistrust is to be looked for in the distortions of time (absolute and perceived by the Subject).

Confidence and mistrust are the main manifestations of memory and forgetfulness. In this respect, they are global because they irrigate all facts, phenomena and events in the economic and the financial spheres. A genuinely global theory acknowledges the global nature of the manifestations of memory and of forgetfulness in confidence and mistrust, and, thereby, the power of time and of its perceptions in the formation of what is called economic or financial.

§ 84. Our global theory is concerned with totality. As we stated in a previous book (*Tractatus*), only the totality unifying Being, Subject and world matter for what claims to be the foundation of the economic. This totality is the cornerstone from which action, which is the purpose of our theory, unfolds. Being concerned with totality entails an endless concern for thought to respect that guideline. It is definitely not easy to think about action by drawing on what, apparently, barely resembles it. Indeed, action seems very remote from everything related to totality as well as duration. Action always comes under the guise of particularity, uniqueness, and within a temporal spectrum of narrowness and the ephemeral.

Our global theory includes action within the triptych formed by Being, the Subject and the world; integrates most of the conventional distinctions drawn by economic questioning in a unitary approach of repository and regime based on time; widens all definitions (inflation, etc.). In this respect, our global theory puts the finishing touch to an effort and a trajectory outlined in our previous books by adding an action-specific dimension to the house built on the foundations laid in said books.

Our global theory is based on the totality that links Being, the Subject and the world. A theory that would develop exclusively the action on the world by the Subject and would consist only in the technical description of such an action-related purpose, would not be genuinely global. As we have extensively shown, this is how Economics has formed itself as a scientific discipline in the modern era, to the point that it has blended into nothing more than the study of the Subject's technical and action-related purpose aimed at transforming the world. The key theoretical bias in the contemporary period consists in this very transformation of what is economic, which has been literally grasped and stormed by the Subject. This transformation is, in its deepest essence, the destination of the relationship between mankind and the world in the West. Little by little, the economic framework and the theoretical environment have stopped being global and become unique and local to an extreme extent. They are now local, in the sense where the Subject and his/her acting consciousness are the link, indeed the only link from which the economic, and subsequently the financial, have been thought. This dramatic shrinking of the theoretical spectrum is perceived only to a weak degree, because of the dramatic extent to which the discipline has focused on, and restricted itself to, the technical description of the confrontational nature of the Subject's action aimed at transforming the world. A global theory must break with this dual focus (Subject, technique) and such a break is a direct consequence of its global nature. This very break, because it entails widening once more to a radical extent the field and the multidisciplinary – foundations of the economic, and because it leads to new forms of questioning and fresh questions, this very break consecrates the global nature of our theory. Our purpose in this book does not include describing in detail this renewed widening of the economic field, but this fruitful development leads to an Economics at last better established on its legitimate foundations.

Note, furthermore, that a theory that would merely propose a (technical) description of the world as it presents itself to us, a passive consciousness restricted to observing the occurrence, admittedly would not lack any interest because it would grasp facts, events and states, in the form of a landscape that is more or less changing. However, when the theoretical bias leads to such a form of focusing, one cannot talk of a global theory, just like focusing on the (technical) description of the Subject's actions cannot either provide a global foundation. On the contrary, the local dimension dominates when either the Subject or the world dominates *per se* the technical purpose of the description provided by the theoretical effort. Both biases sometimes appear in a pure form but, increasingly, in the modern era, theory has mainly focused on the pair formed by the Subject's face-to-face with the world insofar as the Subject aims to modify the world. Moreover, while the modern period – which lasted until the past century – tended to witness an increasing importance granted to describing the Subject's action (often on the world although the Subject's action as such has increasingly monopolized the interest of economists), the most recent period of the contemporary era has displayed its fascination for "external" descriptions of the world, i.e. so-called "globalization". Nonetheless, such a kind of fascination remains merely local, and in every case strayed slightly more from the prospect of a genuine global theory.

We have shown elsewhere that the effort aimed at achieving a global dimension found its roots in the articulation between Being, the Subject and the world, and because it failed to try to think the economic (with) from Being and its modalities, theory was dooming itself to being gradually confined to studying the Subject, or the world, or both and their relationship; with technology (and its descriptions) accompanying this evolution.

Without wishing to recap precisely the key points of this theoretical approach, we would like to emphasize to what extent this cornerstone underpins our global theory. We refer the reader to *Tractatus*, *Genealogy*, and *Value and Time*. A genuinely global theory must have foundations that are not restricted to studying the Subject and the world although it will not ignore them nevertheless. Faced with a technical absolutism exerted by the Subject and a kind of pantheism, which is just as technical, consisting in a description of the world, we need to reassert the serene trinity of Being, the Subject and the world.

For a genuinely global theory, all the other theories are not global and are merely local, particular, efforts (in the sense where intellectual geography allocates a conceptual site, which eventually imprisons the theory). The theories developed in the modern era consecrated the omnipotence of the Subject and his/her confinement in a single relationship consisting in a creative and destructive face-to-face with the world. They have described this relationship in such a technical manner that technology has become the very corpus of this relationship. Then Keynes, who rightly believed his theory was a generality whereas classical observations were merely particular cases, nevertheless merely raised the Subject's omnipotence to its crescendo and its end (without transcending it). Keynes puts the finishing touch, but does not break with classical economics.

§ 85. A global theory must be able to express itself in a few simple and elementary contentions. As far as we are concerned, the first contention establishes that everything economic is, always and everywhere, reducible to a time differential; the economic dynamics that sets facts, phenomena and events in motion is based on memory and forgetfulness, as well as the value granted to time.

The second contention notes that the cycle unfolds from the value granted to time, which is value itself. The preference and substitution functions between goods, services and financial assets result from value defined in this manner. These functions govern the traditional concepts of growth (investment, consumption) and prices, as well as trade-offs between them. These functions also govern the various states or moments or periods of cycle, regardless of its duration, from the most ephemeral to the secular. Each state forms a repository or a regime with its own characteristics.

The third contention holds that the equilibrium is determined by the temporal repository i.e. by time, time-matter, memory and forgetfulness. The equilibrium is absolute (time is absent), restricted relative (stability of functions as well as memory and forgetfulness coefficients within a repository), relative (instability of said, cyclicity). The absolute equilibrium describes a (static) state; the restricted relative and relative equilibria characterize a dynamics that is closer to reality. In a restricted relative equilibrium, the time-matter repository maintains (temporarily or by hypothesis) a form of stability (memory and forgetfulness coefficients). In a relative equilibrium, the dilatations and contractions of time in the repository are permanent. All economic states can be described in one of the situations of absolute or relative equilibrium.

Fourth contention: economic facts, phenomena and events can, always and everywhere, give rise to a monetary description. There is a deep analogy between money and time-matter. Just like a piece of wax, money is informed by memory and by forgetfulness. The phenomenon of interest consists in this information. Interest expresses the distortions of memory and forgetfulness for all so-called economic variables, facts and events. The immediate interest rate comprises the memory interest rate and a risk premium, as each element is defined within a repository or regime, and therefore by reference to a situation of absolute or relative equilibrium.

Fifth contention: economic policy action is pertinent and efficient when it takes full account of memory and forgetfulness dimensions, regardless of its objective. Action can consist in wanting to draw on memory/forgetfulness effects or wanting, on the contrary, to modify these effects just like a river is diverted. Economic policy action, although it seems destined to managing the immediate, in other words contemporary immediate states, is always in fact, in the best cases, the management of a thicker temporal dimension that must be recalled, or on the contrary needs to be forgotten, and therefore ultimately forgetfulness or memory can be wished for or not and thus be the purpose of action. One acts on the immediate only in appearance, in fact one always has to set some older stone into motion.

CHAPTER 5

THE MONETARY DYNAMICS
OF LIQUIDITY

§ 86. Money can buy goods as well as securities. Or, more precisely, goods can, also, eventually buy money. Turning around the fundamental proposal that establishes the causality running from money to securities enables us to unveil the role played by the securities market. It also enables us to shed new light on the crucial link that unfolds from the monetary dimension towards the real sphere, by showing that this link is not only intermediated by the securities market (the stock market we could say for the sake of simplicity) but, far more importantly, that the financial dimension (here the securities market) retroacts with, interacts with, the real sphere. Money attracts goods toward it and the latter move towards it by heading down the path of securities.

An approach that would take into consideration the (quantitative) causality acting from money towards the real sphere but would ignore the one that includes, so to say by the way, the financial sphere, would remain essentially incomplete. Far more, this approach, to be complete, would need to have a premonition of back links that send back, like a boomerang, the financial toward the real in a sort of symmetry.

§ 87. The stock of money circulates in the real sphere (goods and services) and in the financial sphere (securities). With a given monetary unit, goods and services can be bought in the financial sphere; and securities in the financial sphere. The acceleration in the pace of circulation of the stock of money (its velocity) in the real sphere fuels inflation in the price of goods and services; the acceleration in the circulation of the same stock of money (its velocity) in the financial sphere fuels inflation in the prices of securities. The ballooning of transactions within either of the two spheres takes place in proportion to the deceleration in the mobilization/circulation of the monetary stock in the other one. That is true in theory. Theoretically, therefore, one should see a distortion in relative prices (goods and services *versus* securities) and not a global phenomenon of inflation (rise in the general price level). This is true for a purely domestic economy, and is also true for an open economy, or should be. For instance, the increase of balances in dollars held by non-resident investors should be offset by a decrease in the circulation of the monetary stock, in particular for consumption purposes, in the United States. If this is not the case, for it is not the case, this means that there is monetary creation at the two ends of the chain.

Theoretically, by consequence, the real and financial spheres exchange in a fashion a stock of money deemed given. Thus there is a first, fixed, variable: the stock of money (M_oS). There is next velocity of circulation of the stock of money (its velocity) in the real sphere and, also, in the financial sphere. We will denote velocity V_m (of the stock of money). The number of real or financial transactions (related to securities) by monetary unit of the stock of money determines the intensity of the mobilization of the stock of money, the velocity of money in the real sphere or in the financial sphere; this velocity determines *in fine* real and financial inflation.

In such an approach, we have a single and given stock of money that "turns" just like the hamster in its cage, in two wheels in the occurrence located in the cage. There is only one cage (stock of money) but there are two wheels, and the hamster cannot get the two wheels to spin at the same time. In this approach, the stock of money circulates in one sphere then in the other; circulation phenomena are not simultaneous. There is only one stock of money and only one player (the hamster in our example). It feeds inflation in prices of goods and services *or* financial inflation by setting in motion (i.e. because the pace of circulation accelerates). We are insisting here on the non-simultaneity of the sequences in a somewhat light-hearted manner in order to emphasize the phenomenon of distortion in relative prices. A single monetary stock is set in motion in two asynchronous (desynchroniszed?) spheres for single global inflation phenomenon that integrates two states (one real, the other financial). Inflation is correctly, i.e. globally grasped, once it is subdivided into real inflation and financial inflation.

$$M_oS \cdot Vm = Inf(r, f)$$

with: $M_oS \cdot Vm_{(r)} = Inf(r)$ and $a\left(\dfrac{Vm(r)}{Vm(f)}\right) = \dfrac{Inf(r)}{Inf(f)}$

$$M_oS \cdot V_m(f) = Inf(f)$$

In this approach the ratio $V_m(r)/V_m(f)$ determines the distortion of relative real and financial prices and, accordingly, gives the orientation of global inflation. In a fashion, we are in a process of transfer from the real sphere into the financial sphere and *vice versa*. The acceleration in the velocity of circulation in the financial sphere, for instance, means in this approach that substantial sums are transferred from the real sphere in order to finance the financial sphere's growing needs against the backdrop of a rise in $V_m(f)$; we therefore have, symmetrically, a double weakening of borrowing requirements of real transactions (in the real sphere) and of the means required to meet them (whether we are in a domestic closed economy or in an open global economy operating in dollars, this implies or means a contraction in real activity). Furthermore, the increase in $V_m(f)$, necessarily, implies a decline in $V_m(r)$. Lastly, we have, and this is a strong hypothesis of this approach, stability of the stock of money (there is neither monetary creation *ex nihilo*, for instance, nor destruction of money).

§ 88.   In such an approach, there is so to say general regulation of the overall system because, as a trend or at cruising speed, the distortions in the $V_m(r)/V_m(f)$ ratio are eventually compatible with stability of $Inf(r, f)$. We therefore definitely have cyclical distortions (in the cycle) of $V_m(r)/V_m(f)$, within the unfolding of a global economic and financial cycle global during which real sequences and financial   sequences follow one another in a relatively not very synchronous manner. However, the $V_m(r)/V_m(f)$ ratio or, more precisely, $Inf(r)/Inf(f)$ (the stability of the relationship between velocity and inflation is another question), remains inscribed in forms in which compensation effects play. $\left[Inf(r)/Inf(f)\right]$ describes a trajectory through four quadrants, ranging from value 1 (total inflation) to value 1 (deflation total), i.e. between two values that lead to the unconnected rationales operating in the real and financial spheres joining one another at the extremes. At the extremes, there is a contagious reconnection of the two spheres (i.e. positive correlation of monetary velocity and inflation rates): we are tending toward a unitary value of velocity and inflation ratios, and therefore, a movement in the general price level. These two unitary values correspond to breaking points ruptures (bursting of financial bubbles with a deflationary impact/retroaction on the real sphere; general inflation in prices of goods and assets), in particular caused by the response of monetary and fiscal authorities. Between these two unitary values that velocity and inflation ratios can take, we face distortions in relative prices. One leads to inflation in prices of goods and services being combined with moderate/depressed prices of securities, while the other combines moderation in prices of goods and services with a surge in prices of securities (this situation was anything but theoretical when the financial bubble of the 1990s rose, as when the credit bubble did likewise at the beginning of the following century, as the decline in interest rates fuelled the movement; conversely, the inflationary surges of the 1970s badly hurt markets of securities, whether bonds or equities). In both cases, the initial theoretical situation undergoes a dynamic evolution once the reaction function of monetary or fiscal authorities starts to operate.

We therefore have:

$\left[Inf_{(r)} / Inf_{(f)} \right] = 1$ if inflation or deflation $\left(Inf_{(r,f)} \right)$.

§ 89.   In such an approach, we therefore have:

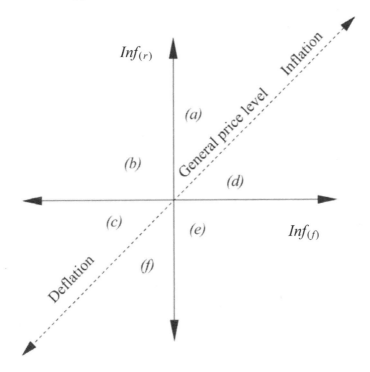

We can clearly see in the Chart the various scenarios that could eventuate in the approach we have described take shape. The unitary values of the inflation ratio (i.e. neutralization of distortions in relative prices) are set out on an equivalence line. Inflation and deflation phenomena (in the complete sense where the general price level is affected) are the extreme phenomena. All the other values indicate a state of the general price level within which the real and the financial neutralize one another's effects, and this does not mean that there are no links between one phenomenon and the other, far from it in fact: when a financial bubble bursts, it leads to deflation in prices of goods and services for instance. Such a ratio can record negative values.

On the left of this equivalence line, we find three situations *(a)*, *(b)*, *(c)* in which inflation in prices of goods and services undergoes a relative increase in comparison with financial inflation (in prices of securities). These three positions, looking beyond this common point, are dissimilar in the sense where they correspond to very distinct moments of the economic and financial cycle.

• *(a)* does not call for any specific comment apart from the fact that by drawing closer on the right-hand side of the equivalence line, we find ourselves in a logic of diffusion of inflation from the real sphere to the financial sphere and therefore a significant increase in the general price level (which requires action from the policy mix). By the way, a noteworthy point is that there is a dynamics in the progression from one quadrant to another and within a same quadrant. Likewise, there is a dynamics of the situations in comparison with the equivalence line.

• *(b)* corresponds to a contraction in the value of securities (financial disinflation) in a context of inflationary strains in the sphere of goods and services. This sequence can correspond to inflationary phases, which are unfavorable to long-term financial assets, because of tensions on (short- and long-term) interest rates and the rebuilding of a high risk premium on the asset class of equities.

• *(c)* sees simultaneous deflation in both the real and financial spheres. The decline in prices of goods paves the way for a fall in prices of securities, toward a drop in the general price level. On the right-hand side of the equivalence line there are three situations sharing a relative increase in financial inflation in comparison with conventional inflation, however dissimilar they may be.

• *(d)* sees, in its dynamics, the financial sphere benefit from price restraint in the sphere of goods and services. The dynamics can lead to the vicinity of the axis / *Inf (f)* that plots a trajectory of financial bubble underpinned by a lack of inflation/disinflation, therefore probably resulting in a rather accommodating monetary policy. The dynamics can also lead to the vicinity of the equivalence line that, like in *(a)*, is the area of a rise in the general price level, in inflation eventually, in hyperinflation possibly. *(a)*, the point is worth noting, also hesitates between the equivalence line and the axis *Inf*(*r*), between general inflation and inflation in prices of goods that anesthetizes any (positive) dynamics in prices of securities.

• *(e)* combines a fall in inflation (disinflation/deflation) with inflation in prices of financial assets, a combination that can be located close to axis *Inf*(*f*), i.e. low inflation/increase in asset prices. When we move along axis *Inf*(*r*), on the contrary, the situations that diverge to the right of the axis seem to correspond only to highly theoretical positions.

• *(f)* leads from the bursting of the financial bubble to deflation in prices of goods, to general deflation in the level of prices.

Such a Chart enables us to visualize the position of the distortion of relative prices in the global cycle and, furthermore, to detect the problematic zones that draw extreme points closer, situations of a rise (inflation) or decline (deflation) in the general price level.

§ 90.   Building, analyzing and interpreting the curve *Inf*(*r*)/ *Inf*(*f*) provides significant information about whether there are trade-off possibilities (or not) between the two main forms of inflation. For a study consisting in estimating over a long enough period the couple [*Inf*(*r*)/ *Inf*(*f*)], should allow us to estimate the general shape of the curve as extracted from reality. The length of the period, if it provides evidence of statistical solidity, will perhaps have to draw a distinction, however, between sub-periods corresponding to different price contexts and regimes.

§ 91.   In the approach we have taken until now, we had as it were a known and constant stock of money, two economic spheres (the real one including goods and services; the financial one including all securities, which at this stage we tend to understand as long-term securities) and a circulation of the stock of money (in other words, the velocity of the stock of money, defined as the number of real or financial transactions, by monetary stock unit). Circulation occurs, on the one hand, within both spheres, in a "closed" manner, as well as from one sphere into the other under the form of what we have called a transfer, which leaves the global stock of money unchanged (velocity is not a multiplier, does not result in any multiplying effect, a point we will discuss further in this book, when looking at multiplication as monetary creation). The stock of money is unchanged, it is neutral (on S_{M_o}), the borrowing requirements in the real sphere must be covered by a "transfer" from the financial sphere, and *vice versa*. There is therefore neutrality in the sense of a general equilibrium with the principle of offsetting in one sphere in comparison with the other one. The way a financial bubble builds up, for instance, within the financial sphere, will require transfers of means of payment from the real sphere that will be put up with only as long as the real sphere will be able to do so, i.e. as long as the creation of means of payment will benefit from an accommodating monetary policy. The financial bubble will be fed by this accommodating policy, until the point where, in the real sphere, normalization sets in, and there is a return to the equilibrium (for instance, a rise in interest rates) that will impose a readjustment of the "levels" of stock of money in circulation (i.e. liquidity, which is money in circulation) in the two spheres. A sort of asphyxiation may occur in the financial sphere (and the bubble will stop rising) because returning to the compensating equilibrium in the real sphere will trigger an adjustment in the general equilibrium of the two spheres. There is an offsetting mechanism in the sense where the expansion of demand for means of payment in the sphere of goods or in the sphere of securities supposes/ imposes cutting expenditure in the other sphere. An imbalance in either sphere ends up by being corrected by the return to a neutrality of equilibrium in the other sphere. This dynamics of adjustment in the two spheres ensures a general macrofinancial equilibrium. As it were, this is made possible, in theory at least, by the fact that

S_{M_o} is given and V is neutral (no monetary creation *ex nihilo*). Of course, this proposition deserves to be confronted with reality.

By the way, one understands in such an approach that as regulation is to a quite large extent the result of corrective processes located in the real sphere (including, primarily, monetary policy), the financial sphere is seen to "depend" on the real sphere and it is believed it can easily be adjusted once an imbalance appears. In fact, in such an approach, everything is seen to take place as if financial imbalances were "residuals", excrescences, and externalities of the real sphere; as if the phenomena operating in the financial sphere were hardly autonomous (causality unfolds from the real to the financial, in the way symptoms are built and the imbalance is absorbed). This approach, which dominated economic thought for a long time, continues to irrigate most approaches. Nonetheless, observation shows that the financial sphere enjoys significant autonomy and that transfers between spheres are not always governed, far from it in fact, by various forms of neutrality and of general equilibrium. On the contrary, the return to the general equilibrium is not at all spontaneous once either sphere is in imbalance.

§ 92. Lastly, in what we call the "traditional approach", not much is said about the dynamics of the monetary stock and its determinants. "Liquidity" is defined as the specific dynamics of the stock of money, which can measure the speed or the velocity of the stock of money. There can be a liquidity effect only for a stock of money that begins to move, set in motion by a certain number of objective forces (in the sense where they are "external" to the Subject) and, for others, given an impulse by the intimate dynamics of the Subject's consciousness.

In the "traditional" approach, the stock of money is unchanged. Everything happens as if the phenomenon of liquidity, by bursting in via speed/velocity, did not change, did not modify (as a backlash) the stock of money. As we shall see, the phenomenon of liquidity is at the origin of a second birth (creation) of the stock of money. There is definitely a type of monetary creation that encompasses the phenomenon of liquidity.

And the phenomenon of liquidity, which encompasses the phenomena of speed and velocity of the stock of money, ultimately the inflation phenomenon, itself obeys determinants that are, entirely or partly, those of action, of Time, of the Subject, of the world that leave an imprint on it. Why does the stock of money, suddenly, in a temporal discontinuity that characterizes its regime or repository, begin to accelerate, decelerate, split up, dilate?

§ 93.   If we were to summarize the main affirmations of what we have called the "traditional" approach, we can write:

- M_oS = Cte (Inv) (constant = invariable), at $t = 0$ (static; the system can become dynamic through an increase in M_oS).

- $V_m = \dfrac{T}{M_oS}$ with T = transaction and $T = T_r + T_f$; V_m is
  neutral (V_m does not modifiy M_oS).

- $V_m = V_m(r) + V_m(f)$ with $V_m(r) = \dfrac{Tr}{M_oS}$ and $V_m(f) = \dfrac{Tf}{M_oS}$.

- $Inf(r, f) = Inf_{(r)} + Inf_{(f)}$

  where $Inf_{(r)} = f\big(V_m(r); M_oS\big)$

  and $Inf_{(f)} = f\big(V_m(f); M_oS\big)$

- $Inf = Inf(r, f)$

  $M_oS \cdot V_m = Inf \cdot T$

  $\Leftrightarrow M_oS \cdot V_m(r, f) = Inf \cdot T(r, f)$

  $\Leftrightarrow Inf = \dfrac{1}{T(r, f)} \cdot M_oS \cdot V_m(r, f)$

  $Inf = \left[\dfrac{M_oS}{T(r, f)} \right] \cdot V_m(r, f)$

V_m is not determined, or not sufficiently, in the approach. Its role appears, as it were, through a balance.

We can see above that the inflation phenomenon is apprehended as a total and complete phenomenon (a "general" one in the sense of the general price level). Inflation definitely results from the velocity of the stock of money (liquidity) but velocity expands, and must therefore be simultaneously recorded, in the real and financial spheres. We are typically in an approach where the lack of inflation in the real sphere leads to (in the sense that one has to, by construction) looking at the financial sphere. Inflation, it is sometimes argued, mutates (from the real to the financial sphere); while others (legitimately) talk about a simple distortion of relative prices. What matters, first of all, is clearly seeing the generality of the inflation phenomenon; and, subsequently, affirming the role of money (its stock, its velocity) in the appearance of inflation whether real or financial, or real and financial.

§ 94.   To move forward, we need to surmount the inertia of the stock of money and substitute, as it were, liquidity for money (as a stock) as an operational concept of action and transformation (monetary creation), and this entails revisiting the determinants of $L = (V \cdot M_oS)$. To move forward, one has to imagine that the two spheres are not governed by a general equilibrium of compensation (general neutrality of monetary transfers, adjustment in either sphere for a general equilibrium of the system), that excesses in one sphere necessarily end up triggering a return to more neutrality and equilibrium in the other for, as it were, the system as a whole and therefore both spheres. To move forward, thus we need to imagine that the two spheres sum up, overlap, more than they offset or neutralize one another, imagine that their links are governed by a sort of cumulative dynamics of creation (monetary creation for instance), imbalances and destruction (of value for example). To move forward, one has to imagine that the financial sphere is unshackled, and has its own existence and rationale, as well as its own dynamics. The nature of this dynamics is characterized by Otherness and is far more specific than we continue to think because, *nolens volens,* we continue to see the financial sphere, in its nature as in the processes that have to prevail in its adjustment, as an adjunct of the real sphere, admittedly growing and increasingly acknowledged, but an adjunct, from an intellectual viewpoint. To move forward, lastly, one has to be able to reintroduce time, time of action, of the Subject, of the world, in the specific movement that prints the stock of money like a book is printed or one leaves a footprint, a specific movement of a temporal repository of contractions, dilatations, discontinuities and non-linearities. To move forward, we thus need to take into account the memory of what, precisely, "prints" the stock of money and brings it to life under the form of so-called liquidity.

§ 95. Consequently, we must manage to substitute L (for liquidity) to M_oS, a rigid and inert approach focused exclusively on the stock of money. By the by, this means shedding light on the determinants of L and we can clearly see that Keynes was on the right track when he forged a bridging concept, i.e. one that included the reality of the matter, money/liquidity, but also the Subject's action, with preference, as this all together formed preference for liquidity. More precisely, we need to highlight the links between L and V_m as well as their determinants; because the very motion of the stock of money results from Vm, which contributes time. V_m is a function of time that gives M_oS a referential framework in which the stock of money is going to move. L furthermore is a function of $M_oS(L = a\ M_oS)$, with an upward and/or downward multiplication coefficient. We therefore need to understand why V_m suddenly starts to take increasing or decreasing values. We accordingly have to look into the stability of V_m.

Subsequently, we have to build for the real (T, Inf) and more monetary (M_oS, V_m, L) values memory effects (of real or monetary variables). This is a crucial development because monetary phenomena are phenomena in which memory leaves its imprint. Money is what remembers and forgets. Memory is a stock just like M_oS is also a stock, and the analogy is striking. By getting into motion and setting in motion a stock of memory, the stock of money becomes liquidity and circulates. The very movement of circulation (V_m) activates a memory, and forgetfulness, function. This can be seen in the intensity of real or financial transactions in proportion to the stock of money, i.e. of transactions by monetary unit $\left(\dfrac{T_{(r,f)}}{M_oS}\right) \cdot T_{(r)}$ unquestionably is linked with a final demand, itself a function of income or, even better, of an idea of income (expected, i.e., a memorized/forgotten approximation). If we denote income Y (what results from activity), we have $T_{(r)} = f(y_M)$. Likewise, $T_{(f)}$ undoubtedly integrates, to a certain degree, the memory and forgetfulness of relevant determinants. We can see from experience that the massive acceleration witnessed in transactions during the phase when a financial bubble builds up on the market of securities (the increase in $V_m(f)$) seems to result from forgetfulness phenomena (precisely, what is called "irrationality" of behaviors in a bubble). If there is forgetfulness, by definition a memorized lesson from the past or stock is eroding.

This is a crucial point of our approach. All monetary phenomena are determined by memory and forgetfulness links with all relevant variables. We shall discuss this further later on but one needs to bear in mind that immediate or contemporary changes in many real or monetary variables are meaningful only for the underlying, deeper and more discreet, movement of heavier strata of memory that displaces the Earth's crust while the lapping of surface water seems to be playing another kind of music.

§ 96. The postulate of the stability of V_m contradicts the characteristics of the temporal repository of L, in other words discontinuity and non-linearity, acceleration and breaking points, dilatations and contractions of time-matter, discontinuous memory (duration) and forgetfulness effects.

In the "traditional" approach, the invoked instability of V_m (in particular to refute the pertinence of the quantitative approach of steering money) results exclusively from the fact that V_m is an incomplete element, i.e. $V_m(r,f)$. $V_m(r,f)$ is more stable than $V_m(r)$ or $V_m(f)$ taken separately. And $V_m(r, f)$ is more relevant in terms of establishing the dynamics of $Inf_{(r,f)}$ as the general price level.

Having said that, one fails to see why and how V_m could prove to be stable in the sense according to which it is understood in most criticism; and, on the other hand, in what manner that would discredit a general monetary approach based on V_m. It is in the nature of V_m to be determined by a temporal repository of discontinuities. Can a more "disciplined" version of V_m be reached, and consequently a variable that could integrate systematic steering and some kind of rule. In other words, we need to draw a distinction between an incompressible nature of discontinuities and the possibility of achieving a certain form of stability in the relationships between major variables, for instance between L, V_m and $Inf(r,f)$.

§ 97.   We have to replace the principle of separation and compensation with respect to real and financial spheres by the principle of addition and autonomy, and this does not prevent the possible existence of links (causality links notably) and a form of general system, perhaps enhanced by a (general) equilibrium. However, we need to discard the idea according to which the financial sphere is not autonomous and, *in fine*, what matters is the dynamics of expansion and contraction in the real sphere. We therefore need to break with the idea that the financial sphere reflects, "masks" the real sphere, in a sort of mimesis. The core of the, descriptive or critical, analysis of the financial sphere starts off from and always comes back to the so-called "fundamentals" of the real sphere (this is the very conceptual architecture of so-called "financial" analysis, the very principle of the explanatory approach of what occurs on the market of securities, the very principle of the quest for value, which is an "unveiling", i.e. the need to pull away the veil put up by the financial sphere, to mask a value determined by causes located in the real sphere).

We therefore need to break with the idea that the financial masks the real, that the financial sphere is a veil put on top of the real sphere; and consequently also break with the idea – which is deeply rooted at the heart of economic theory and the approach taken to interpret and analyze value – which holds that in the medium/long term the financial veil ends up by dropping and the financial dynamics is a temporary veil on goods. Goods are not recovered by a financial veil. In fact, the financial transforms the real to the same extent as the reverse.

We therefore, also, need to break with the idea that regulation of the financial sphere may be determined from the real sphere, by drawing on its rationales and its tools. The autonomy of the financial sphere means that its regulation processes can be specific.

Lastly, we need to break with the idea that there is a general equilibrium of the whole that, mostly, would be the general equilibrium of the real sphere; and accordingly a return to neutrality (equilibrium) in the real sphere would suffice to adjust (balance) the whole. Instead of the stock phrase "the veil of money (on goods and trade)", we prefer the idea that liquidity is not a veil on the real sphere. The only way to account for this is to integrate, in a same approach and therefore in a single monetary equation, the phenomena of liquidity and time (velocity, speed) and the dynamics of the two main spheres at the heart of the economic.

§ 98.   The financial sphere looks forward to/anticipates the future just like one (the financial sphere) remembers the past. This fundamental analogy allows us to grasp in what manner the financial veil, the veil of the financial sphere is in fact made of time-matter, i.e. memory and forgetfulness in the occurrence. The market of securities is primarily a veil of memory and forgetfulness of the real sphere that retroacts on the real sphere. In other words, the market of securities keeps (or does not keep) remembrance of real. By consequence, far from being a useless veil, the financial is the real sphere's necessary veil thanks to which it perpetuates and transforms itself. The way in which this veil operates, its dynamics, is primarily linked to the operation of liquidity as a differential of the stock of money. It is by "differentiating itself" that the stock of money (thanks to its speed) sets in motion memory and forgetfulness effects. The phenomena of speed/velocity of the stock of money – which are at the heart of the dynamics of liquidity – and the phenomena of remembering/forgetting the real are fundamentally related.

§ 99.   If, now, we try to place end to end a few links, what kind of a chain can we then see take shape? We have:

$$M_oS \cdot V_m(r,f) = Inf_{(r,f)} \cdot T(r,f)$$

which becomes: $L = Inf \cdot T$

where we lay down the principle that liquidity is the product of the stock of money by its speed, i.e. by time. Speed, or velocity, is the time factor in this part of the equation $\left(M_oS \cdot V_{m(r,f)} \right)$ and this time factor represents all the present, memorized or forgotten temporal elements. What we are saying here is that V_m is a memory and forgetfulness function. The determinant of V_m is not risk appetite, risk aversion or the preference for liquidity, although these concepts are not ill-founded and are found in cause-and-effect sequences. However, these concepts tend to be consequences (preference for liquidity for instance). There is a deep analogy between V_m and memory/forgetfulness from the viewpoint of the temporal repository, which dilates or contracts over and over again. V_m is an airlock giving access to time that opens and closes, dilates or contracts in discontinuity, breaks and non-linearity.

We therefore have $\left(V_m = y_{M/F} \right)$ or a memory and/or forgetfulness coefficient y.

We still have $\begin{cases} L = M_oS \cdot V_{m(r,f)} \\ L = Inf \cdot T_{(r,f)} \end{cases}$

L (liquidity) is therefore defined as the product of the monetary stock by a memory/forgetfulness coefficient (y). The more or less swifter speed of circulation of the unit of the monetary stock in the real and financial spheres reflects, in fact expresses, the more or less strong dilatation (forgetfulness) or contraction (memory, duration) of time (although the terms dilatation and contraction do not necessarily and directly refer back to memory and forgetfulness).

When the circulation of the monetary stock accelerates (the number and the amount of transactions carried out by committed monetary unit increases), there is a rise in the demand for cash in hand for purposes related to transactions in the real sphere (goods) or the financial sphere (securities). Whether in order to buy goods or securities, the need for cash in hand to carry out transactions involves a projection, an expectation based on what has subsisted from the past in memory. The inflationary process is a process of forgetfulness that does not operate progressively but by leaps. The recession/deflation process is an awakening of memory, recalling. In a second recall process, which we have explained above, we definitely have, by moving toward what will become recession or deflation, a deceleration in $L = M_o S \cdot V_{m(r,f)}$ with $V_m = y_{M/F}$; the value of the memory coefficient y decreases ($\frac{1}{y}$ increases, i.e. the forgetfulness coefficient). This adjustment of the memory and forgetfulness coefficient results in the same effect as the rise in the preference for liquidity, which remained for its part above all a pure psychological process. With $y_{M/F}$, we can link the movements of L and the memorized determinants (with a forgetfulness coefficient) of the demand for cash in hand. L plummets during the recession (contraction/ decrease in $M_o S$). L increases during the expansion of the sphere of real goods or the dilatation of the financial sphere.

Liquidity in the sense of L plummets during the recession because a representation of the determinants of the demand for cash in hand for transactions is literally recalled. It is either more realistic after a phase of euphoria and bubbles, or more downbeat and even more pessimistic than what should prevail, in memory, as an average (asymmetry of memory, with the worst being selected in the occurrence). Appetite for risk or risk aversion phenomena stem from this process. L must therefore be distinguished from "liquidity" in the sense given to this word in the Keynesian expression of preference for liquidity. On which variable does (y) bear? We shall discuss this point further on.

§ 100.   In what is called the quantitative money equation, V_m is the most mysterious variable, the toughest to grasp and determine. Nevertheless, we clearly feel that the general monetary dynamics takes shape around it.

In this book, therefore, we propose interpreting V_m as a memory and forgetfulness function, a variable coefficient that leaves its imprint on the stock of money. This coefficient $(y_{M/F})$ plays a role in terms of routing, distributing, orientating M_oS for a stable, constant and given M_oS and does so between the real and financial spheres and, within each sphere, between the various segments of goods, services and securities, in particular between what focuses on the short term and what relates to the longer term. This coefficient $(y_{M/F})$ also plays the role of a multiplier of liquidity (L), i.e. an accelerator of money and, by consequence, of *ex nihilo* monetary creation. Whether we are in the real sphere or in the financial sphere, the product of the stock of money by time (speed, velocity, $y_{M/F}$ in the definition we give) is not neutral for M_oS: there is an effect of creation or destruction (of liquidity). At the end of each sequence, M_oS undergoes a change.

We therefore have two effects: a distribution effect; and a multiplication effect. $(y_{M/F})$ is both a coefficient distributing the stock of money and a coefficient multiplying the monetary stock. At the end of the sequence, M_oS thus has undergone a twofold transformation, one in its structure (distribution effect between spheres and within each sphere) and the other in its amplitude (multiplication effect, which can also be a destruction of the monetary stock effect). We can therefore break down $y_{M/F}$ into (y_d) and (y'_m).

The distribution function on its own enables us to understand the transfer of liquidity from one sphere into another within the framework of a "closed" schema ($y_{M/F}$ is neutral, there is no multiplication effect). By adding the multiplication effect, we can imagine simultaneous liquidity creation ($M_oS \cdot V_n = M_oS \cdot y_{M/F}$) in the real and financial spheres without any correcting phenomenon. Means of payment grow because of the acceleration in the monetary stock without, in exchange, any symmetrical reduction in the means of payment in the other sphere. This process of *ex nihilo* monetary creation, underpinned by the dollar's status, structured the United States/Asia financial axis at the turn of the twentieth-first century. We have described this at length in our *Monetary Notebooks*.

By interpreting V_m as a time factor and, in the occurrence, a memory and forgetfulness coefficient, we are led to reword the issue of the stability of V_m. This stability, which apparently is lacking in the traditional approach, must be redefined as the stability of a memory (forgetfulness) coefficient ($y_{M/F}$) within a macrofinancial regime and therefore a temporal repository.

We postulate that ($y_{M/F}$) is stable within a given macrofinancial regime. A strategy aimed at targeting $y_{M/F}$ in relation with M_oS *is* therefore possible. And this is the case provided (*y*) is estimated as a general variable (just like there is a general price level), i.e. from real and financial components, i.e. $y_{M/F}$ (*r,f*).

§ 101.　We therefore have, at the end of this initial investigation, established *L* as a concept of liquidity, the product of time and the stock of money.

We therefore have: $L = M_oS \cdot V_m = M_oS(y_{M/F})$.

By substituting liquidity for money in the equation, we have landed again on the dynamics through which money is molded by action and by time. *L is* always and everywhere characterized by a coefficient (*y*) that gives the more or less strong intensity of expansion or contraction (these terms recover distribution and multiplication effects). As a result, we pull liquidity out from an immense ambiguity about its definition and its role, without losing the Subject's action and preferences, aversions or appetencies. Any monetary phenomenon comes with a memory and forgetfulness coefficient, similar to a signature. We also pull V_m out from ambiguity and somewhat tautological definitions (defined by everything around it, apart from itself). Its theoretical and operational necessity at least finds a partial answer.

We have looked into one branch of the equation tree ($M_o S \cdot V_m$) by reducing it (L) and by introducing an interpretation of $V_m(y_{M/F})$ via memory and forgetfulness, in other words time more fundamentally.

The direct elucidation of V_m by the association with a memory and forgetfulness fact (analogy-based reasoning conducted above) still leaves unresolved the issue of what is memorized or forgotten. As an initial analysis, we would be tempted to say "everything", given the extent to which what "molds", "sculpts" the monetary stock is in fact the total environment of money. (y) is the environment of money.

More accurately, we can use the second branch of the equation to grasp Vm from a slightly different angle. We have:

$$M_o S \cdot V_m = Inf_{(r,f)} \cdot T_{(r,f)}$$

or: $\left[V_m = \dfrac{T}{M_o S} \cdot Inf \right]$, or alternatively $V_m = \left[T \cdot Inf \right] \cdot \dfrac{1}{M_o S}$

We use this branch of the equation, because we suspect that V_m is of an $aM_o S$ type. This resembles the form reached via analogical reasoning drawing on the first branch. We had $V_m = y$ with $M_o S \cdot V_m = M_o S \cdot (y_{M/F})$. By isolating ($a$) we certainly have a clue as to what, precisely, is memorized or forgotten in the mechanism that molds the stock of money, which is both distribution of the stock of money in its various possible utilizations and forms of demand, in the real sphere as in the financial sphere, and multiplication (possibly destruction) of liquidity (and, *in fine,* of the stock of money), i.e. monetary creation.

We started off from the idea that time, under various guises (memory, forgetfulness, duration) was the element that, fundamentally, molded the monetary dynamics. This time, that of memory, applies to some of the most general variables of. These general variables, general because they concern the real as well as the financial sphere, are the backbone of $y_{M/F}$. One needs to keep in mind that $y_{M/F}$ is a general coefficient, a global one in fact, and this is definitely a point made in this book. However, at the same time, the term "general" continues to characterize crucial elements, in particular in the monetary issues we are focusing upon, for instance the well-known general price level ($y_{M/F}$) is a general/global coefficient insofar as it integrates memory and forgetfulness in both the real and financial spheres, governing all aversion and appetency regimes.

The extraction of (a) enables us to see that $y_{M/F}$ can be analyzed by the remembering (and forgetting) of $a = T \cdot Inf$. (y) carries a memory and forgetfulness coefficient of activity and inflation into all real and financial spheres because it does consist in $T_{(r,f)}$ and $Inf_{(r,f)}$ In a very approximate approach (y) can be analyzed by $T_{(r,f)} \cdot Inf_{(r,f)}$ by integrating, and this is crucial, duration, memory and forgetfulness for these activity (demand) and price variables, i.e.:

$$V_m \approx y'_{M/F} = \left[\left[T \cdot Inf\right]_{r,f}\right]_{M/F}$$

This initial and unrefined approximation can be replaced by a second one since:

$$V_m = a\, M_o S = T \cdot Inf \cdot \frac{1}{M_o S}$$

The path seems open for a possible memorization of the $\left(\dfrac{T \cdot Inf}{M_o S}\right)_{(r,f)}$ set. Only testing can ascertain whether it is more relevant. One fails to see, on the contrary, why the (activity/inflation + stock of money) pair may not have a memory that plays its role. Instead of $y'_{M/F} = \left[T_{(r,f)} \cdot Inf_{(r,f)} \right]_{M/F}$ we can have:

$$y''_{M/F} = \left[\frac{T_{(r,f)} \cdot Inf_{(r,f)}}{M_o S} \right]_{M/F}$$

§ 102.   We thus need to grasp $\left(\dfrac{T \cdot Inf}{M_o S} \right)$ both as a global (general) set, i.e. a totality of real and financial (r, f) sub-sets, as well as a temporal repository of duration, i.e. of memory, and therefore of forgetfulness. Whether it is T, which encompasses real activity, i.e. activity related to goods and services, and financial operations on all markets of securities; or whether it is Inf, which includes all the prices that form the general price level, prices of goods, of services, of financial securities; in both cases, we are looking for a memory coefficient, by consequence a form of inertia, on the basis of the equiweighted past or not. The memory (and forgetfulness) coefficient can be seen as an expectation given the strength of the analogy between recalling the past and expecting what is yet to come.

The variable $y_{M/F}$ is, in pure theory, the perfect and pure reduction of a micro-financial economic regime to its simple temporal expression of memory and forgetfulness. This variable synthesizes as a simple element the relationship with time within the regime, at what pace and with what intensity one remembers and one forgets in a given economic regime, *hic et nunc*. This variable ($y_{M/F}$) also describes how, in a given economic regime, what is yet to come (the future) is expected, anticipated, in view of the striking extent to which this is the same process as the one that enables us to remember.

There is no reason why, in theory, the variable ($y_{M/F}$) should not be stable in a given economic regime macrofinancial. In fact, on the contrary, it is precisely because there is such a coefficient (y) of the relationship with time that an economic regime is possible. And, mostly, a change from one macrofinancial regime to another results from an evolution in the relationship with time and from a change in the way we remember and we forget and, consequently, in the way we anticipate. We should talk about a break rather than evolution given the extent to which the dynamics of regimes (the monetary regime here) results from discontinuities, threshold, growth and also acceleration effects.

There is speed, there is velocity, because there is time and difference. Grasping and understanding this time factor may be said to be at the heart of the monetary dynamics.

§ 103. The initial equation $\left[M_o S \cdot V_m = Inf \cdot T \right]$ can therefore be reduced to the writing of a simple equality as there are simple elements simple, or $L = M_o S \cdot y_{M/F}$ and $y_{M/F} = \left(\dfrac{T \cdot Inf}{M_o S} \right)_{M/F}$. We have $L = y'$ with $y' = \left(T \cdot Inf \right)_{M/F}$. The equality sets out the equivalence between liquidity and the time factor of the regime of activity and of prices, as this regime encompasses the real and financial spheres.

L can be steered. By assuming the relative stability of the coefficient y within a given macrofinancial economic regime (hence the expression "relative" stability), L must grow in proportion to y' if a relative neutrality is to be reached in the adequate setting of the means of payment in comparison with the general level of activity and inflation in the total set that encompasses the real and financial spheres. We understand "in proportion to" with a narrow room for maneuver because neutrality is given by the unitary relationship.

§ 104. We cannot look for a general or global equilibrium by drawing on the fundamental money equation as long as all markets are not integrated, within the same approach and the same dynamics. The integration of the real and financial spheres, as well as of their various segments means the same. Transcending relative truths, i.e. truths specific to dynamics of relative values (for instance the dynamics of relative prices, within each of the two spheres and between them), this transcending toward general truths (for instance, the assertions that can be made about the general level of activity or of prices) entails simultaneously taking into consideration the sub-sets (markets) of goods, services and securities. The simultaneous taking into account, in contrast with an approach consisting in taking these sub-sets into account successively, admits the apparent paradox of autonomous dynamics combined with deep interdependences, transfers or compensation but also additions and accumulation rationales.

Transcending relative truths means substituting, in the corpus of monetary equations we are concerned with, general variables (T, Inf, V_m) for what, until now and far too often, has remained local variables, local in the sense where each time it relates to just one aspect, one segment, of one of the two spheres, or of both. This is how the study of the general inflation phenomenon, a phenomenon of a general level if there is one, has been flawed by an extremely restrictive interpretation of T, V_m or even Inf, as these variables are restricted to just the real sphere, and in fact to only one part of the real sphere. If there is indeed a single stock of money (M_oS), and this nonetheless does not mean that we know how to measure it in a satisfactory manner or that the available variables defined in this way are fully satisfactory, there is a multiplicity of T, of V_m, of Inf, of real and financial markets, of values of ($y_{M/F}$) which therefore balances every market. Nevertheless, there is a value of ($y_{M/F}$) that enables us to balance

$$M_oS \cdot y_{M/F} = L = T_{(r,f)} \cdot Inf_{(r,f)} = y'$$

We have a y and a y' that guarantee a general equilibrium.

§ 105.   Let us now move on to the second branch of the equation and continue to mine it by fiddling this so fecund equation; this time by taking inflation as our angle of questioning and of approach.

We have: $M_oS \cdot V_m = Inf \cdot T$ soit: $Inf = M_oS \cdot V_m \cdot \dfrac{1}{T}$. The traditional approach, or rather the interpretation made of it, does not qualify Inf and accordingly lets the interpretation get bogged down in just the real sphere of goods and services (the inflation it then discusses is not the general price level but exclusively inflation in prices of goods and services). For our part, from the very outset, we position ourselves on the general price level and therefore on an absolute (and not relative) definition of inflation. This does not mean that inflation is not a relative phenomenon since, on the contrary inflation is precisely that. However, we have a different objective. The present situation of analysis and interpretation of the monetary dynamics equation is unsatisfactory in many respects. First of all, as we have said, only goods and services that make up the sub-set of the real sphere are taken into account. As a result, the dynamics operating in the financial sphere are not accounted for, at the very best the building up from time to other of financial bubbles, and their bursting, result in amazement that suspiciously points to the flaws of traditional monetary approaches; an amazement that is itself startling since the very purpose of this approach to reading the equation is to ensure it cannot account for phenomena that occur "outside" the real sphere (the term "outside" is certainly not very satisfactory because it may lead to the belief that the two spheres are hermetically sealed off from one another; whereas everything is in everything). When, after this startling amazement, the financial sphere is mentioned (often when bubbles lead to widespread media coverage), the financial sphere is discussed at a relative level, at the level of relative prices. The two spheres are discussed but we remain within the relative order without reaching the general price level.

We therefore have: $Inf_{(r,f)} = M_oS \cdot V_{m\,(r,f)} \cdot \dfrac{1}{T_{(r,f)}}$;

This equality opens the way to several possible interpretations. The first, perhaps the most instinctive, can consist in seeing the inflation phenomenon as the relationship between transactional activity (goods, services, securities), or $T_{(r,f)}$ and a stock of money M_oS; in the occurrence, the transactional intensity of M_oS is given by $M_oS/T_{(r,f)}$ or a ratio of transactions per monetary stock unit. In line with what we established above, we can replace

V_m in $\left[\dfrac{M_oS}{T_{(r,f)}} \cdot V_m\right]$, by the coefficient ($y_{M/F}$), a time variable of memory and forgetfulness. (*M* stands for *memory; F* for *forgetfulness*). Inflation (general price level) is then defined as a circulation of the stock of money in the real and financial spheres (r, f). The intensity of this circulation depends on ($y_{M/F}$) which is the temporal (and stable within a given macrofinancial economic regime) coefficient of the regime. A given type of monetary circulation may be more or less inflationary (or deflationary) according to the characteristics and the parameters of the regime's temporal repository. Thus, a regime in which there is more memory (more forgetfulness) will have a different inflationary propensity.

The form of inflation (general price level) is $\left[y_{M/F} \cdot \left(\dfrac{M_oS}{T_{(r,f)}}\right)\right]$ where $y_{M/F}$ signifies and measures the regime's memory (forgetfulness) coefficient.

In all likelihood, monetary circulation will be all the more susceptible of producing inflationary effects as, for instance, there will be a vivid and deeply rooted memory of inflation; while, moreover, there can be just as powerful forgetfulness of the "reasonable" relationships that form the equilibrium or what may take its place (periods of *hubris,* with real inflation, financial bubbles, and to a larger extent periods in which the general price level surges, are often periods dominated by euphoria and forms of forgetfulness). What we are suggesting is that memory is not more or less inflationary than forgetfulness, and *vice versa*. A lot depends on what is stored in memory or forgotten. The specification of ($y_{M/F}$) is a very wide and very fruitful research field. We will suggest, however, in what is finally a quite simple approach of (y) that ($y_{M/F}$) can be seen as memory (affected by more or less pronounced forgetfulness) of the inflationary impact of $\left(\dfrac{M_oS}{T_{(r,f)}}\right)$. The stronger the link between the general price level and $\left[\Delta \dfrac{M_o S}{T_{(r,f)}}\right]$ has been in the past and subsists in memory, the

higher $y_{M/F}$ will therefore be, the greater the probability of an inflationary-like cause-and-effect sequence for a given change in $\dfrac{M_o S}{T_{(r,f)}}$ will be. $y_{M/F}$ is then defined as

$$f\left[\frac{M_o S}{T_{(r,f)}} \; ; \; Inf_{(r,f)}\right].$$

We can also maintain our afore-mentioned approach of $y_{M/F}$ where $y_{M/F}$ is primarily the memorized function of general activity and price levels in the real and financial spheres.

§ 106.   We have accordingly written $Inf = y_{M/F} \cdot \dfrac{M_o S}{T_{(r,f)}}$; which can also be written in the following manner:

$$Inf_{(r,f)} = \left(y_{M/F} \cdot M_o S\right) \cdot \frac{1}{T_{(r,f)}} \quad \text{avec } L = y_{M/F} \cdot M_o S ;$$

We can therefore introduce into our approach of inflation and the general price level the liquidity variable, as it has been defined above, i.e. the product of the stock of money multiplied by time (action), the Subject's psychological time since memory and forgetfulness effects are essentially those of the Subject's repository. This psychological time, in which we renew in a fashion with certain Keynesian functions, is the time of action.

By defining in this way time in the Subject's repository of action, we are simplifying our approach from a methodological viewpoint. The relationship between the formation of economic concepts and the temporal repository is undoubtedly more complex. We have sought to show how it could be studied in *Genealogy* and in *Value and Time*.

We thus have $Inf_{(r,f)} = L \cdot \dfrac{1}{T_{(r,f)}}$; the inflation phenomenon can be defined with a $\alpha \cdot L$ form; inflation is the product of liquidity (i.e. the setting into motion of the stock of money in and by time) multiplied by a coefficient (α) given by the general level of activity $T_{(r,f)}$. We have $Inf_{(r,f)} = \alpha L$. Inflation, the general price level, rises when L increases (i.e. a rise in the product of the stock of money multiplied by a memory and forgetfulness coefficient; this means that an increase in the stock of money is not enough to be inflationary *per se*, this depends on the time function within the regime) and coefficient α needs at least to be neutral. Inflation rises when liquidity L grows faster than the general level of activity T. In this regard, inflation remains a monetary phenomenon in the sense where L molds it, i.e. remains within the dynamics of the stock of money $\left[M_o S \cdot V_m (= y) \right]$.

In other words, the (monetary) liquidity effect is what, ultimately, fuels the increase in the general price level. One way of monitoring, as it were, inflation is to make certain that L is not growing at a noticeably divergent rate (we mean is not outpacing) the growth rate of $T_{(r,f)}$. We can reword the foregoing by saying that one would need to aim for stability in the coefficient☐ to ensure that L and *Inf* grow in a reasonable and proportional manner.

We have written: $Inf_{(r,f)} = \left[M_o S \cdot V_m (= y) \right] \cdot \left(\dfrac{1}{T_{(r,f)}} (= \alpha) \right)$; we can now set out the terms in the following manner:

$$Inf(r,f) = M_o S \cdot y / T = M_o S \left(y_{M/F} \cdot \alpha \right)$$

with: $y_{M/F} \cdot \alpha = V_m / T_{(r,f)}$

hence: $Inf(r,f) = M_o S \cdot y''_{M/F}$ with $y''_{M/F}$ the time factor coefficient of the general activity and price levels.

We therefore have: $Inf = L'$.

We land back on the simple idea according to which the inflation phenomenon is primarily linked to a change in L, which in turn is a distortion (contraction, dilatation, molding) of the stock of money $M_o S$, a distortion resulting from a stable time factor within a given economic regime, a time-factor that gives the intensity of memorization and forgetfulness of the framework repositories of activity and prices. This time factor is given by a coefficient $\left(y'' = y\alpha\right)$ that aggregates memory duration and erosion effects and, therefore, past values $\left(y''_{M/F}\right)$.

§ 107.   Inflation expectations are closely linked to the monetary dynamics and, above all, the monetary dynamics (of liquidity one should more certainly say, in the sense of L) results from inflation expectations. In the approach we have taken, the stock of money (M_oS) is not what fuels inflation expectations since, as we have said, the stock of money, *per se*, does not have any life, any action. It is. Everything starts to move and becomes an economic dynamics in the transformation we have described of money into liquidity. This transformation needs a go-between that literally "informs" the stock of money. It is time, which we have primarily defined by the repository of remembering and forgetting of general activity and price levels of the macrofinancial regime. This is where "expectations" are found (we use inverted commas for expectations here because, in our approach, these are past values, as the link is directly established between expectation of the future and memory of the past). This means that time (expectations) have an impact on the stock of money M_oS, and this impact on M_oS can eventually trigger a dynamics of inflation, but M_oS does not have an impact on inflation expectations.

Inflation expectations are initially given by a memory and forgetfulness time function. They trigger the action with M_oS (the stock of money). This can then lead to an interaction between the two but, at the outset, there is the memory and forgetfulness of an activity and price repository that will set up a dynamic relationship with money (M_oS). At the end of this dynamics, there may be inflation.

We are therefore in an approach where expectations precede money (the stock of money). Expectations precede money because the structure of expectations is based on memory and, by consequence, a representation of the past that might be more or less exact, more or less intense, and thus is combined with erosion due to forgetfulness. We are not denying that money as it were fuels (rather than triggers) expectations because there is definitely an interaction between M_oS and variable (y). However, this means something else, in other words that expectations (including those related to inflation) are linked to liquidity (L) rather than the stock of money M_oS). Expectations have their origin in the time factor, i.e. the time matter made up of the past and which is expressed by y, the memory and, accordingly, forgetfulness coefficient. Expectations are therefore given, in any economic system, in any macrofinancial regime. They are given in the sense where they have a status we could describe as "external". Expectations come from far back, i.e. from the past.

This point holds for the origin of expectations, in other words what they are and where they come from. As for the life of expectations, i.e. their changes, their respirations, this is somewhat different since a change in expectations very directly depend on the product $\left(M_oS \cdot y_{M/F} \right)$ i.e. on the impact of time (to be understood as a memory that forgets general activity and price levels, which must be seen as an expectation of the future, since the analogy of the memory and forgetfulness processes is crucial, as Maurice Allais first pointed out). It is by interacting with the stock of money that the souvenir of the past (expectation of the future) is going to be set in motion.

We could reword the foregoing by saying that there are, really, expectations (about activity or prices) only for a given stock of money and whilst expectations precede money, the latter is what gives them meaningfulness and life. The interaction between money and the psychological forms (i.e. resulting from the Subject and his/her consciousness in action) of memory and therefore of expectations, is a cornerstone of the monetary dynamics, which we will prefer to call the dynamics of liquidity.

§ 108. Liquidity is money (M_oS) increased by expectations (y). And this liquidity gives the key we need to decipher the inflation phenomenon (L, *Inf*). We have shown, by drawing on the plasticity of the fundamental operation of the quantitative dynamics of money, how the various contentions, as well as cubes withdrawn from the equation's original wall, could be assembled and reassembled.

§ 109.   There is a necessary articulation between the real and the financial spheres (r, f). We have said that, in reality, the two spheres add up (multiply one another would be a more appropriate description) rather than they offset one another. We have also stated that the processes of liquidity transfers from one sphere into another are not neutral, in any event far less than is commonly thought and that the cumulative effects of liquidity creation (L), which also increase the stock of money, are   simultaneously witnessed in both spheres (the endogenous increase in the stock of money results from changes in $L = M_o S \cdot y_{M/F} \, ; \Delta M_o S = \Delta L$).

(r) and (f) form a necessary whole. This whole, which acts as a system and a regime, owes a significant part of its regulation of the interest rate — admittedly of the current, visible, "immediate" interest rate as we have named it above but, also of the memory interest rate that, like in a perfect interplay of reflections, refers back to the fundamental liquidity equation determined as we have seen by memory, the strictly symmetrical image, by including in the determination of the memory interest rate the same temporal components. By aligning on a same necessary trajectory of meaningfulness and determinations, the fundamental liquidity equation (this is what we will call this rewording of the quantitative theory of money) and the interest rate theory, both within the consistency of the determinants of the macrofinancial sphere which is specific to them, we are providing ourselves with the tools needed for a more global interpretation of monetary phenomena and, to a larger extent, economic ones.

§ 110.   We have pointed out that the financial sphere, far from being a reflection, or even more tellingly a veil put on the real sphere, had *de facto* acquired its autonomy and the conventional approach that postulates causality operating from the real sphere into the financial sphere needed to be called into question because it is now blatantly rather unrealistic. The fact that the financial sphere has gained its autonomy does not mean, far from it in fact, that there is no link with the real sphere. There is autonomy (which has been won), there is interaction and retroaction (initially from the financial sphere, as a backlash, into the real sphere but now in both directions in the new macrofinancial economic regimes), and there is causality (mainly and until now heading from the real sphere into the financial one).

We have written (r) and (f) to refer to the real sphere (r) and to the financial sphere (f). We also have systematically integrated r and f in the global/general variable that dominated them $\left(Inf_{(r,f)}; T_{(r,f)}\right)$. The time factors y and y', for their part, also apply to the two spheres. Lastly, liquidity L is a concept that stems from the reunion of the two spheres.

When reference is made, in our interpretation of the fundamental liquidity equation, to $T_{(r,f)}$, this indicates that a general level of activity is involved, just like $Inf_{(r,f)}$ refers to the idea of the general price level. This is not real transactional activity in the universe of goods and services (consumption, investment, stocking, trade – nor GDP or one of the measures of its components). Likewise, this is not financial transactional activity in the universe of securities, or the overall activity related to securities, insofar as it can be measures, or any individual gauging of a segment of activity related to securities: equities, bonds, short-term securities, long-term securities, everything that can claim the status of asset class.

In other words, defining $T_{(r,f)}$ and being able to measure it in order to get the liquidity equation to live is a tricky and ambitious task! Likewise, we need to define and manage to estimate $Inf_{(r,f)}$. If we add the just as daunting ordeal of defining and estimating $y_{M/F}$ and, more generally, the memory and forgetfulness coefficients that characterize, through their (relative) stability, a macrofinancial regime, we can see the main sources of concern and work ahead of us for the foreseeable future. The liquidity equation lies above the individual realities of r and f; from the very start, it positions itself at the general level that encompasses r

and f, which are now referred to only individually in our denotation (e.g. $T_{(r,f)}$; $Inf_{(r,f)}$). This is because $T_{(r)}$ or $T_{(f)}$ do not belong to the same level as $T_{(r,f)}$. Reasoning exclusively on global variables (in the sense where we have defined "global" in *Theory*) is crucial.

We call $S_{(r)}$ and $S_{(f)}$ the real and financial spheres, respectively. The approach we have called "traditional" holds that $S(f) = xS(r)$ where the financial sphere is a function of the real one, a residual or even deteriorated form (veil, reflection) of the real sphere. Coefficient x is < 1 in a limitative interpretation of the financial sphere; $x \geq 1$ in a contemporary interpretation where, without letting go of the causality link, the financial increases the real manifold, with a sort of lever effect that is also found in the very formation of financial bubbles. However, in both cases, we remain in a link that could be described as filial or paternal. In this approach, ultimately, imbalances always have a real origin but can manifest themselves through forms of financial inflation (in asset prices) that can lead to inflation in prices of goods and services. This form of inflation remains, in this approach, inflation measuring the general price level. However, this is inexact since its movement consists exclusively in that of relative prices (with the real sphere acting on the financial one). The general price level is definitely more general than is usually thought. If the leap toward $T_{(r,f)}$ and $Inf_{(r,f)}$ is not made, one continues to reason in relative terms and in a manner of reasoning that grants causal preeminence to the real sphere; and accepts only as a serious and final inflation phenomenon the one that affects prices of goods and services (financial inflation is believed to be intermediate).

By shifting into the level of $T_{(r,f)}$ and $Inf_{(r,f)}$, one stops calling inflation what is only a relative shift of prices (the same point holds for activity). By showing the role played by relative changes, we open our approach to a field of reflection about the links between r and f. For instance, experience has shown us that real inflation and financial inflation did not always come hand in hand: inflation in asset prices has often been based on a decline in inflation in prices of goods and services; this was one of the key factors behind the bubble in stock markets in the late 1990s; we have described this process in our *Monetary Notebooks*. We have seen that inflation in prices of financial assets could result from disinflation in prices of goods and lead, when the bubble concentrating all imbalances burst, to a dynamics of deflation. From the viewpoint of the general price level (of all prices), there is a distortion of relative prices in phase 1 (real disinflation; financial inflation) and not an increase in the general price level (at least that is what occurred in the 1990s). In phase 2, there is financial deflation (bursting of the bubble) and retroaction into the real sphere (for debt, via investment or consumption depending on whether companies or households are the most affected by the imbalances, via the overvaluation of an asset class, e.g. equities or real estate in 2000 then 2007 to mention a couple of recent examples). This retroaction is deflationary in the real sphere. We are therefore, in phase 2, in a potential situation of an absolute decline in the general price level, although the situation at the turn of the century was slightly more complex, since the decline in interest rates propelled real estate prices upward.

If we return to the fundamental liquidity equation, we thus definitely have a shift in L (or $M_o S \cdot V_m (= y_{M/F})$) and in $T_{(r,f)}$ that triggers the inflation process. $Inf_{(r,f)}$. $Inf_{(r,f)}$ does not rise in the configuration described in phase 1 because:

1) $T_{(r,f)}$ is hit by two impacts that neutralize one another as it were (even though $T_{(f)}$ accelerates in proportion to the deceleration in $Inf_{(r,f)}$), since real disinflation and bubble are linked;

2) $\left[y_{(r,f)_{M/F}} \right]$, which is the temporal memory/ forgetfulness coefficient, integrated, in the afore-mentioned situation of the 1990s, a memory of disinflation. In the configuration mentioned in phase 2 $T_{(r,f)}$ recorded a homogenous decline (in the early 2000s in the case mentioned above) that was consistent with the

similar homogenous fall in $Inf_{(r,f)}$. Moreover, L (or $M_oS \cdot y_{M/F}$) decelerated, as the two components of L sagged.

§ 111.   We therefore have drawn a distinction between two levels. In the first, we find $Inf_{(r,f)}$, $T_{(r,f)}$, $y_{M/F}$, L (as well as y' and L' as they have been defined), general levels of variables considered in their absolute movements: S expresses the absolute and totalizing sphere that encompasses S_r and S_f. The second level is that of segments, of "cuts" (just like wood is cut) practiced in the various parts of economic and financial units that interact with one another in an interplaying of relative values.

The traditional approach traditional links r and f by setting, in one way or another, that $S_{(f)} = xS_{(r)}$. There are several interpretations of this link defined in this manner, which range from one viewpoint that could be called fundamentalist or unrealistic to another school of thought, at the other end of the spectrum, which is closer to what we can learn from the startling development of the financial sphere that has occurred above all in the past two decades. The first argument is what we will call the neutral veil one; the second is the lever reflection (or multiplying reflection). These two variants form a single corpus, i.e. the causal reflection argument. The expression of causal reflection clearly expresses the direction of the logical relationship and the financial status (the ambiguity of the term in comparison with those of money and liquidity has to be emphasized). Said financial status consists in an image-reality stemming from the real sphere: the financial sphere is an "effect" generated by the real sphere. In this central corpus of causal reflection, we can see an offsetting relationship with a neutral effect, since what has to be financed on one side implies a transfer of liquidity and an adjustment, in other words expenditure on the other; what is inflation on one side implies disinflation on the other; while the stock of money is constant. This compensation implied by the neutral veil is asymmetrical, as it were, since the rationale unfolds from the real sphere toward the financial one. The second relationship takes note of the fact that the financial sphere multiplies the reflection soaked up from the real sphere (lever effect); liquidity, the circulation of money, the temporal repositories of money and liquidity (in the sense where the velocity of circulation and multiplication effect are linked), now play a role they did not play previously, but the theory of causal reflection dominates the overall approach.

§ 112.   Alongside this approach that we have called "traditional", there is a somewhat different approach based on two pillars. The first is the multiplication/creation (of liquidity); the second pillar is the equivalence of the two spheres (to be contrasted with the causal dependency of the financial sphere on the real one and various forms of asymmetries in the link defined by the traditional approach), an equivalence that can include forms of autonomy of either sphere in comparison with the other. This approach is the creative equivalence thesis (a short-cut for a longer and more precise wording: thesis of creative liquidity under condition of equivalence of the real and financial spheres). We have developed above a few key characteristics of this regime.

We have *ex ante* a situation in which there is S, a general/global sphere in the sense where this theory understands it. S *is* unitary, is the unit (1), and $S_{(r)}$, $S_{(f)}$ structure, under various possible combinations, this unit, or $(S_r, S_f) \leq 1$. The liquidity dynamics is going to generate, via the impact of time (speed, memory/forgetfulness because there is a fundamental analogy between forgetfulness and speed as seems to be suggested by the situations in which financial bubbles build up) on the stock of money (i.e. $M_o S \cdot y_{M/F}$), a shock on the stock of money and a cause-and-effect sequence in $T_{(r,f)}$, and their combination starts the inflation process. $S_{(r)}$ and $S_{(f)}$, as their *ex ante* combination may not exceed the unit, or S, and for which the individual value may not, in either case, exceed the unit, are going to, as it were, lead to a shift in S into S' with $S' = wS$. There is equivalent expansion (thesis of the equivalence of spheres) of the two spheres $S_{(r)}$ and $S_{(f)}$ but, above all, S dilates (or contracts) at a global (general and absolute) level $(S_{r,f})$ that is the same plan where $Inf_{(r,f)}$, $T_{(r,f)}$, $y_{M/F}$ project themselves.

The liquidity dynamics is creative, cumulative and non-linear (discontinuities of dilatations) in its expansion phase; while it is destructive, cumulative and once more non-linear (discontinuities of contractions, always with an acceleration) in its contraction phase.

§ 113.   The way in which the stock of money is distorted in the liquidity dynamics is a significant subject of observation and analysis because the liquidity dynamics is the dynamics of the allocation of monetary forms in the cycle (allocation is what drives the cycle). In fact, we are not dealing so much with the allocation of a given, constant and finite stock of money, as with the very process of transformation of money in and through its utilizations, i.e. by the contact of money (M_oS) with the time of the Subject's action, that of a projection, an expectation, and, therefore, necessarily, that of a memory.

The crucial point of liquidity dynamics L consists in the irruption of time into the stock of money, which will give meaningfulness and a structure to money. When we say structure, we understand the molding of a temporal repository (short term/long term) and of a project establishing value on the basis of an expectation. $L\left(= M_oS \cdot y_{M/F}\right)$ records more or less substantial distortions of "liquidity", for instance, covering a wide spectrum ranging from pure cash to long-term asset classes with a pronounced risk-to-return ratio. L forms a changing rainbow of liquidity understood as movement (there are no liquidity "conditions", there is only a movement that carries the name of liquidity).

In the liquidity rainbow, we can find again the more or less marked preference for liquidity described by Keynes (and, therefore, the resulting trade-offs between cash and other asset classes, between long-term asset classes also), as well as the different motives for holding liquidity. Nonetheless, our approach is noticeably original. First of all, and this is not a mere issue of wording, that liquidity cannot be "held" because liquidity is always and everywhere a *per se* holding mechanism (part of the stock of money); liquidity is the very holding of liquidity.

When the stock of money M_oS is broken down into a certain number of sub-sets (M_0, M_1, M_2, M_3, etc.) the statistical accounting form reflects in its calculation and measure the distortion of liquidity resulting from the so to say exogenous impulsion of monetary creation by the central bank and/or by the shift in preferences and the change in trade-offs. One of their prime movers, which we have discussed at length in *The Theory*, is the value granted to time. We find once more, having come full circle, a fundamental element of the dynamics of the cycle.

§ 114.   We have seen that the origin of the dynamics of the cycle was found in the value granted to time, the source of changes in preferences and trade-offs within *S,* in absolute terms, i.e. also within the real and financial spheres and between spheres, within and between the segments of goods, services, securities, and so forth as far as the infinity of any possible breaking down. What we call consumption or investment, in the real sphere, for instance, are the names given to the expression of preferences and a certain value given to time. What we call financial markets are, in the other sphere, the name of a spectrum of preferences.

The economic dynamics, to a noteworthy extent the cycle of the dynamics in particular, results from changes in the value granted to time. In our study of the (monetary) dynamics of liquidity $y_{M/F}$ or $y'_{M/F}$ are time variables that, via their fluctuations, are going to set in motion, the stock of money M_oS, in an expansion or a contraction direction, and lead to the appearance of *L* as such. In the global dynamics of the cycle, the modifications in the value granted to time are intimately linked, when the economic process is set in motion, to $\left[M_oS \cdot y(y') \right]$. The monetary foundations of the economic cycle are located in $L(L')$ and, ultimately, in the interaction between the time repository of an economic regime and the stock of money. This temporal repository includes memory and forgetfulness, duration and discontinuities.

The monetary liquidity dynamics stems from and governs inflation and activity (the global activity and price regimes). There cannot be, *stricto sensu*, a preference for liquidity because liquidity is what appears when a preference, precisely, is expressed with respect to money. This preference, or the blending of the Subject's action with time, is expressed in $y_{M/F}$ as defined. It is (y) that will, by modifying M_oS, lead to the differentiation of the stock of money (more or less liquid, more or less short- or long-term, etc.). The preference for liquidity as defined by Keynes is interpreted here as a moment, in the cycle, when M_oS becomes $M_oS_1 = M_oS.(y)$ with y the memory coefficient suddenly leading to something being recalled in memory for instance (remembering something once more after a period of euphoria is a helpful analogy in terms of understanding the foregoing). M_oS_1 sees its liquid sub-sets grow to the detriment of its long-term sub-sets, the structure of assets undergoes a relative distortion because the expectation has changed within the regime, mainly because the past has been remembered once again.

§ 115.   Our approach does not underestimate the need to know the motives for holding liquidity as defined by Keynes (in our approach, liquidity is born from the very fact of holding it) but Keynes' definition of liquidity, in our opinion, is excessively narrow (the risk-free asset) and, therefore, defined in relative terms with respect to other assets: we consider liquidity L to be a vast field of money in action. Holding liquidity (in comparison with the fact of not holding any) is admittedly one of the driving forces of the developments of the economic cycle, as Keynes rightly saw. However, holding cash (the risk-free asset) in comparison with all sorts of assets that, for their part, include a more or less significant component of risk, is merely one of the situations, one of the structures of liquidity L as we understand it ($M_oS.y_{M/F}$ and not just the risk-free asset or cash). Furthermore, it has not been demonstrated, even though this relative value structure [risk-free asset/assets including risk] is undeniably significant, that other structures (or sets of structures) are not just as significant if not more important. In other words, our approach diverges from the Keynesian one because of its definition of liquidity L as a global set of structures of relative values of all real and financial assets, and not as the only risk-free asset, and, at the same time, by highlighting the fundamental difference between money and liquidity. We will be more interested in the motives behind changes in liquidity understood in the sense of L, than in the reasons why just the structure of cash (risk-free asset) is held, which is the main Keynesian definition of liquidity. The motives behind changes in liquidity (and therefore in the holding of all assets, whether risky or risk-free) are the preferences included in $y_{M/F}$ as we have defined it. The Keynesian motives of precaution, transaction or speculation represent one of the possible combinations in the global approach we propound, motives that determine one possible structure of liquidity L among others, i.e. the risk-free asset, in other words one allocation solution (among others) rather than the "forming", the setting in motion, of money. Money is "informed" by time and each (M_oS, $y_{M/F}$) couple corresponds to a structure of liquidity L and a more or less complex combination of real and/or financial assets. The "risk-free asset structure" is one of them, nothing more and nothing less.

§ 116.   The crisis, when we draw on elements of the fundamental liquidity dynamics, gains renewed relevance. In its key determinants, we find once more monetary excesses defined in a broad sense. When we talk of "monetary excesses", we mean that a crisis affecting the entire economic sphere (in the sense of S, i.e. encompassing the real and financial sub-sets) is, always and everywhere, a revelation (what appears) of a hypertrophy of money (volume criteria, the overabundant monetary stock, credit excesses, for instance, have not overshadowed the way in which the purpose of monetary signs as contractual signs founding the social contract that establishes society has been perverted). Thus, the idea reappears according to which the monetary (credit) cycle plays a crucial role in possible imbalances, and *in fine,* subsequent unavoidable adjustments.

The monetary equation of liquidity highlights, in its first new contribution, the fact that imbalances in the monetary order manifest themselves in a global manner, i.e. at the level of S, including imbalances in the financial sphere (bubbles), with financial imbalances becoming more important (hence the principle of equivalence between the real and financial spheres), while the financial sphere gains in autonomy, although this does not rule out retroaction effects operating toward and on the real sphere. Simultaneously, inflation, defined at the absolute level of the global (general) price level, finds its full meaningfulness in a complete set of relative real and financial values (goods, services, securities). In this respect, the liquidity equation overhauls the monetary interpretation of the cycle and of the crisis by widening it to the financial sphere via a consolidation of the two major spheres at a single level and, above all, by setting out in this level the necessary absolute approach of inflation and activity phenomena (global level).

The liquidity equation suggests that the crisis mechanism does not result necessarily (and directly) to such an extent from monetary hypertrophy (M_oS) as from a malfunctioning (*hubris*) of L defined as the product of the stock of money by time, the time factor within a memory and forgetfulness repository that founds any macrofinancial economic regime. Monetary overabundance is not enough to create the crisis rationale, even though it remains a prerequisite in most cases (although one could imagine a crisis breaking out from the ($y_{M/F}$) coefficient and for a stock of money without any significant excess).

The liquidity equation states that any crisis is the product of M_oS by $y_{M/F}$, i.e. a change in the temporal coefficients of the repository/regime that gives rise to a disturbance. For an equilibrium value of $y_{M/F}(y_e)$ within the regime, we have a malfunctioning of $L(M_oS \cdot y_{M/F})$, with y_0 shifting to y_1 where $y_1 < y_e$, i.e. another value of y indicating an increase in forgetfulness, a characteristic of the crisis rationale. Simultaneously, M_oS_0 shifts into M_oS_1 with growth in the stock of money through an *ex nihilo* endogenous accumulation within S, a double movement of *ex nihilo* monetary liquidity creation at both ends of the S chain, in other words the real sphere and the financial sphere. The fact that $yd'y_0$ shifts into y_1 ($y_1 < y_e$) expresses a shift in expectations because, in the liquidity equation, there is a deep analogy between the expectation of what is yet to come and the memory (renewed recall) of what has been. In the occurrence, the rise in inflation expectations (global price level), as we have emphasized, can result from a forgetfulness process (this is the central and dominant process of crises, with the cycle peaking, and excesses foreshadowing forthcoming drops) and, also, from a memory process (memory of inflation here, which has taken deep roots); in fact, in this case, the forgetfulness process is the first one to occur and the dominant one – leading to, in a second phase, when inflation has set in, a process consisting in remembering (inflation) and self-perpetuating causes of the crisis. Because, at each stage, what is forgotten (the equilibrium) is not what one remembers (the imbalance) (in the incipient phases of the crisis here). Nor is what is recalled (the equilibrium) what is gradually forgotten (the imbalance) (in the turnaround of the cycle here). Memory and forgetfulness build a complex combination in the cycle because what is forgotten or remembered once more is never quite the same or stable.

At the equilibrium, the equilibrium is what is held in memory (we understand equilibrium to mean an average reference value in the regime/repository), $y = y_e$. By moving away from y_e, y is going to call for more memory and forgetfulness than is required to hold the equilibrium. In the cycle's upward phase, y will drop below y_e, and this is analyzed as an increase in forgetfulness that will peak in the euphoria and the *hubris* of the top of the cycle. When we talk of forgetfulness, we definitely mean forgetting what is necessary for the equilibrium (for a certain reference equilibrium in a given regime). Forgetfulness is the key factor in the cycle's upward phase, and in fact the most important. The erosion of the memory of the equilibrium is at the heart of the forgetfulness mechanism at that moment. The increase in the forgetfulness rate is reinforced, after a given point in time, by a

memory effect that is endogenous to the crisis (only characteristics of the crisis and imbalances remain in memory).

In the cycle's downward phase, y is going to rise back above ye
(discontinuous increase in $y_1 < y_e$ à $y_2 > y_e$), and this is analyzed as
a recalling of the equilibrium into memory, which will culminate
in the recession/deflation at the cycle's trough. We definitely
understand memory as memory of what is required by the
equilibrium as defined below. Recalling into memory is the key
factor of the cycle's downward phase, and the most important.
The increase in the memory rate is fuelled, from a certain
moment, by an effect of forgetfulness with respect to imbalances
at the cycle's peak. We therefore have for an equilibrium value y
defined in y_5.

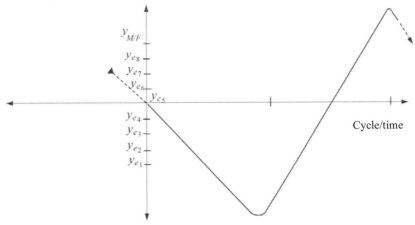

This is because there is an infinity of equilibrium values of y_e
for as many macrofinancial economic regimes. And as a result,
there are as many cyclical configurations combining one and only
one value of M_oS, y, L, T and *Inf.* For every cycle carries within it
an indelible trace of memory, just like a kind of DNA.

PART 2

THE DYNAMICS
OF THE STOCK MARKET

CHAPTER 6

THE DYNAMICS
OF STOCK MARKET SPACE-TIME

THE TIME REFERENCE FRAME. DURATION, MEMORY RECALL AND LOSS

§ 117.   To what extent and in what manner does reality depend upon the past? And, consequently, what is the effect of the past on finance, since it is hard to see how it would not be similarly dependent.

Most of the time, it is established that events have an effect on other events. This is how the phenomenon of *continuum* is analysed, even when dealing with the most innovative developments in fractal finance. The phenomenon of *continuum* evolves within a homogenous reference frame of events and time, each event being supported by others in order to proceed. With such an approach, one can legitimately reduce the world to simple elements such as economic and financial facts and events. It has been noted, within the said frame of reference, that facts and events can be closely connected even when they occur years apart. When considering Stock Market movements, no variation can be said to be independent of the preceding variation.

There is no Subject within such a reference frame. This lack of Subject means it cannot be said how events are connected in so-called long memory processes. Everything seems to take place as if the memory were that of the events themselves, which can, after all, support a legitimate theory that market prices are self-referencing and more generally, although with more difficulty, that economic facts and events are also self-referencing. However, it is hard to uphold such a theory when faced with the evidence: the event is, strictly speaking, the name of the point of impact between consciousness and the world.

Consequently, it is the memory of the conscious Subject who provides the structure for the temporal reference frame in which the events and facts are connected. This time reference frame is "psychological", i.e. made up of the temporal matter of the (Subject's) consciousness, matter which is fundamentally formed of memory-triggers and lapses of memory. Such triggers to the Subject's conscious memory, dotted with memory lapses, provide the unity, coherence and the meaning behind the connections which are observed between economic and financial events.

Accordingly, preference is given to an alternative interpretation of long memory processes. Faced with the contingent and ultimately absurd or incomprehensible nature of unpredictable continuing fractional phenomena, the introduction of the Subject as a basis for the time reference frame restores an overall sense of meaning. Consciousness (the Subject) considers the real world through a process of memory triggers which are affected by lapses of memory, such triggers and process being the very essence of finance as it has developed in the modern age and of the Stock Market, in particular. Finance (the Stock Market) is therefore the means of intermediation and the place where the Subject's aims are summarised, the storage area (memory, duration) for intended plans and projects. Strictly speaking, it is not events which are closely connected at a distance of some years but rather the unitary memory of the consciousness which literally holds them together by providing meaning and coherence to each, and to the whole, by means of reminders within a "psychological" period of time. It is because the Subject remembers (and, therefore, expects, since memory, memory lapse and expectation/anticipation are fundamentally similar processes) and, moreover, acts as a result of remembering (and also forgetting), that the simple elements represented by facts and events manage to connect.

The *continuum* phenomena can consequently be explained by memory storage (whether conscious or unconscious - the question of the unconscious in long memory processes is an important one, since it introduces in addition to the unadulterated freedom of the free, conscious Subject, a more opaque and not less active dimension): something continues when it is remembered, whether in full or in part (memory lapse); that which continues accumulates and forms time-matter (stock); that which continues is a feature of certain economic phenomena, such as inflation and, also, certain financial movements: as shown in *Théorie*, the cycle, in both its real and financial components, owes its dynamics to the effects of memory recall and lapse. In particular, the phenomena of sharp (or long-term) rises or falls in market prices are caused by memories (of other rises and even the current rise itself, if sufficiently long-lasting) and from memory lapses (possible decreases, which, after a certain level of increase, push the prices into a time reference frame within the consciousness, which we have called "psychological" above, where only the increases are remembered and there is no memory of any decrease. This applies up until an event or fact, which is often insignificant, triggers a fresh reminder, a recollection which basically, on activation, operates in the same way as a decrease, before it then in turn feeds upon the memory recall and lapse until it is reversed, in the same way as an increase).

Conversely, the so-called anti-*continuum* phenomena can be analysed and explained by memory lapse. *Continuum* is a developing, non-linear function of memory. Non-*continuum* (or relative *continuum*) is a non-linear function of memory lapse.

This means that, at any given time, a stock price expresses a certain memory and a certain lack of memory, primarily of the real world. In fact, the price already expresses a summary position (we are unable to tell whether the market is a sort of passive summary of individual human consciousness which is expressed at any given time in the market, or a supra-supra-consciousness which exists independently over and above the consciousness of the human Subject – the market as a collective Subject, which is an audacious and attractive theory). If this theory is put to one side for the time-being, we have a stock price which at any given time summarises the memory and lack of memory of a certain number of actual events, held by an infinite number of individual consciousnesses. What is remembered or forgotten (real world) constitutes a fairly stable reference frame for so-called "critical" stock market price variables. This reference frame for duration-memory/lack of memory is characterised by a fairly high level of inertia and only evolves in proportion to the capacity of a contemporary event or fact to call the long-term "regime" into question: the said event/fact is an element of non-information with regard to the trajectory of the stock market price, unless it calls into question an element of the "regime", but settles like an almost invisible film on the layer of time/long memory.

It is therefore memory and lack of memory of the real world which govern. However, a stock price can still to some extent "recall" another stock price which is distant in time. This correlation does not equate to a self-referencing system of stock prices or a reflexive loop of market dynamics but highlights the fact that a distant stock price which is recalled is in fact a slice or sequence of real events and facts, which is stored in the memory and associated with this stock price. A reminder within the time reference frame of the Subject's consciousness always takes place by comparison to the real world and its variables.

§ 118. Bachelier did not adopt long memory processes, Mandelbrot does not say who remembers, no one says who forgets or how, since the memory process cannot exist without a loss of memory process. The two movements of memory recall and lapse show a strong similarity to the process of anticipation and expectation (Allais). The theory of a Subject who remembers and forgets is lacking in Mandelbrot's work.

If one assumes that each price variation is not independent of the preceding one, then it is relevant to look for "remote" correlations between prices and blocks/series of prices. Any forms of resonance and echo will thus be highlighted and a time reference frame will also be introduced in which causality can be considered. There exists what some call "clock time", in which linearity goes hand in hand with a traditional causality of the relationship between cause and effect (prices react as a consequence of something happening). There is a chain, movement, a series of sequences running from an *ex ante* to an *ex post*. There is a past, present and future and the threefold structure of past/present/future is necessarily a symmetrical reflection of the chain structure of causality, running in sequences from the cause to the effect over a segmented period of time called the "clock". The very existence of these two structures, which are fundamentally connected in terms of time and causality, allows us (leads us) to think of the Stock Market as a receptacle of "consequences", of "effect", stemming from causes, sources of shocks, events or facts which originate in the real world. Causality inherently moves from the real world towards the Stock Market.

This dual approach [temporality/causality] which governs the link between the real world and the Stock Market (between the fact/event and the stock market price) can be contrasted with an approach which aims to isolate the special nature of "stock market time". This involves the study of a specific non-linear time reference frame where non-linearity is dominant (dilations and contractions, the price movements of an asset being, for example, compared to the physical process of diffusion of heat in a substance; we discussed this ourselves in *Théorie*, borrowing Descartes' analogy of a piece of wax). This time reference frame is therefore characterised by various (infinite) comparisons of scale within an object or a group of objects and goes hand in hand with an alternative causal structure where there is a total, inter- and intra-influence (dependency): each part of the object influences any other part. Finally, the relationship [temporality/causality] which is thus constituted does *not necessarily* maintain a link with the real world, since the causal structure used is not linear and sequential, running from *ante* to *post*, from the effect to the consequence. Nothing much can be said about the relationship between the real world and the stock market price. It is completely possible that there is none. The two spheres are autonomous and the Stock Market refers back to the Stock Market within a temporal and causal reference frame which includes erratic (jumps) and continuous long memory processes. It is also possible to show that the real sphere and the financial sphere are both closer than might appear, if one places them both in front of one Subject and one sole time reference frame.

This brings us to the question we want to consider. It is not stated where this time (and causal) framework comes from or how it is formed. Although its features appear at first sight to be strange, they are essential if we are to try and reach a better understanding of stock market phenomena. We consider that there is a time reference frame, which has similar roots and features to those described by the so-called fractal approach. This time reference frame is fundamentally structured by time-matter, made up of duration, memory and memory lapse. Duration is an essential matter for economics and finance and is closely linked to the way in which the Subject views the World and makes projections (facts, events). Economic and market facts and events only exist if there is a Subject-consciousness to interpret them. This means that the two dimensions of the real world and the Stock Market are both present within a time reference frame of memory and lack of memory, governed by the profound analogy between memory/lack of memory and expectation (non-linearity, no past-present-future segmentation). There is both an incomplete causality between the real world and the Stock Market (by "incomplete" we mean intermittent, non-linear), a retroactive effect between the stock market and reality and independent causality of stock market prices (internal retroactive effect within the stock market sphere).

There is a general phenomenon of the Subject's perception of the World. This perception is formed within the fundamental time reference frame of specific matter (duration, memory, lack of memory) which is the background for the connection between consciousness and the World (Allais' "psychological" reference frame). All economic and financial phenomena are governed in the same way. The Stock Market is the connection between consciousness and perceptions, and perception itself. All real facts and Stock Market facts are governed by this time reference frame of perception. The Stock Market is the incarnation of the means of perception and also the empowerment of such perception.

Mandelbrot does not establish what forms the fundamental matter of this "stock market time". There is a need to think of time differently, in any event to distinguish it from the so-called conventional measures and norms of time, even though it is not clear whether such a notion of conventional time actually exists (or corresponds to a reality) since it has all the appearance of a convention. The Stock Market, by making itself a major economic and financial institution of the modern age, enables the apprehension of reality to be denoted physically and in an organised manner (the connection between the real world and the stock market price) and provides a more fundamental means of perceiving the Subject i.e. within a specific time reference frame. It is uncertain whether the Stock Market transforms time, as is sometimes stated (transforming conventional time into stock market time). The Stock Market seems instead to be governed straight away by its own time reference frame which is, in general, the means of perception within the economic and financial spheres. The arrival of the Stock Market in the modern era did not strictly speaking "transform" conventional clock time: the Stock Market showed that, in all likelihood, the time reference frame which governs it is the only valid one for the purposes of reality and observation. The Stock Market therefore demonstrated that the traditional pairing of temporality and causality was probably not appropriate.

THE DYNAMIC BALANCES

§ 119.   The Stock Market, stock market prices and their echoes of *continuum* are dominated by time-matter which sustains what are known as the long memory and *continuum* processes. This time-matter is duration, called upon by the memory with a certain erosive coefficient of memory lapse. The said duration, memory and memory lapse are features of the Subject and its consciousness. Ultimately it is always a Subject who, in the Stock Market, recalls or forgets a stock-matter which is sustained by the real world *and* the past movements of the stock market prices themselves, since the Stock Market dynamics draw upon both the facts and events of the real world, the history of stock market prices and finally upon the specific time reference frame of each Subject operating on the Stock Market, such reference frame being made up of items which have been remembered or forgotten, which are recalled or effaced.

It is not certain whether conventional clock time exists and if there is anything other than the time observed in the Subject's reality (since, and this is a fundamental point, stock market time is the Subject's time) within the process of perception. The mechanics of redistributing time, whether by means of compression or dilation, are those by which the Subject perceives the world. We cannot deny the existence of clock time; one just needs to watch the hands move on the dial placed on the front wall of a station while waiting for a train in order to feel that this is the rule. However, the person facing the said clock dial also carries a different internal time reference frame, which enables him to perceive the time before the departure of his train in a non-linear fashion.

Non-linearity and the phenomena of points of concentration or acceleration form part of a specific time reference frame which differs from the conventional model. In this reference frame, the essential question is what took place, in the real world, in the Stock Market sphere and with stock market prices, as well as the interactions between the two. Since the essential time-matter is the stock formed by what took place (the cold wax). This stock will be reheated, informed by the memory recall or memory lapse.

It can be understood that stock market dynamics are independent of immediate facts and events, unless such facts and events reveal something which is likely to have a material impact on time-matter, the stock of the past, by recalling something forgotten, or on the contrary by forgetting other items, or finally by dominating all the stock of a new form of logic which makes the stock outdated. It can be understood that any such immediate element has to be particularly important and decisive. Most of the time, the facts and events of the real world, the stock market prices themselves (i.e. the most recent changes starting with today's) are non-events and enormous means and considerable sums are involved in an immediate process of hedging and research which, quite simply, fail to recognise the matters at stake. Whether one is dealing with facts and events of the real world or changes in stock market prices themselves – both as determining factors of Stock Market dynamics – it is the long sequences and the memorised stock which provide the real movements for anyone wishing to observe them with an element of hindsight.

The price of a share will thus be determined, not by the body of real, financial or stock market (i.e. the movement of stock prices themselves) facts and events which are immediate (immediate perception) but, within a static dimension, by the stock of time-matter linked to the said market value (general, memorised items which are interdependent since the market value is a fractal-type object governed by multiple causes) and, within a dynamic dimension, the way in which this stock (the cold wax) will be "driven" by the process of memory recall or lapse directed by the Subject, whether consciously or unconsciously, and whether such Subject is individual or collective, since there may be an association of beliefs, memory and memory lapse. The manner in which the stock of time-matter is informed (or distorted), i.e. the actual dynamic dimension of the process, is the true source of interest (discount rate).

Stock market dynamics are completely involved in the process of memory recall and/or lapse, using an initial stock of time-matter, which itself regularly increases over time, as new facts and events occur, whether real or relating to the stock market (i.e. the very changes to the stock market prices themselves), i.e. immediate facts and events. The process of memory recall and/or lapse is based on an expectation that can be estimated. It applies to corporate results but, more widely, to anything affecting the existence of a company listed on the Stock Market. The value of a share is contained in the stock of time-matter and the time differential within the time reference frame of duration, memory and lack of memory, provides the dynamics. There are discontinuities in the process of memory recall and lapse, i.e. contractions and dilations, and therefore concentrations, which lead to very asymmetrical distributions of movements, alternate periods of apparent tranquillity and thunder claps in clear skies. This is because the process understands the threshold effects. Everything takes place as if there were an accumulation of immediate facts and events, none of which at that instant can produce an effect which might suddenly result in a switch to a new regime, i.e. to another type of stock of time-matter and another system of perception, whether bullish or bearish.

The threshold effect is specific to the economic and stock market time reference frame. It is a purely mathematical point of view, involving certain points above which a new mathematical relationship takes over. This is true of an individual financial asset (a share, a bond), it is also true of a group of macro-economic and financial items which define a regime. For each stock market "item" the dynamics stem from the information and distortion process affecting a stock of time-matter by means of memory recall or lapse. When the said dynamics call into question the characteristics of the "past" item (since the item is considered by what has been), they provoke a threshold effect and a change in the item's regime. These threshold effects are the source of extreme variations in prices, of crises. But even during calm periods, stock market dynamics advance by means of discontinuities, concentrations and dilations. The said advance is exponential when compared to the conventional laws of scale which struggle in any event to take account of the reality of economic and financial phenomena as they are observed. The concentration points of the volatility are fundamentally based on breaking barriers, i.e. on reminders or memory lapses (which are themselves triggered by an accumulation of facts and events which we have called "immediate".) There is therefore indeed a link between the concentration of volatility points and dependence but the threshold effect occurs when a certain level of dependence is crossed, i.e. the breach of a regime of memory and duration.

§ 120. Memory recall, which shortens the distance between the immediate and what has been, increases the force of attraction between the two poles. It is at this point that intense price variations concentrate, which means that time is in the dilation phase. Memory lapse brings the dynamics back to the immediate moment and results in a concentration of the time reference frame.

§ 121. A review of duration as fundamental time-matter, the information or distortion of which are initiated by memory or memory lapse, means that the idea of relative balance can be brought back within the practical reflection, i.e. the idea of a mean value, a number which to some extent is unique, with – only in part – a rational function. Since reflection within the world of finance, from Bachelier up until the arrival of the fractal approach, became increasingly detached from the concept of balance, first since it segmented time in a very watertight manner – thus excluding duration and *continuum* – and second because it transferred the capacity to state a value at any given time to market immediacy. Although the value is still linked to a relative balance, this approach has led to a relativism according to which the very fraction of utility of the value is in question: the value is that which is attributed to it by the market, it may change at any moment and is of little use.

The distinction between the "intrinsic" value and the instantaneous value requires a fundamental analysis of the very bedrock of economics and finance, a genealogical approach which we have discussed in other works. The thinking behind the said bedrock is fundamental, since it dictates the definition of economics and finance. Finance, due to specific factors which are connected to the manner in which it has been conceived from the outset and up until very recently, but more generally because of the position of economics in the modern age, was unable to define its absolutes, and therefore its points of reference, including value and balance. Finance therefore lacks a theory of balance and accordingly of value. This in turn fostered the process in which it is extremely difficult to standardise events during times of multiple volatilities and dispersals, in the context of an increasing lack of understanding and failure to accept the market "autonomies".

Also lost with the "intrinsic" value or the "ideal" mean value is the idea that the market, by means of an approach which is not devoid of fluctuations and rumours, converges towards such values over time. The foundation of market dynamics is lost, the dynamics of multiple, miniscule convergences towards multiple mean values which themselves evolve (relative values) around absolute values. The understanding of the dynamics of financial markets is deprived of an essential element. The very meaning of the Stock Market is lost together with the dynamics, making the Stock Market more absurd, more contingent.

It is in the context of absolute and especially relative balances, defined on the basis of a time-matter comprising duration and a time reference frame governed by the functions of memory recall and lapse, that stock market dynamics can be understood as a regression to "the" same thing (a relative, i.e. evolving, mean value), which is often observed as the phenomenon of a regression to the mean. One can then hope to demonstrate that what changes Stock Market prices is, in the final analysis, the movements of the value within the meaning of relative balances which are created within a time reference frame and a regime and not the price variations. It is both the balance (dynamics) and the arbitrage (and not either one or the other, as one often hears), since the dynamics of the absolute and relative balances is provided by the value accorded to the time, which governs preferences and arbitrages between goods, services, financial assets, places or moments. A value's utility function is accordingly restored or preserved (see *Théorie Globale*).

§ 122.   When it is said that the best estimate of tomorrow's price is its value today, it is said that there is a *continuum* of duration. Finally, when one accepts that tomorrow's price is dependent upon past prices, one is also saying that tomorrow's price is dependent upon the past, nothing more or less, and on the functions of memory recall and lapse. One is also saying that intensities are continuous. Accordingly, it is often the duration, the dependence on the past and the points of concentration or dilation (volatility) which announce a change of regime (crisis).

What is the source of energy in Stock Market dynamics, the energy which diffuses heat within a substance in the same way as a change in price is driven by the financial asset? How are the changes in the time reference frame (or stock market time scale) linked to the variations in Stock Market prices, in terms of intensity and direction? Within the particular universe of the Stock Market, which element governs the force of attraction between facts/events and Stock Market prices or the variations therein, between the Stock Market prices themselves or their variations? Which element governs the force of repulsion? To what extent are the intensities, and also major movements, governed by memory recalls and/or lapses?

Memory recall and lapse dilate or concentrate time within the time reference frame which is specific to the Stock Market and which is made up of the following raw material, namely duration and a stock (of facts/events, prices) which represents the past. Market dynamics are fundamentally driven by memory recall and lapse. Large intensities may be caused in the same way by memory recall and/or lapse, in a non-linear mode. The intensities of price variations are connected to the intensities of memory recall and/or lapse. The more intense the memory recall or lapse, the quicker one moves through the market time reference frame.

§ 123.　The observation appears to associate sequences of intense price variations, interspersed with calmer periods, with the phenomena of long memory and *continuum*. The concentrations of volatility move in the same direction, themselves progressing as it were by means of concentric circles. It is now customary to distinguish between market time and "clock time". Is this distinction really necessary or, moreover, relevant? Adopting this approach, there is as it were a reference time, "clock time", which is linear and largely defined by the usual manner in which it is measured. There is, *furthermore*, another reference frame, that of market time, which redistributes time by means of dilation or compression. Consequently, the Stock Market price is a function of market time, which itself is a function of "clock time".

The question is the following: does there exist anything other than what is here referred to as "market time"? What we mean is that everything related to economics and finance, facts, acts or events, is governed by a time reference frame which we have described. This time reference frame is specific to the Subject and in particular the temporal structures of consciousness (memory, memory lapse), which leads Mr. Allais to talk, for example, of a *"psychological* interest rate". By *"psychological"*, we mean "related to the *modus operandi* of the consciousness". Taking such an approach, one is essentially saying that the encounter between the consciousness (of the economic Subject) and the world will structure the economic and financial facts and events. The comprehension of the world by the consciousness (projection) is based upon a temporality which is non-linear in duration, interspersed with memory recalls and lapses. This describes the time reference frame of the consciousness. Accordingly there is only one, unitary time reference frame. Clock time is irrelevant to the manner in which the consciousness operates in the world of economic and financial facts and events, or more generally in the world itself. This specific time reference frame, called market time by some, is fundamentally different from clock time.

This time reference frame adopted by the consciousness and structured by duration, memory recall and lapse seems naturally suited to the reporting of activities, facts and events which are largely based upon expectations, as is true of the Stock Market. It is a particular form of time-matter which can easily be compared to the active consciousness (projection/expectation) and with the phenomena of memory recall and lapse.

Clock time has no reality in the economic and financial sphere. The only reality is the perception (projection) of the conscious-ness. There is a time reference frame of duration, memory recall and lapse which at least acts as a filter for clock time, and indeed more probably directly governs any economic and financial perceptions, namely the temporal structure of the consciousness or the very framework of time which stimulates the consciousness and to which it refers.

This time is primary in the sense that it is the one where objects and the world are perceived. Whether it is the product of the consciousness or precedes it in some way, this time is the foundation of economics and finance.

This time reference frame is not limited to the market. It governs all economic phenomena. If "economic" is understood in modern times to mean all dealings of the Subject and the world, it can be seen that the scope is wide. This time reference frame helps explain the mysterious process of price-formation. A price expresses at all times and in all instances a function of time, not of clock time but of the time reference frame for economics and finance, i.e. the value given to time, an initial duration (which can to a certain extent be compared to clock time by means of the passage of time, although duration also expresses the idea of matter, stock) which is informed and distorted by memory recall and lapse.

The price of a stock market asset expresses at any given time a certain value given to time, the expectation of what will come to be and *therefore* that of the memory of that which comes to the Subject from the past.

MARKET ENERGY AND SPEED

§ 124.   What is the equivalent of energy in a financial market? What can be deduced from the assumption that one moves as quickly within the time reference frame for economics and finance as the occurrence of memory recalls or lapses? Everything seems to take place as if, at the outset, there was duration, which is both matter and the passage of time. Duration refers back to an ontological foundation of economics and finance, a primary time which exists before the temporal structure of the consciousness. The passage of time which is a feature of duration bears some relation to clock time when, at times, linearity and symmetry dominate and define the "calm" periods. In this sense, clock time is a particular instance of a general (overall) regime of a time reference frame (as suggested above, there cannot be two forms of time, clock time and market time). The general regime is "market" time; clock time forms the exception.

If the passage of time can be a feature of duration, then the *continuum* (perseverance of existence) of a matter is an even more legitimate feature (but note that it is *continuum* which forms the matter). It is the duration which elapses but which also concentrates and stretches as a result of memory recalls and lapses. At the outset, there is a stock of memorised past, and that is what makes it last, continue. There is no duration without a primary memory. Although an internal memory of events and facts can exist within the economic and financial sphere, a *continuum* which binds facts or groups of facts together, there is above all a memory for a conscious Subject.

Energy, in respect of a financial market, lies within the duration. This continuing time is the driving force of financial markets. It is not so much the volatility itself – although the phenomena of *continuum* are accompanied by volatility – but that which lasts and continues: this is where the source of energy lies. It can give rise to a number of interpretations. One can first link it with the phenomena of concentrations of price variations (volatility), since such variations are not independent and identically distributed. In addition to price variations, the direction of the same prices shows trends which are fairly long and continuing, both bullish and bearish. There accordingly exist both continuing concentrations of price variations and continuing trends of price increases and decreases. The two types of phenomena represent a distortion of the time reference frame. The more intense the price variations and the more market prices rise or fall in continuing long trends, then the more the temporal scale within the time reference frame can be seen to stretch, as it were. The stretching of the temporal framework (a large increasing number of price variations per unit of clock time; a large increasing number of bullish or bearish trends per unit of clock time) means that for one "traditional" unit of time (clock time) there is a concentration of phenomena of *continuum* (variations in price, price trends). The dilation of the temporal framework therefore also represents a phenomenon of concentration of variations and trends. The concentration, which is a feature of the distribution in space of the price variations and directions, can be accompanied by acceleration (speed). There is a dilation of the reference time and an increase in the density of time-matter of each unit of reference time within the time reference frame (speed and acceleration resulting from the compression effect).

The phenomena of concentration of continuing price variations and trends, the phenomena of dilation of the reference time and, symmetrically, of densification of the unit of reference time (compression of time-matter), can all be compared and connected to the distortions of time-matter which make up duration and are sustained by memory. Such phenomena are the result of memory recalls and/or lapses. The memory recall creates the *continuum* and basically brings closer those events which clock time (and conventional space) may at first sight have placed at a significant distance. Memory recall transmits energy and exercises a force of attraction which serve to reduce the distance between events, facts and prices. The distance, in the time reference frame, between facts, events, prices or groups of prices separated by a significant distance in the light of *clock time*, is compressed, reduced or even eliminated. The dilation of the reference time is accompanied by a compression of the distances in the time reference frame (one can move around quicker). This also applies to the distance between two facts, events or prices which are in immediate proximity (the price for a day and the price for the following day), which are as it were brought even closer and furthermore accelerated. Memory lapse produces a phenomenon which is theoretically similar (although asymmetries between memory recall and lapse cannot be excluded: does one forget in the same way that one remembers? Yes, undoubtedly. Does one forget more quickly and in a less direct manner than one remembers? It remains to be seen!). The force of attraction between two market prices depends upon their distance-time, the latter being a function of memory recall and lapse. The same is true of the connection between a price and a real event or fact. This force of attraction, governed by phenomena of memory recall or lapse is also a force of meaning (and of direction). The "meaning" of a market price lies in the *continuum* (duration) which creates a connection within the time of the duration and of the memory with another referent of the financial sphere or another price) or a referent of the real sphere (a fact, event or economic act). The dynamics depend upon energy, which is a differential of the duration (memory recall and/or lapse).

§ 125.   The value, in the Stock Market, is limited. "Limited" is understood to mean something which refers to one or more relative (and not absolute) balances which were considered in *Théorie*. The sudden emergence of time, of the time differential, imposes a reference frame of relative balances, which maintain an essential link with the limited value. The value of the relative balance is a value whose very structure is the time which continues. It is less an average as such than a reference (that which lasts is average) in dynamic movement, the said movement resulting from new events which can alter the duration-matter of memory recall and lapse. It cannot be an ideal (absolute) value, since absolute involves to some extent the cancellation of temporality. The instantaneous values of the Stock Market cause a stir and move towards a limited value, i.e. a series of relative balances in movement.

The instantaneous event or fact only has meaning, with regard to the relative or limited value, insofar as such fact calls into question the block of the past which is continuing and which constitutes the reference. However, all the events and facts which constantly lap against the block of duration, like drops of rain, ultimately end up in turn forming a block of the past which continues.

Accordingly, only that which remains unseen or is not immediately commented upon is of relevance for anyone who wants to understand how the Stock Market operates, i.e. the non-instantaneous component, and relevant events, facts or factors, for the Stock Market price (results, interest rates…), and the past history of the Stock Market price itself.

The present, instantaneous fact (such as an economic figure, a quarterly publication of results) – allowing for exceptions – has little meaning for the understanding of a Stock Market price. What is significant – and important to know – is the relative balance duration-time regime which establishes a limited or relative value. Moreover, the instantaneous Stock Market price, which seems to act or react in sympathy with instantaneous facts, reacts in reality in accordance with the distortion of this regime of relative balance or limited value. Such reactions can be significant and concentrated (periods of volatility).

Over time, it is submitted that the stock market price is moving towards a limited value, that it is as if magnetised by a force of recall towards a value, by a memory trigger. This limited value is continuously distorted and eroded by memory recall and lapse. The distortions and erosions of relative or limited values are exactly equivalent to the manner in which expectations are formed. The future has no real substance in the Stock Market reference frame. In particular, expectations and forecasts operate in exactly the same way as the past makes itself present, using more or less memory recall or lapse. There is only the past making itself present.

The immediate present (facts, figures, events…) may assist, stimulate, encourage the past to make itself present. The immediate market price is fully intact during its variations and movements, the dynamics by which the past, the real, the financial, the price itself) are made or make themselves present.

The more the duration (that which lasts) makes itself present, the greater the degree of *continuum* and the dilation of the time reference frame. The function of memory recall, by reducing the distance between past facts and events and the immediate market price, creates *continuum*. Dilation is understood to mean the stretching of a *continuum* of primary duration matter. This *continuum* process is also a moment of concentration of the fundamental energy of memory: one can move faster within the reference frame because the distances are reduced. Speed within the Stock Market is a function of the time-matter of memory. The function of memory lapse encourages segmentation, the contraction of time and its depletion of energy. One moves more slowly within the reference frame, the distances become longer, the duration diminishes and the meaning along with it. The segments of time become autonomous. The concentrations, *continua* and volatilities decrease into periods of memory lapse.

§ 126.   It is inaccurate to state that "each fact or event, no matter how distant in space or time, has repercussions on all other events". This formulation by Mandelbrot does not take into account the idea that distance is a function of memory recall and lapse within the time reference frame. Accordingly, distance is dilated or reduced according to the strength of action of memory recall or lapse. Moreover, it is not a question of "all other events" but rather those which, for some reason or other, can resonate at a given moment in memory of the fact or event in question. However that leaves considerable scope for crossed memory connections. It assumes that the time reference frame, in which distance is a function of memory recall and lapse, is global in two senses, since it brings together that which seems distant in conventional space and time.

The Stock Market time reference frame contains both "quick" time and "slow" time. Quick time, which represents a dilation of time, is linked to an acceleration of transactions. Not only the volumes of transactions but the speed of circulation of money in the financial sphere (number or volume of transactions traded per monetary unit) experience a significant increase. The phenomena of speed of money (and therefore, ultimately, those of inflation, disinflation or deflation) maintain a connection with the time reference frame. The increase in speeds seems to correspond to the periods of dilation of the Stock Market time scale, such periods being themselves linked to a stronger intensity of memory. Or, in other terms, speed evolves as the memory recall/lapse ratio is distorted, since the dynamics seem to be linked to the distortion.

The function of memory is not linear, which explains the points of concentration, the asymmetries and the discontinuities. Memory is selective and hazardous. Speed, which is a function of memory, is itself non-linear, since memory is selective (the function of memory is revealed both by memory recall and lapse, since memory recall and lapse both belong to the same phenomenon: what is remembered always includes a certain amount of that which is forgotten).

The principles which seem to be essential can be formulated as follows. Distance, within the time reference frame of economics and finance, depends upon the duration, and dynamic movement is a function of memory recall and lapse, i.e. distortions of the duration by memory recall and lapse. The duration is time-matter. Although it can evoke a *continuum*, the dynamics which drive it are not governed by continuity but, on the contrary, by discontinuity, a non-linear and asymmetrical concentration, since memory recall and lapse are themselves non-linear and discontinuous functions. The extreme values are concentrated in time and mark the memory, which explains why asymmetrical distributions will be noted later (as well as the fact that long-term interest rates seem to rise faster than they fall, undoubtedly due to the recollection of the years spent fighting inflation, up until the memory fades and memory lapse takes over). Extreme values leave an imprint on the memory and there are concentrations in time of extreme values because extreme values have effects on memory (*continuum*). Extreme values sustain themselves in a manner akin to a memory learning process where in fact nothing is learnt (the mandatory corrections do not occur because the risk of inflation is established but because it has occurred and is therefore expected) but rather recollected (i.e. expected). The fact that extreme values are clearly remembered does not mean that non-extreme values or "mean" values are not remembered and/or forgotten by means of the same process. However, since memory recall favours extreme values, it will produce further extreme values just like a wave, gradually losing intensity as memory lapse increases, until it fades out.

§ 127.   All the above makes it possible to estimate quantities or variables. But what are we dealing with? Is it a path towards the absolute value, a fixed point towards which floating values, after some fuss, end up being magnetised? Or, more probably, are they relative values which are moving, creating infinite numbers of floating and moving balances, while still magnetising rumours around a reference quantity? The term "relative balance" has been explained.

When one tries to harness the multiple facets, the market multiple – the rain star-studded with points which seem so contingent, so absurd – to a number of unitary fixed points – which is itself a risky step -, the functions of memory recall and lapse in the Stock Market's time reference frame offer a path. Everything seems to take place as if, like torches planted in the night, the memory of companies (their profits, certainly, but even more) were tracing a delicate path. One by one, the trembling torches of the memory are extinguished as the stroller walks by, whilst others immediately light up.

What burns at the heart of such torches is the memory of results and therefore includes a certain degree of memory lapse. At any moment, the current market price emerges surrounded by a considerable degree of contingency and risk but subject to a twofold requirement: this price still maintains a continuous connection of varying strength, not only with past prices (to be more specific, certain memory sequences for a certain type of sequence of actual events, i.e. corporate results, for example, since the *continuum* of Stock Market prices is the *continuum* of a relationship between the price and a certain phase of the event or fact in the real world) but above all with blocks of the past, carved as if in the stone of time, over the duration, with memorised sequences of results, which are therefore published to a certain extent; moreover, each "current" price regularly increases, drop by drop, like the grain of sand in a sand-rose on the block of the past and of memory until it changes the shape thereof, just like the sand and the desert wind patiently create temporary rose shapes; occasionally a "current" price may even prove to be so exceptional in terms of the information which it seems to carry, that it will cause the block of the past to explode, just like a sand storm will dissolve the rose only to recreate it later.

The grains of sand which, one by one, caress or beat upon the sandstone are pieces of information, events or facts relating to the company, principally the latter's results. This regular, hazardous lapping has, in fact, no sense in the light of what happens before it – but from which it ultimately originates, and this results in a certain degree of necessity. An immediate rumour, a fact or event which is usually described as "cyclical" is, in fact, not normally capable of altering the transcyclical block of the past, such as for example sequences of memorised results. Accordingly, each point which laps at the past is unable to alter it. One can say that a "cyclical" fact or event is non-information from the point of view of the relative value within the meaning as defined, i.e. from the point of view of memory recall and lapse within the market time reference frame of duration. However, the point which taps against the window originates in the block of the past, to a greater or lesser degree; moreover, as discussed, a sole fact or event can break the past block of stone just as one cracks a slab with a tap of the chisel, dissolving the past in the lapse of memory or projecting the memory into other past sequences; finally, and above all, a single "current" point will be even more important, if there is a more profound memory lapse regarding what has been: it will then occupy the whole of the space up to a proportion of an increasing rate of memory lapse (or, in other words, only recent increases will remain in the memory). The shorter the memory, the stronger the memory lapse, the greater the place occupied by the immediate fact or event in the financial time reference frame.

The immediate rumour, i.e. the "current" price, does not therefore contain enough information to act upon the block of the past which, in fact, determines it, although it would be possible. The relevant information is therefore, at any given moment, already known and is located in its entirety in the memory and duration which continues to variable degrees. The present of the current price accordingly has no substance of its own. The past and its *continuum* occupy the whole of the temporal field and even structure future expectations which, after all, are extensions of *continuum*. An occurrence is, first of all, the result of an earlier occurrence, which continues to a greater or lesser degree despite the erosive force of memory lapse. The immediate, current price is, in turn, like the glow of distant stars, light which is transmitted from very far away in the reference frame of time and space, until sometimes it is no more than the reflection of a dead star. The stars from which such points of light are created and unfurl constitute the fundamental framework for finance, i.e. the time-matter of duration, the stock of accumulated, past time. Memory recall, which is always a certain phase of memory lapse, distorts, compresses or dilates this matter. The "information" from such matter sets the financial dynamics in motion, that of non-linear financial time. The financial "objects" will move more or less rapidly within such dynamics, in a non-linear manner, according to the forces of memory recall and lapse. In this time and space reference frame, memory holds the key to distance and therefore to space-time. The current and immediate price, although apparently alone, isolated and contingent, can at any time provide light for such distant matter. This past matter, which is stored and remembered can in fact be very far distant, can refer to facts and events which are so far removed from the usual time and space that, at first glance, it is not easy to see the link between matter and immediate price. However, such a link does indeed exist, since memory recall shortens the distances and the memorised financial item will travel quickly towards the present, thus eliminating the distance and altering the structure of time.

The immediate current price is a product of a memorised time-matter (which has therefore been more or less forgotten), which travels within a space-time where the distances are compressed or stretched by memory recall and lapse. At the end of this voyage from a past star, which is sometimes very distant, possibly even dead, a light appears in the present in the form of the immediate price.

Symmetrically, the current, immediate price is ultimately always attracted by the past star from which it originates, a force of attraction which is made stronger by the fact that the distance is compressed by the memory recall. This is the function of memory (and therefore of memory lapse), which brings a series of immediate points back to a block of memory-matter. The attraction is made stronger by the fact that the connection forms between the immediate price (and therefore an environment of immediate facts and events) and a block of past occurrences and meanings, the distance being shortened and the time dilated: accordingly one travels quickly through space-time. This block of past occurrences and meanings, which helps create a relative balance, undoubtedly represents a form of "mean" of facts and events. However, such relative balances are highly unstable and constantly distorted by the dynamic forces of memory recall and lapse. This is the sort of basis on which the concept of value can be analysed within Stock Market dynamics.

§ 128.   So, what should be done? For practical purposes, how can the various points and conclusions of the preceding arguments be used to good account? We will try to give a practical content to the block of occurrences and meanings referred to above. It can be deemed that, at any given time, for any market value or for the market as a whole, there is a point of reference (relative balance) provided by a certain state of memory (and memory lapse) regarding elements, facts and events which have a significant effect on the company. At first, attention will be paid to the corporate results alone or to the results of all companies for the market taken as a whole. There is, at any given time and for each stock market price, a certain state of memory of the sequences of results, a slice of time affected by a certain memory lapse. In terms of dynamics, it can be said that this state of memory (sequences of results which are memorised in a more or less linear fashion, with memory lapse being more or less present in the sequences of results, according to whether one is dealing with the near or distant past) is constantly moving, evolving. There is a multitude of relative, unstable balances, although all can be reduced to a few blocks of past occurrences and meanings with which they maintain relationships which are magnetised by a force of attraction. That being so, under static conditions, one has a certain memory of certain sequences of past results. This memory, under static conditions, can be said to be fixed. One starts from the idea, as discussed above, that there is a connection between the current, immediate price and the financial objects which exist in the Stock Market time reference frame. Such financial objects are pieces of ordinary, past time, sequences of facts and events which can be cut up like pieces of cold wax. It can be submitted that the series of current, immediate prices are not simply the issue of one or more blocks, in the same way as starlight may originate from a distant galaxy or from a cluster of bits of dead stars drifting in space, but also move, as if by means of attraction and magnetisation, towards a value or values of relative balance, all of which have a certain state of memory recall and lapse in respect of key elements of the company whose market price is at issue. There is not necessarily just one block. It is very possible that there exists a form of archipelago or groups of blocks which drift together, side-by-side. The conditions are still static, which means that this block of the past, the block of occurrences and meanings which has been cut out of the time-matter of duration, is fixed (practically speaking, a sort of average, in simple terms, of X years of results; fairly rapidly, in fact, such balances melt away as one steps deeper into the past and the opposite occurs as one approaches the present). It is fixed in the sense that no memory recalls or lapses originate from this block: for example, after establishing that there seems to exist a relevant memory of ten years of sliding results, which of itself already creates a mechanical dynamic by means of the lapse of time which will, progressively, result in the most distant years exiting the memory and being forgotten, therefore after having established this ten-year memory, one can – for example, by means in particular of a fresh, current, immediate, event – introduce a violent reminder of a specific segment of the "mean" ten-year sequence or, even, of another "part" of the sequence which is not located within the ten years in question but twenty-five years further back. The memory recall will eliminate the distance and "stick" the piece of distant DNA to the initial ten-year sequence. The DNA of a market value or of the Stock Market taken as a whole is made up of a central core which represents one or more sequences of occurrences of past facts and events, to which pieces of more distant or closer sequences attach themselves. It all undergoes a dynamic process.

However, we are still at the static phase, the identification of one or more sequences of past results. Only the results have been taken into consideration, since it has been decided, at this stage of research, to choose only the said results from among the universe of relevant facts and events for a given company.

The sequence(s) of results form a block. This block is static. Using this approach, we will look for a block and therefore a point of reference which we assume will remain relevant for the valuation of a company listed on the Stock Market or that of the market taken as a whole. It will be shown that the value adopted by this block is sufficiently stable (although in fact it is a mean and is sliding) for a valid submission to be made that the difference between the relevant and sequential memory of the results and the value of the results which seem to be integrated in the current, immediate price should be reduced in the long term, magnetising the market price towards a value which is consistent with the memorised block. The point of reference is quasi-fixed, with a moderately dynamic process of mechanical memory lapse linked to the progressive exiting of the most distant years. The dynamic process comes in particular from the return to the average market price or, more specifically, from the "results" component which forms part of the ("anticipated") market price.

Adopting this approach of a quasi-absolute balance (it is not absolute, since it allows time to enter; and is instead a strong, relative balance), and, in order to return to the previous metaphor, of fixed stars for which the map of the sky is known.

From a practical point of view, the difficulty lies in identifying the past sequence(s) which can validly be admitted as a relevant, and especially stable, memory of results. To show a certain degree of stability (for example, to show that the market seems to retain an average sequence of ten years of results), and therefore a degree of regularity, constitutes a factual task which is impossible in the long term, which therefore justifies a more realistic but also a more complex approach, by means of permanent values of relative balance. However, the quasi-absolute or strong relative approach has the merit of simplifying to excess the analysis and interpretation of Stock Market prices, by reducing the relevant elements of results to a few fixed or quasi-fixed points of reference, sequences of DNA from the past. Furthermore, the observation seems to indicate that blocks of the past, namely blocks of sequences of corporate results, do indeed exist and are sufficiently stable and continuous (stability of memory recall and lapse) to provide a reference for the value, at least for a time. Accordingly, it is not merely excessive but wrong to deny the existence of any mean, absolute or relative value towards which points or series representing current, immediate market prices move, as if by attraction.

The fact remains that the fixed points discussed above are far more fluid than would appear. How should this be taken into account?

If it is possible to identify fixed points, i.e. sequences of past results which form a relatively stable memory to which the market seems to refer on a regular basis, and which, consequently appear to provide a means of assessing the market value of a company on the basis of the current, immediate price, at any instant, accordingly submitting a form of medium-term reminder towards this point of reference, just like one ultimately remembers a reality which is in some way established, if possible – observation attests to the fact that such fixed points do exist in the Stock Market universe -, however, such stability is relative in two ways: the fixed points, i.e. the stock of time-matter (duration) which is used as a reference, when sufficiently fixed, to what is known elsewhere as a "regime", may change, because the regime changes or because, within a regime, the references will move subject to the flows or occasionally the thrusts, of facts and events which pass according to how prices develop; moreover, without a radical change to the fixed point, the latter may and actually is distorted by the dilations and compressions of memory recall and lapse within the time reference frame: some or other segment of the block of duration which constitutes the fixed point is remembered or forgotten, to a greater or lesser degree, according to and depending upon the events or facts of the current, immediate environment. Accordingly, a fixed point may be constituted from the sliding, multi-cyclical memory of ten years of results, an equally-weighted average which progressively forgets as it were the more distant years. However, some or other immediate fact or event may attract the attention, create a reminder of some or other year or sub-period of such sequence of ten years and cause the rest to be forgotten. It may indeed even reawaken a more distant sequence and group it with the sequence of ten years (a memory composed in the same way as a DNA transplant) or forget everything up until the immediate instant which becomes, over time, the component of a new memory, distorted, since it will only understand something which is identical to the most recent period (Stock Market rises during the period when a bubble is formed, for example). Taken to the extreme, the fixed point may be cancelled by the force of immediate facts and events; either a substitution of the fixed point will then occur (the memory will look for new, more relevant sequences) or complete memory loss; in both cases there is a breach of regime, but such breaches can only be temporary.

There are accordingly multiple levels: fixed points which are relative but strong, which may disappear in favour of other fixed points or nothing (memory loss) and also return; a dynamic movement of the fixed point itself which, while still continuing to act as reference for a regime, is constantly transforming; finally, just like there are multiple galaxies, there are, at any given time, various regimes which coexist in parallel worlds. A regime may be dominant, together with all its features, fixed points of memory recall and lapse, but may in turn be dominated and replaced, without completely disappearing. The parallel worlds exist in a space-time where distances can be reduced or even eliminated by memory recall, which will make the financial objects located in some or other regime or parallel world travel faster. Financial time, due to its non-linear structure, unites these worlds. This makes it possible for a regime to be apparently put to sleep and for another to return or accede (i.e. to make its presence known, since a regime already exists, being a particular section of what has already existed).

The existence of multiple levels makes it difficult to understand what is happening in the Stock Market, the current, immediate prices and the estimated price in accordance with the direction taken by the immediate price (that which may come to pass).

From a practical point of view, the finance industry allocates a considerable amount of resources and time to the analysis of current, immediate information. Although such information cannot be said to be unnecessary, it is not essential to an understanding of what is at stake. Such information cannot be said to be unnecessary since the current, immediate price, together with all the surrounding facts and events, is likely to alter the fixed points which are in turn important. However, since most of the time such facts and events will not alter the fixed points or regimes, it is work of secondary importance. Moreover, the current price is always the light from a more or less distant star which has travelled for a greater or lesser amount of time within the space-time of a financial reference frame.

At any given time, it is a question of trying to understand where the fixed points are located, how such points move, how they are distorted, broken or replaced, in order to put the current, immediate price and the accompanying events and facts into perspective by comparison with the fixed points, to ask oneself whether the immediate price is likely to alter the fixed points and, if not, to try and estimate to what extent the current, immediate price has distanced itself to a greater or lesser degree from the comprehensive logic of the fixed point(s). Such distancing creates value, excess or bubbles.

It is therefore appropriate, when generally distributing resources, to readjust the analysis and research to focus on what is not immediate, i.e. to concentrate on the features of the regimes, the identification of the memorised sequences of past time and also the rate of memory lapse. Although everything relating to the present moment of the Stock Market can prove misleading when analysed on its own, the levels of memory (results and any other direct and indirect variables which may prove to be relevant for a company and, *ultimately*, its market price) can provide points of reference for the understanding of the immediate and the future direction. Since the future for the Stock Market is always the product of a *continuum* of the past and the duration. The Stock Market dynamics stem from the fact that the financial objects (by that we mean all the facts and events which come within the financial time reference frame) continue to exist. Although the Stock Market may often appear, and is often described, as a disjointed and uncertain process, there is at work a deep-set continuity of the past in duration and memory.

The task of cutting the past into relevant DNA sequences which are likely to be memorised (recalled) or forgotten is essential. For market prices, this is undoubtedly a question of the results, but that is too partial an approach. The results must without doubt be analysed in their memory dimension (some will say this is multicyclical, but it goes even further since, often, the multicyclical analyses are confined to mere fixed, sliding means of the nearest cycles, whilst memorised time-matter is in non-linear movement and at any moment may be joined by bits of DNA from other more distant or different regimes.) However the results cannot be the only time-matter which is memorised over the duration and more or less forgotten. If one assumes that, at any given time in Stock Market dynamics, what is relevant is a block of past time, which is cut out in much the same way as one cuts a stone or a carrot out of the ground, it is clear that elements other than the results are also relevant, since they are likely to be remembered. In the block of cut stone, one will find other minerals, fossils and metals mixed in with the basic, dominant stone. In the carrot brought up from the basement, the plant elements will describe a climate, an environment, facts and events. If, as we think, it is sequences of the past which, at any given time, stimulate the Stock Market dynamics, then in principle it could only be a complete past, the elements of which are to a greater or lesser extent recalled or forgotten. The current, immediate price is simultaneously the product of complete past sequences (all that affected or surrounded a company's existence is in principle relevant), one of the elements of such sequence, and, potentially, the element which disrupts the past sequences.

Whilst the essential part of resources are devoted to the necessarily unproductive decoding of the immediate present (which does not exist, in the literal sense, within the market time reference frame), a two-speared effort must be undertaken with regard to the past: to cut out relevant, sequential sections on a vertical axis; and to identify, from the results alone, the other relevant elements.

§ 129.   At any given time, there is an interaction, an energy link, between the current, immediate price and the memorised past sequences. This interaction stimulates the market dynamics. There is an energy link because the immediate present (fact, event, the price itself) triggers (or not, or to a greater or lesser extent) the mechanics of memory recall and lapse. It is these mechanics which set off or set in motion the sequenced past matter within the time-space reference frame. By recalling the DNA of a regime (or parts thereof), i.e. relevant past sequences, the present, the immediate environment and facts will literally make "objects" which are sometimes remote "travel" within the reference frame, by exercising a force of attraction and boosting the speed.

The energy of market dynamics is a source of speed. The source of the market energy is located in what we have named the "fixed points", "blocks of occurrences and meanings", i.e. sequential sections of the past and, more generally, of duration, which come within a temporal reference frame of memory recall and lapse, the dynamics of which are provided by the reminders and lapses of memory of the multiple layers which are superposed in a myriad fragments of "fixed points" of moving facts, in an infinite number of combinations which form, at any given time, pieces of Stock Market DNA, which group together and separate.

Market energy is housed within the time-matter which constitutes duration. This energy is liberated into the market space-time when the financial objects which make up the "points", "blocks" or sequential sections start to move, or literally to travel within a form of psychological reference frame (once again the grand concept of Mr. Allais), the distance being an inverse function of the attraction created by the memory or reminder.

Accordingly, this means that the phenomena of acceleration and speed in the Stock Market are closely connected to the dilations or contractions of space-time and the distances ultimately provided by the action of memory recall and lapse on the essential matter of duration. In particular, the speed of money within the financial sphere, here the Stock Market itself, is intimately connected to such factors. The speed of money within the financial sphere can be seen, in very simple terms, as being the amount of financial transactions effected per monetary unit. With a stable monetary supply, the acceleration of the circulation of money in the financial sphere goes hand in hand with increases. Such increases are not linear, being the result of "jumps", and the distributions of market movements show non-linear, asymmetrical outlines (of movements in general, between rises and falls, and during rises and fall).

The reasons for the speed of money, acceleration or deceleration of its circulation remain largely mysterious. The Keynesian approach is based on ownership, backed by the necessary notions of "preference for liquidity" or, more generally, of "appetite for risk" or "risk-averse" (these two notions are in fact widely used in market analyses of the Stock Market). This approach paved the way and enabled progress to be made. It can inter alia be seen that the phenomena of the increase in market prices are linked to the monetary phenomenon of circulation (of money) in the financial sphere. Such circulation is in turn driven by an appetite for risk, based solely on the best-known Stock Market notion (the connections between real and financial spheres and accordingly the transfer mechanics which may or may not exist, and which we discussed in *Théorie,* are not considered here). Liquidity, here in the financial sphere, is defined by the circulation of money (money is defined by its circulation, i.e. its liquidity, a theory adopted in *Théorie*). This circulation creates money from nothing (the abundance of liquidity which is often advanced by observers in such periods of rising prices reflects the fact that circulation is increasing, and not necessarily that the monetary stock is increasing, even though that is normally the case, because the monetary authorities are accommodating and because, of itself, the acceleration of circulation creates money). Such circulation is, finally, not linear, since the accelerations are dissymmetrical or asymmetrical, which explains in particular why the majority of increases are condensed into narrow sequences of time.

Monetary stock is "informed", i.e. set in motion within and by the financial time and space reference frame described above, and with which it unites in order to produce the Stock Market's monetary dynamics. The meeting of a monetary stock and past sequential sections driven by memory recall and lapse will produce the circulation and acceleration, and ultimately the phenomena of price increases, the opposite being equally true for decreases. What is called "appetite for risk" is, basically, the setting in motion of blocks of duration governed by memory recall and lapse. The time-matter which is duration and the monetary matter are merged in the same reference frame within the Stock Market dynamics.

The same is true of the phenomena of price decreases, of market "deflation", which are closely connected to the deceleration of monetary circulation within the Stock Market's financial sphere, itself caused by aversion to risk, which means, within the psychological time reference frame, the sudden emergence of memory (since the movement is often by jump, by a rupture).

Whether dealing with a rise or fall in market prices, the speeds are dictated by the movements of memory recall and lapse, although memory lapse and memory recall as such cannot individually be associated with the rise or fall; it will depend upon the point of application (i.e. the sequential section of the past which is remembered or forgotten). An analysis of these elements was presented in connection with an interpretation of the dynamics of the cycle in *Théorie*. Moreover, memory recall and lapse are not two distinct dimensions but form one single concept: that which is stored in the memory, is remembered or is recalled always contains an element of memory loss, which can sometimes become completely dominant; in the same way, memory loss (of past sequences which could incite prudence) which seems to be a strong feature of the periods of acceleration of increase in market prices (market bubbles) can be described in terms of memory (only recent increases or an exceptional environment remain "in the memory"; there is therefore a change or breach of the memory regime, to forget – this – is implicitly to choose to no longer remember but that).

Asymmetries which can exist between increases and decreases refer back to the perception of risk, which can be described using the elements of the time reference frame of memory recall and lapse. The observations made on this subject (do shares or bonds rise more quickly than they fall?) in *Les Carnets monétaires* showed thick, asymmetrical distribution tails (accordingly interest rates have on average risen more quickly for the last thirty or so years and, especially, such increases occurred within very short time-frames; on average, shares rise more quickly than they fall, unlike bonds). The memory reference frame for bonds has been marked by inflation and the fight against inflation and what can be called the self-regulatory anti-inflationary function of the bond markets (it is the fear or expectation of a return to inflation which makes it impossible for inflation to appear, since it creates a pressure on long-term interest rates caused by the memory of periods of inflation and central bank intervention). This time reference frame for memory in the bond market is an interesting case in point, since there is an unambiguous observation (distribution of speeds of increases and decreases with thick tails on the right – it rises more quickly – and increases which are concentrated over time, a phenomenon of acceleration and therefore of alteration of the structure of time) and a clear demonstration of an effect of memory. On the one hand, one has the sequential section of the past which remembers inflation and the action against inflation. On the other hand, within the time reference frame, the reminder is activated as soon as an inflationary figure, which is more worrying than others, exerts pressure on long-term interest rates. This represents a rapid movement within the space-time reference frame of the financial object which makes up the memorised DNA. The latter starts to travel very rapidly, the distance is reduced by the force of attraction which the reminder produces between, first, the current, immediate inflationary figure and the sequential section plan of the past. The activation of this energy liberates the speed and causes the acceleration which is observed (most increases in long-term interest rates are effected in less than five months). Dilation or concentration/contraction of time are at work within the space-time reference frame. It can be seen in passing that memory recall and expectation, here of inflation, are strictly the same. One anticipates in the same way as one remembers (and therefore in the same way as one forgets, since all memories involve a degree of memory loss).

This observation is a feature of what we have called a "regime", a period during which there is a certain stability of the principal parameters of the reference frame. In the present case, it can be thought that what has been described as a "paradox of calm" will progressively take hold, an increasing effacement of the original sequential section (the fear of inflation in short), as the current, immediate facts and events, introduce, bit by bit, the idea that inflation is no longer a threat. The memory is then so to speak "put to sleep", forgotten and possibly replaced by another sequential section of the past (e.g. deflation with effect from the start of the new century) and therefore a modification of the risk premia (from an inflationary risk premium to what is instead a deflationary risk premium) and, ultimately, a modification of the price of the financial asset. Here is an example of both a fixed point which remains relevant but places itself in dormant motion (memory lapse) and the replacement of a fixed point which once prevailed by another fixed point. However, and this is essential, the sequential section of the inflationary past may, one day, sooner or later, be suddenly awakened. Like a flash of lightning in a clear, blue sky, a sudden reminder can create astonishment and a rupture, bringing back to the regime a dimension which had, quite literally, become remote (the reminder will result in a sudden acceleration of an increase in interest rates), or, even, result in a rupture of the regime (crisis, explosion of the bubble). Analysis and research have to track precisely these levels, like parallel paths which end up crossing.

§ 130.   The distribution of speeds of rates for the last thirty or so years shows fairly clearly that the quickest and most pronounced increases were more numerous than the quickest and most pronounced decreases. Accordingly, we were able to submit the idea that this thirty-year regime had a time reference frame in which the memory of inflation, and the acts of fighting inflation, were dominant, even though the increasing deflationary risk, after a decade of deflation, very probably leads to a rise in the rate of memory lapse within the reference frame.

What happens to the shares themselves within the Stock Market dynamics? An analysis of interest rates only offers indirect access, provided that the relationship between interest rates and share prices remains stable, which is only true in a given macro-financial regime (inflationary, growth without inflation, deflationary with deflationary trends). On average, since the start of the 1970's, shares have tended to rise quicker than they have fallen, and the distribution of extreme movements, whether up or down, do not show a particularly asymmetrical distribution unlike interest rates. This observation, which is particularly valid up until the end of the 1990's, in the context of a significant rise in the share markets, is fairly clearly influenced by the two sub-periods of market crashes (in 2001 and 2007), while remaining, on average, relevant. The observation remains the same if one includes dividends, in respect of a group which includes the developed countries (the observation does not seem to be altered by the addition of emerging countries). The observation also shows that a quick and pronounced movement (whether up or down) tends to be followed by a movement in the opposite direction, together with a reduced intensity, the speed decreasing from 25 to 65%. There is accordingly a "reactivity" to pronounced movements. One notes, consistent with the idea that share markets rise quicker than they fall (at least during the period, i.e. the regime under observation), that the (bullish) reaction to a pronounced drop is greater than the (bearish) reaction to a rise (these results were discussed in a first *Research Paper* in 1998: *Asset prices: Fall faster than Rise?*, Paribas, 20 April 1998; see Barron's 11 May 1998, Newton Revisited, *How Fast do Markets Fall? A Study Raises some possibilities*; these results were discussed again in *Les Carnets monétaires, 2008*).

How should these observations be interpreted from the point of view of Stock Market dynamics? It comes spontaneously to mind that the appetite for risk involved in shares (the Stock Market) is stimulated by a drop in interest rates (through a preference for shares or bonds, and in particular the risk premium of shares) and the expectations of growth and rising corporate profits. The long period which commenced in the 1980's and continued until the end of the 1990's without a real break, was that of deflation, which had a positive effect on share prices, as a result of the bearish trend of long-term interest rates. It dominated the "results" component in Stock Market behaviour until the creation of a bubble since, during the period from 1982-1998, although rises in profits scarcely deviated from historical long-term trends (of between 7% and 8%), share prices did not stay within the long-term outlines, i.e. 13% for a very long-term average, in line with increases in profits, each sub-period (of about 14 years) of comparable deviation having been followed by a sub-period of deviation in the other sense, during which share prices rose less than corporate profits, thus suggesting overall a return to the long-term average.

It seems, with shares, that the Stock Market dynamics are extremely sensitive to what certain people call the "liquidity effect", which summarises the fact that interest rates drop and that such drops are sometimes structural (a deflationary regime). The notion of liquidity is similar in this context to that of appetite for risk: money starts to circulate in the financial sphere of long-term assets constituted by Stock Market shares, in proportion to the memory prompts or the memory recall and lapse. As from 1985, the time reference frame started to be progressively integrated in the memory, and therefore led to an expectation of a drop in long-term interest rates which sustained appetite for risk.

What has thus been observed of rises and falls in share prices, and the speed thereof, can describe a given regime or period during which a certain number of elements, facts or events have led to the reality of the markets rising faster than they fall. Adopting this approach, there is a time reference frame of duration where a certain number of segments or pieces of DNA, with the meaning defined above, have been memorised. The same is true of the structural drop in short- and long-term interest rates, in nominal and then real terms, in the wake of the great deflationary "reduction". Behind this deflation lie remembered or recalled sequences which take root and which favour a class of assets such as shares in relative terms (a preference for shares or bonds, a function of appetite for risk) and absolute terms (reversal of the inflation sequence, rise in interest rates, drop in profits and therefore the effacement of a block of history from the 1970's). Linked to the macro-financial regime which is then introduced is a memory, a time reference frame which both progressively remembers and adapts essential factors (fight against inflation, adjustment of added value which is more favourable to profits) and also forgets, precisely, what dominated the regime and the previous reference frame, since memory recall and lapse are two sides of the same phenomenon. Facts, events and relationships which might have existed before the very inflationary decade of the 1970's, are then recalled, during the mutation of DNA, over a longer period. When examined over the longer period, this decade was exceptional. The longer-term reality contains cycles and regimes of growth without inflation and a more normal hierarchy of returns and risk as between shares and bonds. It also includes a relationship between interest rates and share prices which is certainly present (negative with a slight advance for interest rates) but certainly not as exclusive as the period after the 1970's (inflation followed by deflation), where the correlation becomes so sharply negative that shares start to resemble bonds and *vice versa*. Between 1970 and 2000 this element dominates the regime of memory and Stock Market space-time, and thus has a strong influence on its dynamics. The "interest rate" factor dominates the real factor of profits, or other factors (in any event the "immediate" profitabilities which almost never have any significance other than to reveal what might jeopardise the memory regime, as has been seen). There is a progressive effacement of the 1970's and a memory of periods which, like the years 1950-1960, witnessed growth without inflation or inflation which was (less or) barely volatile. That said, if the connection of meaning remains as strong between interest rates and share prices in a positive sense for shares in a deflationary phase, it is because there is a continuing memory of the connection forged by the painful experience of the 1970's. In fact, during the better part of the 1990's the inflationary regime was not forgotten: it was because this regime was remembered that the drop in interest rates could benefit shares to such a great extent. However, credibility progressively arrives and a certain memory lapse takes over: the risk of inflation fades from memories, the links between interest rates and shares become looser. The reminder of the risk of deflation with the sudden explosion of the bubbles in 2000 and 2007 (shares, credit) will bring closer within the space-time of the reference frame situations which are in principle distant (Japan in the 1990's, the United States in the 1930's). As has been seen, these events will travel in an accelerated manner within such space-time of the memory, sustaining by their force of attraction, to what then seems to be occurring or emerging, a market acceleration spiral of the Stock Market, accompanied by a reversal of the relationship between interest rates and share prices (positive correlation).

In a regime where the "liquidity" factors (including the interest rate, appetite for risk, speed of circulation of money within the financial sphere) dominate the real factors (such as profits), which was the case during the long deflationary period, it is perhaps not surprising that rapid rises are more numerous than (rapid) falls. The phenomena of non-linear accelerations which are specific to time reference frames where favourable memorised events are attracted to each other like magnets, can consequently be understood (the deflationary regime commencing in the years 2000 shows a symmetrical, downward trend).

A second element should be added to the memory regime for the period from 1970 to 2000. This element is the Stock Market rises themselves, which progressively form duration and support each other, providing the memory with a base for consolidations which progressively accumulate in the same way as stalagmites in caves, drip by drip. The *continuum* of increases means that only the increases are remembered and it is for this reason, among others, that they will continue, for a time.

Is there a more structural reason for the fact that shares, as a class of asset, experience more rapid rises than falls, i.e. is there any reason to believe that, in addition to the features of the various regimes which might have governed or govern the Stock Market, there is a more persistent form of DNA? On the one hand, the speeds are dictated, as discussed, by the forces of attraction between facts, events or any other piece of DNA which is memorised (or forgotten and then recalled), forces of attraction which cause an accelerated circulation within a psychological time reference frame and a distortion of the temporal matter (duration). Since the speeds have been dictated, there is no reason to believe that there may be more rises than falls. It is easy to imagine a very bleak psychological time reference frame by only remembering the worst and recalling only the crashes. The rupture sequences in 2000-2002 and then 2007-2008 have shown this.

On the other hand, it might be that, from among the animal spirits which inspire it, the determining factors of the Stock Market's time reference frame attract more particularly an appetite for risk. Or, in other words, if one accepts the simplistic idea that there is some form of genome or DNA which corresponds to each class of assets, i.e. a certain identity card within the meaning as defined above (facts, events or other elements which have been memorised, forgotten, recalled or effaced), i.e. an identity which dominates the present economic climate (such and such a regime) or which orders it (identity can thus mean that the time reference frames relating to the Stock Market would have a certain propensity to select only a certain type of pieces of duration within the memory recall and lapse process discussed above. If one accepts this simplified notion, which would then apply to any class of asset, the formation of the contents of the Stock Market time reference frames and of the terms of operation would be specific, i.e. would provide an identity). The hereditary phenomenon of *continuum* would form part of a certain *continuum* of identity.

Accordingly, we would unconsciously have a greater or lesser tendency only to select a certain type of information from within the market time reference frame. Moreover, within the very workings of the reference frame itself (circulations, attractions, speeds of memory recall and lapse) there would, once again, be identities, i.e. fundamental *continua*. The "Stock Market" would thus be the name taken by a certain genomial identity associated with a space-time reference frame which divides duration in a certain manner and accordingly also applies memory recall and lapse in a certain way.

The pertinent money matter is a memorized matter.

CHAPTER 7

STOCK MARKET VALUE
AND PREFERENCES

THE GENERALISING ROLE OF THE STOCK MARKET AND RISK PREMIUM

§ 131.   The Stock Market groups together the expectations of future growth, and therefore a form of future consumption and investment function. The Stock Market also represents a waiver of part of the immediate consumption in return for an expectation of deferred profit, consumption or investment. Finally, as witnessed clearly during the unexpected growth period of the 1990's, there is a simultaneous drop in the rate of savings and a rise in the price of assets and in immediate consumption (or investment) in circumstances where the use of indebtedness and various wealth effects, linked to the immediate assessment of the Stock Market price lead, somewhat uncomfortably, to a strong and simultaneous increase in the immediate and future prospects of consumption (investment). This will, in particular, lead to a disproportionately large increase in the offer of goods and services for a future consumption which cannot materialise since, at that moment in time, unless the cycle of debt is extended *ad infinitum* without any damage, households will be forced to save again.

Accordingly there is indeed a link between the consumption function and the price of Stock Market assets. The Stock Market values a future consumption function, which represents a waiver of all or part of immediate consumption. In this simple context, the "risk premium" may act as a link between two temporal strata. Still within this simple context, the immediate (current) Stock Market increase corresponds to a deferred future consumption, which is favourable or better, and which seems to indicate that there is no particular, immediate reason for consumption to increase sharply. On the contrary, the postponement now of consumption to the future (when it is expected to be better), which justifies the Stock Market increase and which is funded by the waiver of instantaneous or immediate consumption and the purchase of securities on the Stock Market, must correspond in part to such waiver, all else being equal. This would, in passing, and still in the same simple context, enable one to understand the Stock Market tendency to rise when the economic cycle is itself rather depressed. The intertemporal consistency means that the signal given today by the Stock Market price for the future (function of deferred consumption and investment) does not lead to (immediate) decisions to consume or invest which, later, turn out to be intertemporally mistaken. Accordingly, as seen above, if the accumulation of favourable signs for future consumption (Stock Market increase) leads to a sharp rise in immediate consumption by real or psychological wealth effects and a drop in savings, the intertemporal consistency of the cycles of consumption, but also of investment are not maintained, since, based on the signal given by the Stock Market at the present time for the future consumption function, the economy may find itself committed to an accumulation of capacities (excess capacities) which will have later be confronted with inadequate consumption, at a time when households have to face adjustments to their balance sheets.

We talk of a "simple context" since it is clear that, in reality, the consistency or alignment of the intertemporal levels, which is one of the Stock Market's roles, effected in particular by means of risk premium, may be seriously disturbed by the credit cycle and, more simply, by money, when the latter becomes uncontrolled. It is (easy) credit which allows for the impossible to be achieved, the funding of the immediate moment without relinquishing the future. The relationship between the consumption function (and growth in general) and the Stock Market price requires minimal interference from money, in order to be as it should. However, the real position is made up of bubbles which we have analysed elsewhere.

Equity risk premium can be distorted by purely monetary phenomena. The Stock Market price is obtained as much (if not more) by the circulation of money ("liquidity" as it is sometimes defined by the trading rooms) as by the value of the company(ies) which make up the Stock Market – and this is true irrespective of the way in which such value is measured. This undoubtedly applies in what can be described as a normal situation (i.e. no monetary excess). The speed of circulation of money within the financial sphere, i.e. the relationship which may exist, for example, between stock market transactions and all the means of payment, is largely responsible for the creation of the Stock Market price. This is even truer when the accommodating nature of monetary creation permits euphoria in the financial sphere and, moreover, a simultaneous expansion of both what is real and what is financial. There is a link between risk premium and the circulation of money within the Stock Market, and in general within the financial sphere, between liquidity and risk premium, the latter being lower the faster the monetary circulation within the Stock Market relating to financial transactions. This circulation may include the phenomena of creation of money out of nothing, of transfers of the means of payment from the real to the financial sphere, of the indebtedness of the market players. The monetary nature of risk premium is underestimated and this undoubtedly contributes to the feeling that risk premium is surrounded by mystery.

Moreover, even though the Stock Market is effectively made up of companies and, consequently, its dynamics should be essentially provided by that which relates (more or less) directly to such companies, the Stock Market has in modern times become the main institutional form responsible for relations with the outside world, for projects (expectations) and risks. This giant form of intermediation between the Subject and the world, which is involved in the manner in which the Subject is projected to the world, has become progressively more independent until it has become a form or type of institutional personality ("the" market, thinks, speaks, considers...) in a potentially conflictual relationship with other institutions (e.g. the central banks) and which may even turn against the Subject. This empowerment of the market means that what is called the "Stock Market" reflects and means something much more than just the companies themselves, even though the companies occupy a prime position in the development of modern capitalism. This empowerment means that the Stock Market is, at any given time, almost the sole form of intermediation between the Subject and the world, i.e. it integrates all the projects, all the facts and events and all the risks. The basis for the formation of the Stock Market price is therefore very extensive and the same is true of the risk premium. Part (another part) of the enigma of the Stock Market risk premium lies in the fact that this equity risk premium bears witness to multiple risks, which are far more numerous than those which objectively relate solely to the companies in question. This is perhaps true since, ultimately, only a few risks are at present financialised, i.e. are covered by a segment of the financial market which deals with forms of insurance and protection and which, accordingly, expands the financial market's investment universe. Man is faced with an almost unlimited number of risks, very few of which are insured by the financial markets (environmental risks, risks of natural catastrophes can, for example, be seen to be processed by an independent segment of the financial markets). In these circumstances, it is the category of assets represented by shares, the Stock Market, which alone encapsulates the whole of the risks and equity risk premium is thus a global risk premium. The more these "other" risks are financialised, the more the equity risk premium may be reduced within the Stock Market to its determining factors (which are more or less direct).

It is because the Stock Market is the most complete and total approximation of future reality, the biggest gateway to the (future) consumption and investment function, that the Stock Market price and equity risk premium are scrutinized and commented upon to such an extent. It may in some way represent what is ultimately a recent development in the financial markets, where the equity market still occupies by far the most imposing place in the representation of the world (as stated earlier, the modern economic Subject projects itself into and towards the world through the market and the world appears to some extent through the intermediary of the market, which is the variance or negativity which permits the said projection/appearance). The debt markets, especially public debt, are indeed imposing, in terms of depth and liquidity, but it is the equity market which contains a striking summary of projects, striking because it is focussed on the flash of indicators which provide clear-cut sections of the world.

This investment universe, constituted mainly by the private forms of the modern project (there are indeed state or "mixed" forms but the modern approach to the economic project adopts the strong symbolic form of the private company, even though state efforts and expenditure are also experiencing continuous, parallel growth), constitutes a living organism which experiences a form of horizontal growth, e.g. by geographical expansion (in particular the emerging markets) – reflecting the future reality which is anticipated by the Stock Market. Horizontal extension is also understood to mean the progressive transformation of new macro-economic subjects in sets of financial themes and segments of the category of assets represented by Stock Market shares; accordingly shares linked to raw materials in the wake of the voracious boom of the emerging economies at the start of the century and of China, in particular. These forms of horizontal expansion of the Stock Market's investment universe are produced by the transformation of the world and the technical means of such transformation.

The principle of vertical expansion is, in turn, based in risk, insurance and protection. Since it contains, in a striking summary, the function of future growth (consumption, investment), the Stock Market also contains all the risks thereof. This global risk premium can be found both in the equity risk premium which is estimated for a market taken as a whole and also in the individual risk premium of some or other share. This either reflects the as yet inadequate development of the financial markets (financialised segmentation of the forms of risk and therefore of insurance), and as the vertical forms of expansion of the Stock Market investment universes are extended, the generalisation of "specific" risk premia (environmental risk, unemployment risk, industrial risk, etc. and all foreseeable risks or risks which may one day be foreseen *ad infinitum*) is accompanied by a reduction in the equity risk premium, a refinement, a cleansing, by means of migration towards new financial market segments and where new forms of insurance by financialisation of the risk correspond to as many categories of assets (e.g. polluting rights, with a significant scope for expansion); or there is indeed a global risk dimension within the Stock Market, attached to the category of assets represented by shares, which is channelled by the famous risk premium, which cannot be compressed and which, ultimately, refers back to the very status of the Stock Market: as a total and totalizing form of the future growth function, the Stock Market bears the aggregate risk attached to such future growth function. The fact that the Stock Market, in its dynamics, continuously produces extensions of universes, both horizontal and vertical in the sense defined above, does not alter this and, as a result, there would scarcely be any mystery surrounding equity risk premium. Equity risk premium would then be expressed, in all instances, as a mix of equity risk premium strictly speaking and an aggregate risk coefficient, a remainder which could decrease as the various aspects of these "other" risks are processed and treated to a financial response by means of insurance or the constitution of a specific category of asset. The formula can therefore be expressed as $Rp = Rp\ (equity) + g$ where the factor g represents the "other" global risks, global because they are infinite and scarcely covered.

TIME-MATTER AND PREFERENCES

§ 132.   We demonstrated in *Les Carnets monétaires* that it was no doubt vain to try to approach the question of the value of equity markets, i.e. the value of the Stock Market, using only the variables of results, dividends or any other element linked to the company's business or the distribution of its results (in part, as we have seen, since the value of the Stock Market encompasses and includes much more than the mere sphere alone of the companies which make it up, whether one is considering activity, profitability or risk), *especially* with regard to fairly short-term, or "cyclical", prospects which last, in the best i.e. the longest-case scenario, from one to two years. It was quite clear: too much time and resources are employed solely in order to analyse the immediate or quasi-immediate moment in time, even though the true issues are essentially contained within what has already taken place and which continues to have a structuring effect, as a result of the effects of memory recall and lapse which make up the Stock Market time reference frame. The immediate moment in time, and by immediate we also mean that which remains simply cyclical (i.e. which only affects one part of a complete cycle, the rise or the fall, while only the complete cycle can even begin to be of any interest with regard to value), therefore is and remains external background noise for the purposes of determining the Stock Market's value.

With regard to the principle of possession of a market asset, which is deemed to be long-term, only the whole sequence of results (at least one full cycle, and probably several) seems to be relevant, in any event much more so than the results of only one year or even of one quarter. Let us deal straight away with the – remaining – issue, namely whether the results of one company, or of all the companies, suffice on their own to exhaust the question of value of the Stock Market thoroughly. We know that the answer to this question is no, but that it not the purpose of our discussion today. If one considers that the results are sufficiently relevant, as such, to form the basis of an analysis of the value of the Stock Market, how then should we structure such an approach?

If one returns to the principle of possession of the market asset (which allows the question of value to be approached from "the outside" and not by means of a form of absolute internal calculation), it can clearly be seen that long-term possession, associated with the Stock Market – and which reflects the long-term gestation of projects of an economic nature – corresponds perfectly to the medium-term prospects of the economic project(s) borne by the companies which make up the Stock Market, and the prospects of memory and *continuum*. Accordingly, it is because long-term possession induces an expectation, which is itself long-term, that it is relevant to take into account a long period of time which has elapsed and been memorised, even if forgotten in part. The taking into account of the phenomenon of *continuum* in its various manifestations seems to satisfy the requirement that the temporality of the project, that of the possession of the market asset, the temporality of the expectation and finally that of the memory, which are linked by a profound analogy, are brought into alignment within a coherent time reference frame,

Consequently there is a time reference frame which is structured by memory (and memory lapse) where, unless the cyclical fluctuation helps update a more fundamental element (and by that we mean the capacity to modify or break a given system of memory), purely cyclical information is non-information with regard to the value of the Stock Market. The immediate moment in time only seems to be of importance. On the contrary, one needs at all times to understand or move some old "rubble". The cycle produces a fuss around something from the past which is maintained in the present. All the particles which together create this fuss largely cancel each other out by means of the symmetrically-opposed nature of the immediate signals emitted around that which remains from the past (in other words, good and bad news cancel each other out).

There is, then, first, an approach which requires one to define or determine a value for the Stock Market based on the memorised flows of companies' business (let us say their results). The dynamics of the Stock Market value are provided by the distortions of time matter, i.e. the manner in which the section of the past (memorised flows) is "informed", or distorted by the memory recall or lapse, non-linear phenomena which are in the process of acceleration, contraction or dilation. The distortions of time matter (e.g. twelve average years' cashflow, net results, dividends) are produced by the shift of preferences, which is governed by the value given to time (memory, memory lapse). When dealing with market matters, the appetite for risk, which merges to a large extent with the preference between shares and bonds (or the preference for liquidity, if one approaches the equation from the point of view of risk aversion), the said appetite for risk (and conversely the said aversion to risk) corresponds to the value given to time: the rise or fall in the appetite for risk *is* a shift of the value given to time, and therefore a shift of that which remains from the past in the present.

The dynamics of stock market time matter (flow of activity and memorised results) are therefore driven by shifts of preferences which merge with the phenomena of appetite for risk or aversion to risk, and which, ultimately, result in distortions or dislocations of the value given to time. The determining factors of the said dynamics can be immediate (flow of information triggering the shift). The more the investor concentrates on short-term prospects, the more dominant the effect of the preferences and their distortions on Stock Market behaviour – causing a stir – and the less dominant the effect of the component part of the results alone (especially when such component part does not itself include a form of memorisation of flows and is only defined as the immediate short-term results, i.e. results which are less than two years' old).

"Long-term" time-matter is informed/distorted by the impulsions of preferences which, in turn, maintain a link with what is "cyclical", short-term or indeed immediate, until it dominates Stock Market behaviour over the so-called "cyclical" periods. In fact, with regard to such periods, the value of the Stock Market which can be described as absolute, namely that which can provide a valid indication of the future performance of Stock Market shares as compared to that of a risk-free asset, can be seen as a combination of that which will determine a preference *for* the Stock Market and therefore a preference *as between* the category of assets of shares and *something else*; the said "something else" can be defined simply by Government debt (but all other categories of assets are eligible), and therefore a combination of the determining element of such a preference and that which enables one to say whether the "something else" with which the Stock Market is associated or compared has a value, for example if the Government debt to which the shares are compared has a value. In such a combination, the determination of the preference for shares is essential and dominates all other possible determinations.

The preference for shares, which is above all a preference as between shares and other categories of assets, undoubtedly results from a certain difference in yield as between the categories of assets (static) and the dynamics of such difference (expectation). It can be seen that this difference in yield tends to precede and to play a part in performance as between the Stock Market and other categories of assets (to keep things simple, Government debt), and that this very performance tends to precede and play a part in the activity, irrespective of its size. It is therefore said that the value of the Stock Market, at least over the short-term, is a relative value; that the so-called absolute value is a direct function of time-matter (everything, which is relevant to the Stock Market, is considered from a non-cyclical angle, according to the principles of memory, duration and memory lapse); that the so-called relative value is equivalent to a preference for the Stock Market and therefore as between the Stock Market and everything else; that this relative value is no doubt directly determined by the past, current and/or expected yield and seems to maintain a link with future activity and growth, but this function of preference (relative value) encompasses or incorporates *the* risks in a wider sense, and by that is meant not only the risks which are directly and immediately connected to the Stock Market, the shares, the companies which make it up, since the Stock Market, as seen above, reflects and incorporates a risk which goes well beyond the specific elements which make it up (a global risk premium which, in the modern era, bears witness to the fact that the world appears and projects/is transformed through the intermediary of the function of finance and particularly of the stock market); that this preference for the Stock Market, this function of preference as between the Stock Market and *something else*, is very close to the function of liquidity, and even merges with the latter in the sense that the phenomenon of liquidity is understood to be the result of the process by which money is "informed", such process setting the money in motion and in circulation, such information including the powerful effects of a time reference frame of memory recall and lapse; that this preference for (or against) the Stock Market is finally not so much determined by those elements which are nonetheless directly relevant to the Stock Market companies, particularly in the non-cyclical, non-immediate dimension (results, dividends...), but much more so by liquidity and by the key role played by interest rates, which is to some extent the price thereof when determining the preference between the two categories of assets; that the absolute and relative conditions of Stock Market equilibrium, together with market dynamics, are based on the value given to time, and in particular memory and memory lapse, and therefore the market cycle advances on the basis of this value given to time, which governs the preferences and substitutions between the Stock Market and *something else*, goods, services and/or other financial assets, the value given to time which both steers, and stems from, the monetary dynamics of liquidity, which is the process by which money is "informed" by means of memory recall and lapse; that the (short-term) cyclical dynamics of the Stock Market, as described on the basis of the preference between shares and something else (debt), corresponds to the fluctuations of memory recall and lapse (the phenomenon of liquidity is present within these fluctuations which distort the monetary stock) and incor-porates in a wider sense a global risk premium for everything which the Stock Market reflects and brokers, over and above the mere companies which constitute it; that in the very short-term, the market dynamics are completely contained within this preference and its determining factors, which relate more to liquidity that to the companies' activity; that in the medium-term, i.e. for trajectories of dynamics which free themselves from the closest cyclical dimensions, market dynamics are provided by the impact of the process by which market time-matter (i.e. the memorised stock of information, facts and events relating to the Stock Market, namely the companies and their environment in the wider sense since, as seen, the Stock Market incorporates a global risk premium) is informed and distorted by the fluctuations of memory recall and loss registered in the time reference frame, and therefore by the dynamics of preferences (accordingly, in the medium-term, there are "real" factors, of activity or results, considered in their density of duration, which dominate the factors of liquidity or preference for the Stock Market, and moreover the two are intermingled); that one accordingly obtains the following equation for the Stock Market price: $Pm = f(Pf, S_{M/F}, rp)$, i.e. a function of preference for the Stock Market (as between the Stock Market and *something else*), of the specific corporate matters and environment which make up the Stock Market within a dimension of time-matter which is memorised over the duration and forgotten to a greater or lesser extent, and finally of a global risk premium which goes beyond the specific component parts of the Stock Market and reflects its global role as intermediary with the world. In the equation $Pm = f(Pf, S_{M/F}, rp)$:

Pm = market price,

Pf = preference,

$S_{M/F}$ = memory and memory lapse of that which is specific to the company listed on the Stock Market - stock (memory, forgetfulness),

Rp = risk premium.

By writing Pm in this way, i.e. as a function of the above three elements, two dimensions and approaches, which are often kept apart, become integrated. First, the approach by which the Stock Market price is determined solely on the basis of the non-cyclical component of the specific dimension of the activity of the company(ies) which form part of the Stock Market, a non-cyclical component which is expected over the long-term. Thus, it can be said, ultimately, that the Stock Market price (or that of some or other company, or some or other market segment) will move towards (convergence) a "value" (which is itself fluctuating, and therefore perhaps better described as a "line" of value, which one follows but which itself moves), which is a function of an expectation which extends beyond the cycle, or even the most recent cycles; this function of expectation, in our approach, is reduced to a long memory function, a function of *continuum* accompanied by a coefficient of memory lapse which acts as a trip rope. In this approach one should, for example, literally cut pieces of duration (the past) relating to a few relevant variables (profit increases, dividends…) and then, chisel, plane and shape these blocks in the same way one carves stone. The whole of this approach lies within this raw material, which stems from a section of duration within a time reference frame running from *continuum* to eclipse (forgetfulness) where the memory replaces expectation (in fact, one anticipates in the same way as one remembers and forgets; one can even go so far as to say that expectation does not exist of itself: to expect *is* to remember (and, therefore, to a certain extent, to forget). It is not certain, as stated rather quickly above, that the Stock Market price necessarily moves towards such a line of value, even if it allows the dynamics to be defined. It can be said, in this initial approach, and without making any further commitment, that there is a value, a line of value, defined as stated above. This value in the universe of ideas to some extent defines an intrinsic value which would be of very little use indeed, if it did not allow one to conceive the dynamics, i.e. a magnetisation, which make the Stock Market price fluctuate around such a value, back towards which some force will bring it sooner or later.

A second, separate, approach, will only consider the preference as between the Stock Market *and something else*, i.e. ultimately, the determining factors of arbitrage and substitution which are something quite other than the traditional variables of company activity. Attention is paid to the determining factors of *future* arbitrage for the Stock Market (as between the Stock Market and something else), to an expectation therefore of preference. In its most basic version, the only part of this approach which will be used is the yield differential of the assets which are compared (shares, bonds or something else). However, once again, the approach can be expanded by introducing a function of *continuum* within the function of preference. The same is true of memory recall and lapse regarding the difference in yield as between shares and bonds, a section of duration and the past which can be expressed as:

$$Pf = [ey - (ay', by'' ...)] \ M/F$$

where:

ey = earning yield,

ay' = yield of another category of asset, of any other category of asset by comparison to which the preference for the Stock Market (and for something *else*) is expressed,

by'' = the Stock Market may be preferred to an infinite number of other assets.

Therefore a second approach is said to exist, by means of the preference as between the Stock Market and *something else*, which does not exclude the phenomena of *continuum*. This approach suggests, ultimately, that the Stock Market price may be known in a relative manner and that once the estimation of the absolute value as discussed above runs into difficulties, the preferences remain available as a compromise. The Stock Market price could, for example, be seen as the combination of the preference for the Stock Market (whether or not accompanied by the time reference frame of memory recall and lapse) and, insofar as the same is available or practicable, the absolute value of the asset to which the Stock Market is being compared (Government debt for example).

However, this distinction between the two approaches goes much further. It can be seen that on the one hand there is an "intrinsic" determination of the Stock Market (e.g. the value resulting from the expected results), and on the other hand a determination by means of the investor's "external" choice, when such investor has to prefer the Stock Market, to choose between the Stock Market and *something else*, a dimension which is much closer to the concepts of preference for liquidity or appetite for risk. These two dimensions basically come from two different analytical approaches. Both can be compared within the same time reference frame and usefully connected within the dynamics discussed above. This is because the Stock Market price results from a preference for the Stock Market *and* from a projection of value in respect of the specific matters which constitute the Stock Market (the companies' business). Both fail to grasp the fact that the Stock Market encompasses, over and above the specific nature of the companies themselves, a global risk premium, which is consequently added to *Pm*.

THE TWO LEVELS OF STOCK MARKET VALUE

§ 133.   There is therefore a function of preference for the Stock Market and an intrinsic Stock Market line of value ($S_{M/F}$). Let us consider the connections between them. There are two levels which appear in principle to be different and unconnected. On the one hand ($S_{M/F}$) holds itself out, or appears to hold itself out, as some form of absolute value "in itself", virtually defined "once and for all" on the basis of a certain type and number of elements which allow the activity of one or more companies to be described and the said activity to be projected into the future. One refers to an "absolute value", since a certain number of points seem to exist, in the form of a skyline, which steer or attract the market and its participants like beacons. These points can, to a certain extent, be said to be invisible or scarcely visible: the market does indeed "cross" them in the same way one crosses a path, zigzagging through the forest around a line of coherence and reason marked out by these points. Their existence is conceptual and, in some ways, it is precisely due to the fact that they were conceived and are the subject of a certain consensus regarding the way in which they are determined and the value(s) which they adopt that, they effectively play the role of beacons or magnets on the skyline where they are located. To put it plainly, it is a form of self-fulfilment. In more specific terms, it is because such concepts are conceived or at least accepted by those – various investors – who are led to express a preference for or against the Stock Market (as between the Stock Market and anything else), that these very concepts become operational. Accordingly, a link can be forged between "absolute value" (which is not in fact that absolute) and preference(s) "for" which are expressed by a Subject-investor.

There are indeed two levels. The level of an "absolute" value and the level of preference of a Subject for the Stock Market (i.e. as between the Stock Market and *everything else*). The absolute value (of itself) becomes, within the very dynamics of the Stock Market, a value *relating to* a Subject (investor), a value relating to someone (to oneself). The market dynamics emerge from the point of contact between these two levels. There is an unwieldy level, characterised by a certain degree of inertia, which is a section of duration and memory, time-matter and a cold block of wax incorporating, in relation to the company(ies), a certain number of relevant elements in order to form an idea of the activity and its future. This block of cold wax which, as discussed above, incorporates facts, events and risks which go beyond the strict definition of a company's activity (and, consequently, should be taken into account in its estimation and calculation), constitutes the level of "absolute" value discussed above, a section of the past and of memory which provides the raw material for a future dimension. It is called absolute because, at this stage, it is not the subject of a preference, or a design of the Subject-investor. It is a pure conceptual object (the only thing to exist will be what "appears" to the Subject during the process of expressing preferences), although its composition and texture immerse it deep within the dense time of duration and memory ("absolute" should not accordingly be understood in the sense of being cut out of the investor's time reference frame and expressing preferences within the market universe, but quite the opposite).

There is therefore a level of values defined in this way but which at this stage has not (yet) overlapped with the Subject's preferences. Faced with this universe of objects, steeped in duration and memory but which are purely conceptual, a second level rises up which contains the driving force of the first level. This second level is that of preference for the Stock Market, which is, from the outset, a level of "relative" value (as between the Stock Market and something else). The preference will invest it with dynamics by taking over and giving life to the block of duration and memory discussed above. It will do so in a number of ways. The Subject-investor's function of preference is the function of memory recall and/or lapse, of breathing life into the original block of duration and memory which suddenly "relates" to someone: it "appears" all at once and, as a result, only its appearances (phenomena) are visible. We only see what wants to appear and make itself known to a Subject. Second, as seen above, the function of preference is driven by elements of arbitrage as between the Stock Market *and everything else.*

All things considered, there are two connected levels and what seems to be erratic short-term noise (function of preference) and, second, an inaccessible and somewhat virtual level of "absolute" value, are in fact a unified requirement: the "noise" always reflects the bringing to life of a level of duration and memory which, in return and simultaneously, drives the function of preference. One level lies within circulation, liquidity, acceleration or contraction, the other provides time-matter with a different structure. All in all, the market dynamics emerge from the superimposition of the two levels which continuously act one upon the other.

Of the said two levels, that which has been described as an "absolute" value by way of simplistic abbreviation, is undoubtedly the more inaccessible. One may even hear from time to time that there is nothing much to be said about this level. This absolute value towards which the Stock Market is supposed to converge can simply be said not to exist and, consequently, in the best case scenario, the Stock Market would be left with a short-term function of preference as discussed above within what we called the initial level and, in the worst case scenario, with an absolute and random contingency. However, the said "background level" (since we are discussing a background world), although not easy to penetrate, provides a great wealth of understanding of the Stock Market and of market dynamics.

This "background level", as such, i.e. as bearer of an absolute value, cannot be seen or recorded. It exists, a vast continent of duration and memory which constitute its structure. From this point of view, it is inaccessible. However, it becomes present and appears when the function of preferences and arbitrages (first level) set in motion by the memory recall or lapse, triggers and drives a set of dynamics which are those of the market. It is no doubt vain to think that one can obtain a complete understanding of the "background level" as an absolute, intangible value. It is, however, possible and necessary to work out what element of this "background level" presents itself upon contact with the dynamics of preferences. In practical terms, it is futile to expend resources trying to define an absolute value for the Stock Market or its individual component parts. It is, however, profitable to expend efforts in two directions. First, with regard to the said background level, to try and highlight certain characteristics, sections of blocks of duration and memory which relate to those elements which directly (companies' activity, environment of results…) or indirectly (we have seen how the Stock Market encompasses, over and beyond its most visible constituent elements and determining factors, the "world" in a much wider sense), form the said background level. By so doing, one only obtains access to what already agrees to be present and to offer itself up for observation, to that part of the "absolute" value which will remain for ever hidden, which agrees to appear and to reveal itself to a Subject. Second, to work on the first level, the visible and observable level of preferences and arbitrages, e.g. as between the Stock Market and *everything else*, since the Stock Market dynamics are for the most part located not so much within that which constitutes it directly and specifically (e.g. companies) but rather in that *which is not the Stock Market*, everything else. Market dynamics are at any one time the result of a relative judgement.

Market dynamics become necessary and split away from pure contingency and chance once the two levels interconnect. The link between the two levels, the common blood which flows through their veins is the unit of a time reference frame, where matter is made up of what has been memorised (and/or forgotten) and which continues to endure, the fundamental matter of the background level to which access can be obtained by observation, even if the whole remains shrouded, where preferences drive the said matter, once such matter is solicited by memory recall or lapse, in the same way as one turns on or starts an engine.

Market dynamics occur for the most part outside the Stock Market since, at any one time, it is a question of deciding, preferring, arbitrating between the Stock Market *and everything else*. It is striking to see to what extent, through a form of blindness, the principal resources and intelligence are dedicated, almost exclusively, to looking for the determining factors of the Stock Market and of market dynamics within the Stock Market itself, with regard to what is most immediate within the Stock Market. This self-referencing approach refers the Stock Market back on itself, to the universe of companies and the interpretation which can be made thereof, based on indicators which are essentially unrefined, to a greater or lesser extent (cash-flows, dividends, results) and which consist, most of the time, once again from a self-referencing point of view, of comparing in one way or another the Stock Market price (or that of its component parts) with the said indicators from the universe of companies. However, one can manage without the Stock Market at any given time and the reason why one may or not be interested in it brings *everything else* into play. The territory of preferences and arbitrages as between the Stock Market and *everything else* largely remains to be elucidated. We still need to understand why, at any one time, a preference for the Stock Market can be expressed before then disintegrating. This calls into play what happens outside the Stock Market and the view which the Subject-investor may form thereof. In practical terms, this means that, based on observation, a much wider range of preference indicators is required than the sparse utensils which are available. The preference for the Stock Market involves a vision of the world and that world – other assets, goods, services but also facts, events, fears and risks – must, by means of observation, analysis and research be placed into contact with the Stock Market in the context of preferences and arbitrages. So long as the approach remains self-centred, seeking to determine the Stock Market and its dynamics based on itself, its essential qualities will probably continue to elude us.

We will therefore study the two levels, as defined, together with the connections between them; we will study in the widest sense the field of preferences and arbitrages which, at any given time, may be preferred to the Stock Market or which may, on the contrary, lead to a preference for the Stock Market, the said field *of everything else* which is not the Stock Market forming an integral part of the background level (background world) of duration, memory recall and lapse, and the first level of the dynamics of preferences, well beyond the simple preference between the Stock Market and the risk-free asset or Government debt.

When it is said that market dynamics are always decided as between the Stock Market and *everything else*, in the order of preference for the Stock Market (which therefore includes the possibility of not preferring the Stock Market and which thus amounts to preferring *something else*), it is said that market dynamics are a matter of relative value. A second field of relative value is therefore opened. A first field has already been discussed, that of the time reference frame, made up of duration and memory, a matter which already contains a relative dimension (that which has come to pass and has made itself present, since that which occurred, came to pass, has already been considered). There is not in fact, strictly speaking, a market "present" (and that is true, as discussed elsewhere, of economics and finance in general): that which is present is the presence of that which endures, in the form of *continuum* which eclipses memory lapse; that which is present is, at the same time, part of nothingness (an expectation or projection which are features of the Stock Market), or negative; there is therefore no room for the present, and all that remains is the presence of duration and memory which merges past and future in the same temporal system (which we have called the time reference frame). If, as discussed, the "absolute" value is not dismissed, it remains invisible, or observable, set in the background; nothing much can be said of this absolute value, and only various forms of this value make themselves visible or present or appear, within a system of relativity and within a discontinuous and plastic market space, where one moves more or less quickly in accordance with the intensity of how one remembers or forgets, based on a relative *continuum* of duration. This *continuum* of duration remains relative, since the discontinuity of the blanks in one's memory, of the memory recalls and of the permanent struggle between what wants to continue and what fades away, introduces and creates the market dynamics in an unstable state, which can in no way be said to be absolute. The market equilibria are relative.

Beside this first field of relativity there exists a second dimension, which is also relative, that of preferences and arbitrages as between the Stock Market and everything else. This second field includes the issue of risk premia, since a risk premium only exists for a given possibility (for the Subject-investor) of whether or not to prefer the Stock Market. This amounts to saying that market dynamics are always expressed as the composition of a level of value where the Stock Market is referred back to, or faced with, its direct determining factors (i.e. those which help understand the companies which, effectively, make up the Stock Market), and a value level where the Stock Market is referred back to that which does not directly constitute it, that which, in literal terms, does not form part of it, namely everything else, the world, this second level being that of the Subject, since it is within this second level that preferences, arbitrages and choices are revealed and expressed, and accordingly that the operational nature of market dynamics is formed. The two levels are enclosed within a unique time reference frame of duration and memory, which means inter alia that that which is not part of the Stock Market but which determines it is, also, governed by the *continuum* of duration and the discontinuities of memory recall and lapse, which breach or pierce it in order to generate the dynamics. That means, in practical terms, that the observation and processing of all the elements and variables which are specific to that which is not the Stock Market but which comes within the operative field of preferences and choices, must be understood in their dimension of duration, memory recall and lapse.

This is how the question of risk premium must be posed. The Stock Market is overshadowed by a gigantic, generic risk premium, in the sense that this risk premium includes everything which forms part of the preference as between the Stock Market and *everything else*. This generic risk premium can be segmented or subdivided into an infinite number of secondary risk premia, like so many pairs comparing the Stock Market with some or other asset, property, event, fact (...) *ad infinitum*. The usual methods of estimation or observation of what is called "equity risk premium" are certainly very far-removed from this requirement, which is extremely fragmented and limited. So long as the attempts to understand the Stock Market continue to be based on a fantastically narrow vision of risk premium, it is probable that very little progress will be made. This limited vision will become outmoded, when we become convinced that market dynamics depend upon a preference between the Stock Market and (the whole of) everything else, that this preference can be expressed by means of a global risk premium and that this global risk premium must be understood not in its immediacy but together with the phenomena of *continuum*, within a reference frame of duration, memory recall and lapse. Although it is not easy to provide a projected estimation of this global risk premium, it remains conceivable for it to be considered with the benefit of hindsight, which, so far as we are aware, is still not the case.

In Search of the Risk Premium

§ 134.   Risk premium expresses a value given to time, through the idea of the expected profitability of risk. In a very generic manner, the Stock Market forms a relationship with time through the risk premium. This relationship is structured as stated above, within a reference frame of duration, memory recall and lapse driven by discontinuities, contractions, dilations and ruptures. In this context, risk premium is a function of the larger or smaller value given to time by a Subject, since risk premium expresses a judgement, that of the Subject. We demonstrated elsewhere, in *Théorie*, that the larger or smaller the value given to time was itself a function of memory recall or lapse, phenomena which are specific to the "psychological" time reference frame of the Stock Market and, more widely, of finance and economics. The distances within the said space-time are also a function of the trip ropes of memory recall and lapse.

Consequently a connection can be made between the risk premium cycle, or at least the simple developments, rises and falls thereof, and memory recall and lapse, with regard to what is necessarily a very large group since, added to the strict, direct variables relating to the companies registered on the Stock Market, is a vast set of facts and events which make risk premium a "global" variable for the determination of market dynamics. A certain number of observations made with regard to risk premium can be encountered and assembled behind this idea. The same is true of the presumed link between risk premium and the predictability of the *whole* of the economy (here it is the word *whole* which is important, containing the idea of a global premium for the whole of world facts and events, whether regarding the capacity to foresee them or more simply to identify them). This predictability of the whole of the economy includes traditional variables (volatility of growth, interest rates, rates of inflation, etc.) and seems to be linked to the quality of the information (the better the information, the lower the premium).

The term "whole" certainly encompasses a good deal more than simply the so-called economic variables. It is a representation of the world, of what is not the Stock Market, of everything else (the risks). Facing this whole is a collective Subject, since it is a collective projection of appetite or aversion (for risk) which is expressed, and which will be encountered in the movements of large economic functions such as consumption or savings (a link can be seen between the preference for the present moment, a drop in the propensity to save and a rise in risk premium).

We are therefore dealing with the expression of a collective Subject with regard to a whole, which can be compared to the world. This expression is a projection towards the future for the expression of a preference. The preference for the future, irrespective of the determining factors (information, comprehension, mere belief, etc), brings the premium down and the preference for the present increases. These preferences are governed by memory recall and lapse within a system of duration. In particular, the projection towards a "future" is a direct function of the past, of what remains from the past or is remembered. The risk premium therefore maintains a link with a future space-time (which comes from the *whole* of the world, what is foreseeable, etc.) which is governed by the structures of duration, memory recall and lapse of a specific reference frame, before even discussing the "future" with a "whole" which is "different", since the risk premium establishes a link with both what will come to pass (the future) and with what is different (anything which is not the Stock Market, *everything else*), the said two dimensions playing their role to the full in the game of preferences (for the present or the future; for the Stock Market or everything else).

The changes in global risk premium as defined are related to the distortions of the space-time reference frame, in proportion with what is remembered or forgotten (the market present is brought together with that which endures by means of memory recall or lapse), the immediate facts and events may possibly have a power to alter or modify although, most of the time, the immediate is happy to flow along like a drop of water over glass.

The "global" risk premium (for a Subject expressing a collective aversion or appetite) will be lower (raised) the greater the preference for the future (the present). We will reformulate this equation by assuming that the global risk premium, in its variations, expresses a certain value given to time, that this time is not simply split three ways into past-present-future, which would bear no relation to the market and financial space-time reference frame, which is a system of duration, *continuum*, memory recall and lapse, that the preference for the present or the future masks the value given to time (which depends upon the strength of density of duration and memory, with concentrations and dilations, ruptures and discontinuities), that the preference is not simply a temporal preference or value given to time but also a preference/arbitrage for the Stock Market as compared to everything else, that the phenomenon of liquidity, of preference for liquidity, in the same way as that of appetite or aversion for risk, is profoundly linked, as demonstrated in *Théorie*, to the value given to time and the process by which money is informed by means of duration, memory recall and lapse. Accordingly, the understanding of risk rises or falls in accordance with memory recall or lapse and what one remembers or, on the contrary, forgets. The increase in liquidity, that of appetite for risk, that of the speed of circulation of money, which is driven and informed, the increase in market transactions and the reduction in risk premium: all these phenomena are interconnected within one specific space-time reference frame which we have discussed and where, in particular, the phenomenon of interest is fundamentally understood on the basis of the process by which money is informed/distorted by memory recall and lapse.

§ 135.   The expected, anticipated profitability of risk and, moreover, the value given to time are two sides of the same mirror. Consequently when one uses the term "expected", the question of risk premium is regarded from the point of view of projection time, which, first, sets a strict limit on defining the premium by means of the excess profitability noted in the past as compared with cash; which contains, second, a simultaneous requirement that the temporal system of such an expectation be defined; and, finally, requests that the specific category(ies) of the source of the profitability be stated (an asset, all the assets, a special feature of some or other asset, several things or some thing other than the assets and which is not directly visible once one discusses the Stock Market, which always seems to be confined only to the companies themselves?)

With regard to the first point (the measurement of risk premium by the past excess profitability of shares as compared to cash), it is not so much the return to the past in order to provide an approximate vision of the future which causes a problem – on the contrary, that is always the most fruitful path – but rather the variable which has to be projected into the past. It would seem more relevant to pay attention to the memory (including a certain amount of memory lapse) which the market retained of the implied measurement which comes from the market itself (and not the instantaneous measurement) rather than the memory of the excess actually noted. This memorised excess profitability may undoubtedly constitute a point of anchorage within the projection and probably plays this role but the *continuum* of the implied risk premium which comes from the permanent prices and which is literally memorised, seems closer to the actual function of expectation in the formation of Stock Market prices. One can always imagine, when examining more closely the structure of memory recall and lapse of the past excess profitability of shares as compared to cash, that one will find a better means of predicting or expecting future profitability. By refining the memorised sub-periods, their weightings, by estimating more precisely the coefficients of memory lapse, by defining the systems, it could be shown that the past excess profitability may be an approximation of the risk premium with a certain predictive capacity. Insofar as the risk premium of shares on the Stock Market can be defined on the basis of the excess profitability of shares as compared to the *expected* cash, the research of memory recall and lapse is not unjustified (but, as seen, this approach is very limited with regard to the expression of preferences, since risk premium includes a factor of arbitrage and preference which is much wider than cash alone). An approach using the memory of "simple" preferences (i.e. merely between simple assets, shares and bonds) based on dividend-style yields or results is more promising.

Approaches based on enquiries fall wide of their target both due to the construction of the structure of expectation (a very short-term fragmented projection which amounts to projecting the most recent past) and to the very unrefined nature of preferences, which are as "simple" as those discussed above. The enquires are not completely without interest: they simply state the near future as a direct function of the recent past; they also state that until the questions and the manner of raising questions have grasped this, until the aim is to try and remove some models of longer memory recall and memory lapse, then the same results will be obtained.

One can see that the three approaches discussed above all suffer from a system of preferences which are too "simplistic" (it is always a question of choosing between the Stock Market *and everything else*) and of temporal reference frames which are inadequately (past excess profitability of the Stock Market) or improperly (enquiries) worked through or defined.

Once a commitment is made to the idea of excess *expected* profitability, a time reference time (actually space-time) has to be defined which, for our part, we have defined within the context of non-linear movements of memory recalls or lapses of relatively unstable blocks of memory and duration, themselves in movement, within the Subject-investor's psychological-style universe where the non-linear movements of time (dilation or contraction, depending whether memory recall or lapse is involved) lengthen or shorten the distances within a market space-time which can be subject to sudden distortions. This forms the first point. Irrespective of its definition, the risk premium within the Stock Market must be considered within a specific system of space-time as described. The said space-time must give rise to research which refines the systems of memory recall and lapse and their unstable dynamics.

The second point concerns the universe of preferences which the risk premium has to digest. This universe, which may be simple or, necessarily, more complex, and which is much more extensive than we had thought up until now, means that the risk premium is equivalent to the sum of (i) a specific premium, where it relates to the immediate Stock Market object (companies, namely their results or dividends; and more widely, a sector or the market as a whole ...), a specificity which itself includes other specificities (per company, per sector, per country...), and (ii) a premium which we have called global, which incorporates much wider preferences as between the Stock Market and everything else (all the assets should include, in addition to their specific premia, a global premium which one may consider should be the same for all the assets).

Furthermore, once one accepts the unrefined idea of risk premium defined by means of the preference between the Stock Market (shares) and a very low-risk asset (cash or Government debt), which determines an *expected* profitability, the second part of the preference equation should be introduced, in whatever form, here cash or Government debt, within the space-time reference frame which controls the whole question of risk premium. It is a question of being able to form an idea of the future profitability of the cash or the very low-risk Government debt. It is imperative to be able to estimate a value-time for such risk-free asset or, for example, by incorporating a memory of inflation in the approach, to be able to estimate the actual values which are being assessed within a system. In any event, the expectation of profitability in the second part of the equation requires a similar treatment with regard to the time reference frame (and space-time). We discussed such an approach in *Les Carnets monétaires.*

Once the question of risk premium is posed, as we are doing, from the point of view of preferences (of a Subject-investor), which ultimately determine the excess profitability as compared to that which contains little or no risk, the research must be directed to the determining factors of the preferences and therefore of the choices and arbitrages. In this context, the arbitrage of yields seems to be a fruitful path since the Subject-investor will tend, in anticipation, to compare these yields. This expectation, as seen above, being largely the result of an experience and memory which may be more or less complete, personal or collective, it seems advisable to adopt an approach within the proposed space-time reference frame. Within this reference frame, an approach aimed at "simple" preferences may, as described in *Les Carnets monétaires,* reduce the equation of the future performance of the Stock Market as compared to cash (excess profitability) to a function made up of the preference between risk-free shares and bonds (or cash) and a measurement of the expected profitability of risk-free bonds (which we have called elsewhere the debt "value"). The Subject-investor determines its preferences on this basis, the "value" of the Stock Market being a function of the preference between risk-free shares and bonds and the debt "value". The first part of the equation (the preference between shares and bonds) will mobilise a memorised function of the instantaneous difference in yield between the two types of asset, the second, as seen above, a value game which mobilises for example a memory of inflation or growth for the risk-free debt asset. It can be seen that this produces a capacity to predict the excess profitability of the Stock Market as compared to the risk-free asset which is fairly robust, although subject to rules which intersect with as many sub-periods which will end one day (the definition of such sub-periods by means of average relative yields as between shares and Government debt or of actual interest rates for risk-free bonds collides with the ruptures and discontinuities which are specific to the market space-time: one can only leave a system by breaking out, which involves a form of crash or rupture).

It can thus be understood that, from among the various approaches adopted by the literature on risk premium, the approach based on implied market values and which states a yield which can be compared with the yield of a risk-free asset, which can be the subject of a preference, a choice and an arbitrage, seems to be relevant (insofar as such implicit values are properly incorporated within a reference frame of duration, memory recall and lapse). The approaches through dividends or results (dividend yield, earning yield) and their yields unsurprisingly appear to be the most solid, although extremely limited and unrefined. However, it can in part be understood why enquiries or studies of past excess profitability as compared to the risk-free asset prove less successful. The answer lies in the definition of risk premium as a system of preferences. This transitory conclusion allows the distinction between at least three approaches which are usually used to be clarified. Two search for the substance, all three search for the spatio-temporal form of expectations, a problem to which we can provide a solution.

The "simple" preferences may also try to describe a performance of the Stock Market which is superior to that of a low-risk asset, *anticipated* by a Subject-investor, as the sum of the Stock Market "value" and the preference between the Stock Market and risk-free bonds. This last preference does not move, it is the common point of the two equations or approaches. However, instead of taking the "value" of the risk-free bond, that of the Stock Market is taken here, which will be assessed using the same principles, within the same space-time reference frame of memory recall and lapse, relating this time not to memorised inflation or growth but to series of, inter alia, companies' activity, results and dividends.

§ 136.   Risk premium is supposed to remunerate the Subject-investor for the risk taken over and above the pure value-time of money. Such an expression of risk premium reveals how this question, which is often posed from the point of view of excess profitability compared to risk, is in fact that of the scale of values given to time and therefore of preferences between assets (cash or Government debt for the main part within the traditional approaches of "simple" preferences) and the more interesting but as yet unexplored territory (that of global risk premium) as between the Stock Market and everything else. We stated earlier that the *expected* profitability of the Stock Market as compared to the risk-free asset and the value given to time were two sides of the same mirror. We have now reached this point. Each object of a potential preference, as compared to the Stock Market, of a choice or arbitrage, whether relating to financial assets, goods or other items which can be the subject of an arbitrage based on risk, each potential subject of a preference is allocated a value given to time by the Subject-investor. This value fluctuates and is sometimes very unstable, increasingly so the further one moves away from the pure value-time of money (cash). This scale provides structure to the space-time reference frame which nurtures its dynamics from the memory recall and lapse of data, facts and events associated with each object of a preference. This structure, to a certain extent, is reflected in the famous "risk-yield" pairs which give rise to the construction of so-called efficient boundaries.

It is this value given to time, as demonstrated in *Théorie*, which is the source of monetary dynamics (liquidity, preference for liquidity, appetite or aversion for risk) and consequently of market dynamics. The heating of the cold wax, which is money, initially as a result of the phenomena of reminders, memory recalls or lapses, will set in motion the dynamics of circulation of money within the financial sphere for the purposes of transactions in financial assets (and market transactions, in particular) and within the actual sphere for the purposes of transactions in goods and services, of communicating vessels which may exist between the two spheres (see *Théorie*). The *circulatory* definition of cash (defined by its circulation and not what it is, see *Tractatus, Généalogie*) is effected by means of such a connection between money and a space-time reference frame which sets it in motion through a Subject actor (investor in the case of market dynamics) which expresses preferences. The said heating process may or must give way to a cooling process, the transition resulting from alterations to the system(s) of memory recall and lapse as a result of sudden reminders or memory loss, given that the procession of immediate events and facts, which in the majority of cases are of little or no importance in the actual determination of market dynamics, may, from time to time, disrupt a system of duration and memory which could believe itself to be eternal, making it change course in the same way an iceberg slowly changes course, causing it eventually, and equally slowly, to melt or sink.

There is certainly, or maybe, a pure value-time given to cash and which expresses, in a very unrefined manner, the profitability of the *expected* risk-free asset (an approach made possible, as discussed, using the actual interest rate, by incorporating a memory or lack of memory of inflation and/or growth). There is above all a value given to time by the Subject in its choices, preferences and arbitrages.

The arbitrage of preferences between financial assets (or, by expanding it slightly, as between real assets and financial assets, as between consumption and savings, in order to go much further), the most conventional and unrefined of which is that comparing the Stock Market and the risk-free or low-risk asset, may be reasonably brought back, reduced to an arbitrage between *expected* yields, for which the past provides an indication (the memory of expected yields and not the memory of recorded yields would be a better approach). This comparison of expected yields between categories of asset suffices to some extent to encompass the perceived/expected risk between financial assets. However, a substantial dimension of risks still exists, apart from those risks which are directly attached to the categories of assets falling within the arbitrages of simple *preferences* and indeed even extended to actual assets. There remains an immense residue of fear, of apprehension but also of hope and projection, of perception of risk, which is altogether something else and which, ultimately, will play an essential role once the Subject has to choose, since it will be obliged to make such a choice, between the Stock Market and *something else*. This substantial dimension, which incorporates multiple sources of risks, will ultimately lead to a variable remuneration which is only an apparition but which is nonetheless vital for the equation of market dynamics.

§ 137.   We therefore have the idea (see *Carnets monétaires*) that the excess profitability of the Stock Market as compared to a risk-free or low-risk asset (over-performance of shares as compared to cash) can be expressed as the sum of a preference between shares and Government debt (a determining factor of excess profitability of the Stock Market as compared to Government debt, i.e. of the performance of shares as compared to bonds) and a preference between Government debt and the pure risk-free cash asset (a determining factor of excess profitability of Government debt as compared to cash, i.e. of the over-performance of bonds as compared to the purely monetary asset). It is therefore stated that the preference for the Stock Market (a determining factor of excess profitability of shares as compared to cash) is the function made up of preferences between shares/bonds and bonds/cash. This equation can also be expressed as the composition of preferences between shares/bonds and shares/cash. Therefore, in this case, there is a preference for bonds (as compared to cash) which is equal to a preference between bonds/shares (the opposite of the preceding function) to which is added a preference between shares/cash. The result is a function of preference for that which is not the Stock Market, even if here what is not the Stock Market is limited (Government debt).

The function $Eq\text{pref} = f(Eq/Bd\text{pref}, Bd\text{pref})$ places the preferences in the foreground by clearly identifying market dynamics as resulting from the choices and arbitrages made by a Subject-investor. Another way of expressing this is to say that the "value" of the shares is equal to the "value" of the shares as compared with the bonds, to which is added the "value" of the bonds (as compared to cash). The term value is to be used here with caution but the preferences of the Subject-investor are expressed through their target or their determining factor (the "value"). There are market dynamics to the extent that the preferences are expressed by comparison to an understanding of the relative value(s), since essentially it involves a comparison of the Stock Market and everything else.

The preference between shares and Government debt is determined and can therefore be expressed by the relative expected yield of two categories of assets, the expectation may be an approximation by a memory of relative instantaneous yields, which may be longer or shorter. This preference between the Stock Market and Government debt, which will take the form of an excess profitability of the Stock Market as compared to bonds, includes expectations such as that of growth (of the general, sectorial or individual activity of some or other company). Accordingly, there is indeed a link between the preference for shares/Government debt and the cycle of growth (of GDP, of production, company results). The shares/bonds preference is brought into alignment with such variables. The difference in expected yield therefore anticipates the relative performance of shares/bonds, which anticipates growth. That is true of the cyclical fluctuations of preference for the Stock Market (which is always expressed by comparison with something else) and also for longer-term direction, for which an assumption is made that the preference for the Stock Market cannot move away from the line of long-term growth (results, general activity…).

In a very simple (simplistic) version of preferences, market dynamics are expressed as the composition of Stock Market profitabilities as compared to bonds (or cash) and of the bonds (the cash) themselves. In this version, market dynamics are close to that of risk premium alone defined strictly (or directly), i.e. as compared to cash or Government debt. The equation can be expanded, if one is able to obtain a long-term "value" for shares as compared to the expectations which are themselves long-term (increase in results, dividends …). The expansion is completed by introducing a variable which is only residual in name, which encompasses everything which, in the world, presents a sufficient risk of diverting the Subject-investor away from the Stock Market and therefore for which a premium will be requested (or will appear). It can be asked whether the said "global" risk premium is not already contained in the expected excess profitability as between the Stock Market and the risk-free or low-risk asset. Once a preference for the Stock Market (as opposed to cash) can be expressed and measured, which is itself determined by a differential of expected yield, does such a preference not contain the whole of what is not, in fact, directly linked to the Stock Market? By adopting such an approach, and by pushing it to the limit, market dynamics are purely and simply defined as the dynamics of preference between the Stock Market and everything else, the expected yield differential for which – within an appropriate space-time, i.e. one structured by memory recall and lapse – between the share market and that of the risk-free asset, incorporates the essential part of the information and the direct or indirect risks involved in preferring the Stock Market. The expected yield differentials between the Stock Market and cash introduce an assessment of memories, which have been forgotten to a greater or lesser extent, of the dynamics of results or dividends, of inflation or growth (in relation to cash), a form of risk premium dynamics adjusted by a few long-term memorised factors.

§ 138.   Another question arises. When referring to risk while discussing risk premium, one means the risk taken of not holding (risk-free) cash. What risk are we discussing? As we have seen, it is both a specific risk attached to that which makes itself immediately visible in the Stock Market, i.e. linked to the companies in some way or another. The waiver of the pure liquidity of an asset which is completely risk-free can be added to this first specific key factor. A second key factor, in our opinion, incorporates all forms of "world" risks, which are non-specific (or, rather, specific *ad infinitum*) and which the Stock Market will remunerate by assuming the role of mirror to the world. The investor is remunerated on the Stock Market, or expects to be remunerated over and above the specific risk of the immediate component parts of the Stock Market. From this point of view, the expected yield differential (required once one expresses this differential within a function of preference or arbitrage) as between the Stock Market and the risk-free asset is expressed as a function of a specific risk premium and a more global premium *PrefEq/cash = f(Rp_s, Rp_g)*.

Up until what point are the concepts of market value and preference for the Stock Market distinct, must they be distinguished? Is preference the energy which sets the value in motion by steering towards it as if magnetised? Or, finally, are there only preferences and their systems of fluctuation, which are identified with the value? This interrogation leads much further than might first appear since, finally, the (philosophical) question is whether, over and above the facts, events or phenomena which appear to a Subject-investor's consciousness, the value itself holds still, towards which converge, without ever managing to arrive, all the apparently hazardous movements, which find an ultimate requirement within the value. A Subject-investor's assumption of power over the world (when considering the Stock Market) in the modern era, as setter of values, creator of values by its "free" projection, which blots everything else out, has brought the value so close to the Subject's preferences that the two dimensions have ended up merging. Above all, in the modern era, causality tends increasingly to move from the Subject and its preferences towards the value (which results therefrom), and the Subject's status is to be that by which the value makes itself present.

Let us return to the "puzzle" of risk premium, this price given to future time. The Stock Market premium remunerates risk, *and something else*. The equation is $ERP = f(R, \alpha)$. The first key factor, namely risk, contains (i) the specific, direct risk relating to the Stock Market, shares and all the facts and events which are immediately linked to the life of companies, and (ii) the global risk, i.e. all the risks which the Subject-investor may have to face and which the Stock Market reflects, more generally a summary of the world embodied by the Stock Market. The equation here is $ERP = f(Rs, R_G, \alpha)$.

§ 139.   A certain number of studies have commented, considering that there is an enigma, that the century-old annual average of the actual profitability of the Stock Market exceeded that of the risk-free asset (*T Bill*) by such a significant margin (7.6 – 1.34 = 6.4) that one could consider either that the very variables used in the calculation of this "premium" were incorrect or at least not correctly adjusted, or that other factors and dimensions in addition to the traditional, specific element of risk alone were contained within the said premium, such other factors therefore to be remunerated by such a premium, or, finally, a bit of both. Before even questioning, for example, the relevance of the T Bill as a relevant marker of the risk-free asset or, an even more delicate question, as the appropriate rate of substitution of the preferences for present and future consumption (as compared to a mortgage rate or municipal bond), the relevance of an average can be seriously called into question, even if projected over a century. If one accepts that the Stock Market is governed within and by a specific space-time reference frame, which is non-linear and made up of sudden dilations and contractions of time and mental (psychological) space, where memory recall and lapse produce shifts of position and determine speeds, then one also has to accept that the risk premium of shares in the Stock Market varies in a non-linear, sudden and exponential manner. The averages – within a world of possibly extreme distributions – are consequently inoperative (moreover, it will be seen that a mere average mixes and incorporates periods, i.e. very different systems, for example the great depression and the period after the second world war, although, within a time-reference frame of duration and *continuum* which are governed by memory recall and lapse, it can be shown that a certain degree of unity and coherence can be achieved by incorporating facts and events which are profoundly different).

Once one admits the specificity referred to above of the Stock Market's space-time reference frame, then beyond the radical limits which are imposed on any approach by averages, one discovers an equity risk premium which is potentially subject to much more extreme systems than one would have thought. One must, in particular, be able to accept the possibility that there exists, within the space-time reference frame of a "mental" or psychological nature, in the sense used by Allais, a risk premium for shares in the Stock Market which cannot be directly observed, and which is suddenly distorted, stretched or contracted by reminders and/or by memory lapses. There would accordingly be two forms of Stock Market risk premium, one which can be observed (the observation of which raises numerous difficulties and which has been the focus of all the literature on this subject up until now), and the other which cannot be observed, which is specific to the market reference frame, the observable premium being determined by the non-observable premium. The relevant equation can be expressed as $ERP = f(ERP_r, ERP_{M/F})$ where ERP_r = real premium and $ERP_{M/F}$ = premium governed within the mental space-time by memory and forgetfulness. Accordingly, there may not be a "puzzle" but rather a reality of extreme positive and negative regimes with thick-tailed and possibly asymmetrical distributions, which would not be understood correctly by the averages but, more fundamentally, would be unsuitable for an approach using averages.

A distinction must therefore be drawn between the recorded (recordable) or observed (observable) premium and the "true" premium (this term is unsuitable and "real" may be preferable.) Accordingly, if a traditional approach is adopted, the equity risk premium is equivalent to the *expected* profitability of the market asset less the *expected* profitability of the risk-free asset. What is important here is the word "expected", which defines a system of "real" risk premium, in the same way as there exists a real and therefore non-observable interest rate. What then matters is what is covered by this expectation. If, as we think, one anticipates in the Stock Market in the same way as one remembers and one forgets, then the equation can be expressed as

$$(ERP_{M/F} = Aer - rfAer),$$

where Aer = expected asset return

and $rfAer$ = expected risk free rate.

Consequently one can, as stated above, try to understand not only the magnitudes of the market risk premium but, above all, the sudden, non-linear distortions of such magnitudes. The "average" risk premium has little meaning, masking large distortions which are concentrated within time and driven by effects of speed which are unique to the market space-time reference frame, fashioned by memory recall and lapse. Added to this, as seen above, is the fact that the concept of risk, as understood by the Stock Market, encompasses much more than the specific elements of the Stock Market and its direct component parts. This does not conflict with the idea of very flexible, intertemporal substitutions which would consequently be recorded by a much more extensive risk aversion coefficient than one might have thought, indeed quite to the contrary. However this requires, first element, that the concept of "consumption" is more loosely defined and, as a result, will ultimately encompass and embody the Subject's global relationship with the world. Moreover, second element, the system of preferences, choices and arbitrages, and therefore of intertemporal substitutions (of "consumption"), is governed by a space-time reference frame of memory recall and lapse, where consequently any utility functions of "consumption" are influenced and determined by past "consumption" or, in the same way as described above for market events and facts, by present "consumption". Accordingly, third element, it can be understood within such a reference frame of space-time and speeds, which are specific to the market reference frame, that the flexibility of substitutions, preferences, choices and arbitrages, which are intertemporal, are marked by appreciable, concentrated and sudden distortions. In such a context, the utilities are decreasing functions of the past world (in the sense of all the facts and events), of the relationship (of the collective Subject or the individual Subject) to the past world, assuming that one understands by this a natural extension of the strict concept of "consumption"; the marginal utilities are in turn increasing functions of the same elements and dimensions.

§ 140. Once within a space-time reference frame which is structured by memory recall and lapse (duration), the link between the concept of risk and time, where the latter is understood to mean within the reference frame specific to the Stock Market, becomes essential. Since the risk is the reminder or memory loss of what has taken place, the whole of the facts and events which are directly or indirectly linked to the Stock Market. The phenomenon of risk is complete within the phenomena of memory recalls or lapses, complete within the principles of the space-time reference frame which are *not* linear or characterised by symmetrical or normal distributions. It is therefore illusory to try to standardise risk based on such distributions. The risk is a section of duration affected by the coefficients of memory recall and lapse. It constitutes in fact the raw material of the market space-time reference frame. The risk is, precisely, the name adopted by the shift of energy within the space-time reference frame boosted by memory recalls or reminders and memory lapses. The risk is an electrical flux whose energy is that described above as "market energy". The risk is not external to the Subject's relationship with the Stock Market: the risk is lodged within the market space-time reference frame and shares all its features and distortions, both non-linear and sudden.

There is accordingly first a temporal (spatio-temporal) cycle of equity risk premium which can be described as "vast", within the Stock Market's spatio-temporal reference frame, which is of a "mental" or psychological nature within the meaning used by Allais ("conscious" in the sense that the Subject-investor is consciousness), vast in its movements, concentrations, expansions and contractions, and also its distributions of extreme occurrences. This space-time is not and never will be the same as clock-time or the geographical space of sports fields. There are, second, *other* risks than the risks which can be imagined as being directly or indirectly linked to market matter and the matter of the companies which constitute the market. These risks are (or will become) insurable or may not be insurable, on individual, collective or global levels. The risk premium provides protection, a cover against this vast and sombre aspect of risk which stretches well beyond conventional measures. The premium will therefore have to increase in environments where such risks are increasing but where, often, no one can determine precisely what risk is in question. This difficulty is largely caused by the mystery (puzzle) of risk premium which may have appeared to be more sophisticated than it should have been (conventionally).

The market risk premium has to be described as "vast" within the dual meaning of the *nature* of risk as has just been stated (the field of insurable and uninsurable risks relating to the Stock Market and the market environment is in fact considerable), and the *magnitude* of the risk within the specific space-time reference frame which has been described. In particular, the extreme, violent and sudden distributions reflecting the probabilities of the occurrence of disasters or, more simply, of plights, are specific to this market reference frame, the extreme distributions being accompanied, as seen above, by the typical asymmetries of speeds, magnitudes and concentrations.

Finally, it has to be understood that the utility functions, which are constructed from intertemporal choices of wealth and consumption and which are supposed to steer, if not to determine, the systems of preferences and arbitrages, can only be of help in understanding or defining the market risk premium provided that there is both a "vast" definition of the functions of wealth and consumption, "vast" in the sense used above (i.e. the world) and, above all, an integration of such utility functions and systems of preferences which they influence within the very market space-time reference frame itself, which is structured by duration, memory recall and lapse, and therefore structured by the non-linearities resulting from psychological matter which constantly distorts, breaks or twists the utility functions. This means, for example, that the phenomena of memory recall or lapse, which the psychological forms of vexation, remorse and regret feed upon, may lead to distortions of the significance given to some or other utility of wealth/consumption in the determination of preferences and arbitrages. Similarly, the observed phenomena of aversion to loss (with the asymmetry of appetites and aversions for profits/losses), seem to be connected to the *past* experience of the Subject-investor in portfolio management, such phenomena referring back to the structure of memory recall and lapse of the market reference frame.

§ 141.   The idea that the Stock Market obtains a protection from, or at least absorbs the shock from, the fluctuations in consumption (together consequently with a possible extension of the life cycle by assuming that the attraction of the Stock Market as an asset depends upon the link or correlation between consumption and the income from the Stock Market which fluctuates with the years), this idea therefore of a smoothing out of the fluctuations of consumption in the context of intertemporal preferences and substitutions (for which traditional T. Bills or Bonds may offer an acceptable approximation of the rate of intertemporal substitution – T. Bills – or of the demand for precaution corresponding to the desire for an intertemporal smoothing-out – Bonds), this idea which forges a link between risk premium and the intertemporal preferences connected to the arbitrages of present and future consumption, must, in order to be accepted, be enclosed within the confines of a specific market space-time reference frame, accept a much vaster approach to the scope and magnitude of risk, consumption and wealth which are used to define the utility functions.

There are accordingly a number of elements which may suggest that there is not, despite what one often thinks, any mystery surrounding equity risk premium. However, the most fundamental issue, in our view, is to take into consideration a specific space-time reference frame which is structured by memory recall and lapse. This is the main gateway for an understanding of the Stock Market, which is always and above all, as stressed above, a preference, a choice or an arbitrage between the Stock Market *and everything else*, the Stock Market and the world, in the mind of an active Subject, who is here an investor.

CHAPTER 8

DOMAIN
OF FINANCIAL IMAGINATION

§ 142.   Finance, and especially stock market finance, organises the exchange and trade of images. These images, which are produced by expectation and projection, represent the very "way of being" of a Subject, Subject-investor or *homo economicus*. It is the nature of finance to base itself, unlike the majority of other sciences, on projects, i.e. on that which forms part of nothingness and not on objects or simply on facts and events alone. The presence of what will come to pass together with the project form the very essence of finance. This means that negativity constitutes the principal (non-)matter of the space-time of finance, the Stock Market and numerous sections of the economy. This non-matter or negativity which inhabits the projected objects, the expectations, within this space-time, is the result of the interplay of the Subject-investor's consciousness. By means of projection, this ultimate product of non-matter or oblivion therefore effaces and deletes that which effectively exists but simultaneously calls something else into nothingness. This effacing capacity lies at the heart of any economic theory of the Subject, which remains to be constructed.

Finance and the Stock Market therefore organise the circulation of foreign objects and images, which stem from an imagination, that of the Subject and a domain of imagination, that of the consciousness. The constitution of the conscious Subject projecting itself into the world, i.e. an understanding of the

Subject as being that which allows the world both to make itself present and be transformed, this modern understanding of the Subject make it possible for finance to appear in the form in which we now know it. The creation of (financial) objects which are not yet in existence can only be made possible by the appropriation of the world by a Subject who becomes aware (i.e. surpasses, imagines) and as a result seeks to transform. The trade of (financial) images is therefore inconceivable without a theory of the Subject based on the Subject's effacing consciousness.

The trade of images is not unconnected to that of commitments and credit, given the extent to which economic and financial space-time is occupied by projection and expectation, i.e. the way in which a Subject-consciousness surpasses itself, each effort involved therein producing images and projects.

The very nature of finance is to describe that which does not exist, to try and capture that which floats, undoubtedly fragile images which are embodied and known but which are essentially inhabited by non-matter or, perhaps more correctly, by anti-matter since the consciousness produces images by secreting anti-matter, i.e. from the domain of imagination. The space-time specific to finance and in particular to the Stock Market is inhabited by, constituted of anti-matter and imagination in proportion to the capacity of the Subject and its consciousness to efface perception and projection or to create images.

Accordingly, no modern finance can appear or be formed without a theory of the Subject and a space-time for such Subject, a space-time of consciousness and its capacity to produce a world of imagination. It is this same space-time, the nature of which is sometimes described as "psychological" and certainly as "mental", which, far-removed from clock-time, from the known linearities of our "real" world of objects, facts and events, concentrates contractions and dilations of matter (anti-matter) which is contorted at whim in sudden accelerations and makes the energy centres of this space travel more or less quickly throughout this strange reference frame, depending upon the extent to which they are stimulated (as discussed in our other works, this stimulation of energy is linked in particular to memory).

Finance is accordingly based on anti-matter which constitutes its basic space-time. As such, finance is filled with nothingness, since, at any given time, it concerns what will come to pass and what remains to be done or accomplished, in respect of which the financial market effectively tries to assess the contours, risk and price. The essential part of the measure or standard will consequently be prospective in nature, attempting to apprehend a future result and assess the future impact of an action. The financial market is, effectively, seeking to allocate a price to an action, which will efface the world or part of it, in order to recreate, transform or alter it. The financial space-time is therefore specific on two counts. It does not contain real objects but only images; the said images (commitments, projections …), which represent future real objects which will, or will not, literally "take place", are projections or representations of an active Subject's consciousness.

§ 143.   The conscious acts of the Subject directed at the world are all financial objects, which float within the financial or market space-time. Such objects are not virtual, since they may become reality after completion of the project which they embody and which they contain; they may also, as such, i.e. as pure financial objects, have an impact on what is real and possibly modify it. Market finance structures the reception, the confrontation, the real life of this space-time of non-existent objects. To an extent never seen before, market finance has physically organised a scene of action, namely a confrontation of the targets of the consciousness, of intentions and designs, aimed like arrows at objects which exist or do not exist, since the targeting seeks to modify or destroy and often creates the object while moving towards it.

Modern finance, by creating the market institution, has given a practical form to the aim of the Subject's consciousness, the nature of which is imaginary. This practical form makes the action visible by institutionalising it and accommodates within the real world a space-time which may seem real but which in fact borrows its features, its workings and its energy from its source Subject. This practical, open externalisation of the aim of the action introduces a potentially conflictual joint existence of at least two reference frames of time and space, one structuring the Subject's method of thinking and acting and the other constructing the linearities of the real world. These two parallel dimensions, which may however be superimposed or even intersect, play a profound role in the structure of the two main spheres at work in economics, namely the real and financial spheres. The essential distinctions now made from observation of clock-time and other specific spatio-temporal forms refer back to these two dimensions, as do the descriptions of finance as virtual, albeit with a significant lack of understanding and criticism.

It is not that no "finished" financial objects exist since, being the result of a process, they may to some extent be observed or described after completion of the work of construction, constitution and emergence; however, the financial object will always be worked upon, driven, distorted, contracted and extended by the project which contains its energy and the structures of consciousness, memory recall and lapse which form the anti-matter, always slightly more remote than might appear, stretching out towards the target which it will never reach, permanently uncompleted and with no prospect of ever being self-sufficient.

By providing economics and finance with a theory of the Subject, defining the Subject as a form of consciousness and design which effaces and therefore creates, one can take into account not only the modern context which hastens economics in the sense of appropriation by a Subject who is now central, but also – consequently – the emergence of a specific spatio-temporal reference frame which is, for the most part, that of the active consciousness itself. This active consciousness, which only exists, strictly speaking, by extricating or removing itself during the action which constitutes its way of being, will manufacture imaginary objects (and, more generally, an imaginary space-time) which give physical form to the target in the same way one lights a track at night, but are absolutely not the actual point of impact with the world. This space-time which comes between us and the world, as soon as the action plans appear, is essentially that of economics and finance. By coming between the Subject and the world, this space-time is both the form through which the world is effaced (creator/destructor) and the form through which the world appears.

§ 144.   We are trying to demonstrate that the financial space-time is structured like a world of imagination, that the objects which inhabit and drive this reference frame are images which are separate from real objects, that such images are produced by an image-making consciousness of the Subject and that such objects are present-absent, since they render present something real which is absent. Within the financial universe, and specifically the financial securities market, we are therefore interested in mental images. Such images, in our mind, inhabit the reference frame of expectations and projections which form the very means by which the Subject's consciousness and action open up to the world. This projection focuses on the real object by means of creative negativity. The real object is effaced and then left behind during the ensuing projection towards something which does not yet exist. Accordingly, this projection is accompanied by (produces) mental images, which represent a certain way in which the object can be absent within its very presence. Within the Stock Market sphere, and more generally the sphere of finance and economics, the vast majority of concepts and indicators which are presumed to be useful are intersected by expectation, i.e. a form of effacement of the real object which is intended to be appropriated (results, company cash flows, growth ...), and this effaced form constitutes the image which is, effectively, traded and negotiated. The real objects are not themselves discussed or traded: but rather the projections, i.e. the mental images which make the real object present to some extent, even though this real object does not (yet) exist because it is not there, because it is projected into the future. When I try and imagine what the growth, prices or activity of some or other sector will be, or the geo-political environment, I am focussing on a series of real objects which do not yet exist, because I am projecting myself into the future, or which are, quite simply, in the present but on which I am focussing through an image-making consciousness. Both real contemporary objects which exist or future anticipated objects – which are the dominant means of organising financial structures – pass through the image-making consciousness and mental image, a form of *analogy* by means of which, or through which, the real targeted object – whether existing or projected – will appear (make itself present) to the consciousness.

The mental image of a company, its resources, organisation or results, the mental image of oil and gas resources, of prices, political and military tensions, there are mental images of objects X which can be described as real, in the sense that they inhabit the normal reference frame of clock time and standardised space, whether present or future. Real objects are transformed into mental images by the image-making consciousness and it is in this form that they come to the market. When we consider the determining elements of the financial market, we do not have access to the real object as such but to images. The mental images of real objects called X cannot be confused with the real object X itself, which is to some extent a reduced model. One must overcome the illusion of inherence in order to state clearly that the financial and market reference frame (which can be extended to include economics) is not a reference frame of real objects, whether existing or projected, but a reference frame of mental images governed by its own temporality and spatiality, the phenomena of memory, *continuum*, belief, memory lapse, by non-linearities and sudden contractions and dilations. This reference frame, which we have described within the context of market dynamics and the particular features of the space-time, stems from the way in which the Subject's consciousness operates (whether that Subject be economic, an investor or *homo economicus*). It is an effacing consciousness, which takes possession of the world and of its real objects by leaving them behind (thus by rendering them absent, literally by imagining them) and is simultaneously image-making, since an image corresponds to each effacing and creative design of the consciousness. It is a mental universe lined with (mental) images, which will constitute the fundamental framework for the financial and market action and dynamics, a universe of anti-matter which reflects the transforming action plan, within the real world.

The images which inhabit the space-time reference frame of the Stock Market and of finance are "filled" with knowledge, to differing degrees. These dynamic images of expectations, which are more or less remote and which are specific to this reference frame, are what they are, no more or less. They summarise a certain depth of knowledge, rather than constituting an additional or new dimension. Since the mental image (and by "mental" we include everything which refers, in literature, including our own literature, to a "psychological" dimension, to the effects of memory recall and lapse, to everything which expresses the intricate existence of a particular spatio-temporal dimension which is specific to economic, financial or market phenomena), is to some extent "charged" (recharged) by present and past knowledge, where blocks of time-matter perform their role by means of permanent tensions between memory recall and lapse, the whole within a *continuum* of duration. This is where the link between the act of image-making consciousness and the constitution of a financial imagination is formed. It is based on a structure of time-matter and spatial speeds, which is determined by the various states of duration, its accelerations and contractions, duration being understood to mean the time-matter which contains the knowledge discussed above and which will foster the mental image.

§ 145.   The domain of the economic, financial and market imagination results from the relationship between the object and a consciousness. This relationship constitutes the essential form of understanding of modern economics, confronted by tension, acquisition and transformation as between the Subject and the (real) world. The mental image, as we have described it, is the manner in which the real object appears within the specific space-time reference frame, where the financial dynamics are formed. More precisely, the (real) object is targeted – one considers all the objects of discussion, trade and calculation which drive the financial markets throughout the day – in a form, an overall packaging of tangible and perceptible elements which have been perceived (a particular company and its directors, its brand, its building, this knowledge of memory recall and lapse which mixes everything which has been perceived in respect of a company, which surrounds the company, these mysterious blocks of duration and time-matter which will procure, within the mental image at a particular time, that some or other elements, which are past or present concretions, become fixed. This will result in an image becoming fixed in the same way as one momentarily freezes knowledge); since expectation is a mental image which fixes a state of time-matter; to this static vision should be added the dynamic dimension, where the time-matter will be stimulated by memory, extended by memory lapse, or shortened, compressed by one or the other.

To expect is to imagine and one imagines in the same way one forgets or remembers. The real object targeted by the image-making consciousness and delivered by the mental image is a summary which compresses within itself a layer of duration. It is within this layer that the various temporal and spatial strata for one and the same objet lie (the same company five years ago, ten years ago, in a particular area for a particular market or product) and will be put into play, set in motion, from memory recall to lapse, from deletion to juxtaposition. The real targeted object only rarely appears in its pure and most immediate present. The real economic, financial or market object always appears to the consciousness surrounded by an obscure halo, mixing various archaeological layers, and the face which it presents to the image-making consciousness may, often, be that of another clock time or, more often, a mix of several faces. Memory recall and lapse will, as discussed, have the power to move these strata at great speeds and therefore these images as well, within the space-time reference frame.

The consciousness of the economic Subject, the Subject-investor, and the *homo economicus*, targets an object whose contents are directly or indirectly linked to the financial matter, targets an object through its image and is not therefore the consciousness of a targeted image. It is the object itself which is targeted (the company, the director, the product …) and which will accordingly make itself present from the point of its absence, since the act of targeting it brings into being the absence of the object, which will be represented by the image. The object as an undifferentiated *whole* is targeted by the consciousness of the economic and financial Subject, the image therefore assuming an undivided nature. The image is one and is fixed, saturated with the knowledge that the consciousness has injected it with (this static vision then makes way for a set of dynamics of mental images, since the economic, financial and market dynamics are fundamentally a set of dynamics of mental images within a space-time reference frame structured by the Subject's image-making consciousness and whose imagination is structured in similar form to anti-matter, which is stimulated, stretched and contracted by the "knowledge" of memory and duration, and also by memory lapse). The financial image presents itself as an undivided whole with distinct properties; this is how the *object image* appears to the consciousness of the economic Subject and/or Subject-investor. However, this undivided appearance which is the very form of the mental image conceals within it certain blocks of time-matter and space representing the archaeological strata of knowledge, which constitute, "charge" or "recharge" the mental image: these fundamental unitary elements, which borrow heavily from that which has been and continues to endure, are grouped together to some extent by the consciousness in the undivided form adopted by the image.

§ 146.　　Belief constitutes one of the essential structures of the image-making consciousness, within the space-time reference frame of economics and finance. By this one means that it is through belief that one accepts the idea that the real object X is targeted (and therefore appears to the consciousness) *through* the layers and strata of time which are compressed or stretched to a greater or lesser degree. The said strata certainly imprison a spatio-temporal variant of X but, also, as with the layers excavated by archaeologists, numerous other elements within the direct or indirect environment. This evocation of layers of earth which contain the principal trace (by principal one means that of the primary representation or theme of the targeted object, in the same way that oil production cannot be directly confused with the theme of inflation or that the results of an aircraft manufacturer cannot be directly confused with the exchange parity of the dollar or the Arab-Israeli conflict), is of the same nature as the blocks of time-duration-memory, affected by a certain degree of memory lapse, cut out of a long duration and summoned or dismissed within a mental space-time reference frame. We discussed these blocks in *Théorie* and again in *Les Fondements*.

The financial object – whether real and existing, inexistent or absent within time or space – which is targeted and which will give rise to the production of a (financial) object-image by overtaking and effacing the reality, which is then captured as a generalised whole, becomes present in the sense that it appears to the consciousness which targets it and consequently makes it present but only insofar as such object is distanced within its own reality, captured and effaced and therefore literally rendered absent. This presence (of the financial object-image) – absence (of the real financial object), which is the foundation for the operation of the financial and market space-time reference frame, is made possible by the phenomenon of belief which incorporates the idea of a complete and spontaneous adherence but also, and especially, the idea of memory which provides the bases for the adherence.

The real object of financial analysis and interpretation in the daily operation of finance and the markets, which is therefore targeted by a consciousness, becomes the object-image and the essential element for the structure of the market reference frame. The transformation or change of the real object of financial analysis (e.g. the "true" activity of a company) into an image incorporates the whole of an experience, duration or a memory. It relates to the experience of the targeted object and that of its direct or indirect environment. It also relates to the experience of the economic Subject, Subject-investor or *homo economicus*, which effects the targeting, since the image-making consciousness is always effected from a particular point of view. Without ignoring any difference which may exist between imagination and memory (or recollection), we maintain that the structure of the world of imagination, which is that of the space-time reference frame of finance and the Stock Market, is charged, "recharged" and nurtured by memory. One imagines in the same way as one remembers, within the reference frame which is the subject of our study. This means inter alia that the leaving behind of what is real and the conversion into an image, the distancing, rendering absent and projection are of the same nature as the act of remembering, particularly when the image as a total object (complete summary) is full of anti-matter (oblivion), driven by the flows of memory and duration. Memory-duration is anti-matter (oblivion) in the leaving behind of what is real and the constitution of the financial object-image.

§ 147.   The fundamental identification of the memory and imagination through the mechanics of imaginary projection-creation, recollection and, it should be added, discounting of the future (one expects, imagines and remembers in accordance with processes of a homogenous nature within the financial and market space-time reference frame), this very identification of the acts of memory, expectation and imagination of the consciousness and the Subject (we are now distancing ourselves somewhat from Sartre's theories on the world of imagination, which are in other respects so useful) would not be complete without the integration of memory lapse: since one forgets in the same way as one remembers, expects and imagines. The constitution of the financial object-image by means of effacement cannot ignore the extent to which it is memory lapse which renders absent or inexistent and which can introduce a form of oblivion. However, we will have to distinguish between that which results from the same operation of nature (expectation, memory recall, memory lapse, imagination; from this point of view, memory recall and lapse are the same type of phenomena within the financial and market space-time reference frame) and that which seems similar, at first sight (to forget and to efface, to assume that what is real is absent or inexistent and to forget it). Does one imagine in the same proportion that one forgets? It would seem not. One imagines in the same proportion as the memory which nurtures the creation of the world of imagination and which constitutes the essential background for the game of finance, the financial markets and the Stock Market. This is one of our fundamental theories: duration and memory structure the "psychological", "mental" reference frame of anti-matter or oblivion which targets by rendering absent and which renders present a surpassed, inexistent or absent reality in the form of an image. Memory lapse is more the coefficient of erosion of the axis of duration and memory than the dominant factor of this process, despite appearances which can easily make it seem similar to oblivion. Imagination, expectation, memory lapse and recall constitute the essential structures of the consciousness of the economic Subject and Subject-investor, of the psychological forms.

We have demonstrated that the financial and market space-time reference frame was characterised by an imaginary structure and essence. Therefore there exists a category of objects of the Subject's consciousness, which analyses and participates in financial and economic matters (is it not accordingly wider, more general than we would like to believe?): it relates to imaginary objects which populate finance (and, as we have just stated, potentially all worlds, since any objet of the consciousness is eligible for the processes described here). It relates to financial object-images, unitary elements of the mental or "psychological" financial reference frame within the sense used by Allais. The objects exist *sui generis*, are presented once and for all, as if set in static by the summary of reality which has suddenly been effected, and this is enough to characterise finance by means of this function, which is to some extent a mental one. These objects are moreover contained within a set of dynamics driven by the consciousness, within the group which such consciousness may form from such unitary object-images and within the memory recall or lapse of some or other unitary object-images. This is where the sudden accelerations are formed, which contract space and time or, inversely, the dilations. Everything takes place and is played out in accordance with the Subject's consciousness and it is in this way that all these developments constitute a theory of the economic and financial Subject.

The financial object-image targeted by the consciousness by leaving behind the real object is unitary, a general summary, and as such is always something other than the sum of its elements. This object-image is always located beyond that which seems to be attainable, and each new image moves the perspective further away. This enables one to understand in passing why the Stock Market and the markets may often seem unattainable, since the image, of its very nature, is what is in reality unattainable, since located at a distance and permanently overtaking. Moreover, although the image is always a general summary, which is fixed at the moment of appreciation, it generates its own variants, namely other images, which will bring into play the effects of memory recall and lapse, experience and belief, in the same way as one operates valves or a sail. However, the images which have already been produced will continue to exist within the reference frame as created: the financial object-images will not die within the financial and market space-time reference frame; they continue to float like planets in space, sometimes they are forgotten and confined within another dimension or another galaxy and sometimes they return. The mental world of finance and its imaginary objects is expanding.

Reflection, in finance (in the wider sense), produces images to the same extent as the Subject-consciousness' focus on the world (on companies, businesses and, more generally, the world of facts and events) affirms the appearance of the (real) object as a form of possession. The real object, as we have stressed, must be distinguished from the object-image which is unreal, even when it relates to targeting and appropriating financial or economic contents which do not yet exist, which are only a projection. The object-image is unreal either because it refers to contents or a real object which forms part of nothingness (this negativity is unavoidable), or because it refers to "future" contents, in which case the negativity is even more unavoidable. The financial object-image is non-existent and negativity constitutes its way of being.

Finance, the Stock Market, and economics in general, work and reason within a field of *unreal elements*, a field of object-images which express the extent to which such reflections are based on projection and appropriation. However, the Subject, because it only produces object-images, will always remain at a distance from what is real, placed in front of or behind the window of the image, and this distance cannot be eliminated. Financial or market sciences only deal with what is real behind the window of mental object-images. It is these mental images which, in various forms (analyses, forecasts, projected results, professional strategy, macro-economic or sectorial assumptions, risk scenarii, possible sociological developments...), constitute what is called *the market*, or rather the regulated financial market as we know it; a place where all these forms of unreality (negativity), all these *images* are traded, confronted and sold. The consciousness of the economic Subject and Subject-investor produces projects and plans for the appropriation and trans-formation of the world: these projects and plans take the form of unreal object-images which take material form (thus endowing them with a certain reality) within the enclosure of the market, a sort of external form of the image-making consciousness.

The economic and financial Subject uses the image-making consciousness because economics and finance are essentially based on desire and consequently on the various forms of shortcoming (negativity). This is indeed the relationship established with the world in the economic and financial context, as was amply demonstrated in *Tractatus* or in *Généalogie*.

§ 148.   By assuming that finance – and in particular the financial market – is inhabited by mental, and therefore unreal, object-images (and the same is true of economics as a whole to a certain extent), one also assumes that the determining factors of time and space which govern the real targeted object (whether existing or "future", projected or expected), are the result of such unreality, i.e. the space-time reference frame is absolutely specific. Time and space cannot have the same character or same substance within an image-making reference frame, within a field of object-images. It was demonstrated, in *La Dynamique boursière*, that time-matter acquires an alternative substance, which is more suited to the expansions and compressions; that space acquires a meaning which is more qualitative, to some extent, provided by time itself and speed in particular. The economic, financial or market space is a mental space of mental object-images, where such objects move around by means of stimulations of time-matter moulded by duration (the mental object-images having a complete form, including, inter alia, spatial characteristics). There are accordingly, and this is important, two dimensions, two levels of understanding and analysis: the level of the financial object-image, an enclosed whole, which is to some extent closed into itself (e.g. the forecasted results for a particular company in the coming year; the scenario of sales of products in America; the impact of a 20% rise in the dollar, of a 15% drop in the price of petrol on the net results, on the stock price); each of these options corresponds to what we will call a financial object (mental image), an object for which and within which external relations no longer exist between elements (there is henceforth pure internality and the spatio-temporal dimensions are fixed, without any parts, without any possible segmentation, within the financial object). Moreover, there is a second level, that of the enclosure within which all these object-images evolve, move around, the mental "place" where external spatio-temporal relations are established between these object-images, relations which cannot be those of the world of clock time. This is why it can be said that the time of the consciousness of the image is not that of the object-image.

We therefore assume that all the financial proposals (and, in general the economic proposals), and in particular all the expectations in any form whatsoever, together with all the representations of economic and financial reality (one can therefore distinguish, within that which is transformed into an image, between the representation of the "existing" reality and the expectation-forecast, neither of which differs to the extent that the unreality viewed by the image-making consciousness describes them all together), that all such acts of the conscious reflection of the economic and financial Subject who produce object-images, *are* all object-images.

Each financial or economic object-image, i.e. each unitary element (since one can segment and reduce to an almost-primary element all the complex chains which are represented and expected and which take the form of a specific language of the space-time reference frame of finance and the Stock Market), each block is therefore made up of time-matter which is compressed, reduced or contracted duration. In line with the fundamental theories presented in our earlier works, the pure block or the more complex chains are sections of time, of the time and are therefore presented as intertemporal summaries of sequences, particular lengths of time-matter. It is within this layer of duration that the mental object-image, whose referrer or correlative is the existing real object or the projected object, is cut out and constructed. This means that the block, as described, possesses its own spatio-temporal DNA, which is produced once and for all (and as such the object-image is a closed whole like an oyster closes itself up) and its own energy, which may be released once the memory recall or lapse stimulate this essential matter.

The DNA of financial object-images (an expectation of results, for example) therefore contains a specific structure of duration, a summary of events and facts, which is intertemporal. The time of the financial object-image (the block, the chain), like the time in which all the mental economic, financial or market object-images are steeped, this time of unreality is unreal in the sense that it does not really pass, that it can dilate, unfurl or, on the contrary, contract, at will, in a reversible manner which is specific to the unreality of its structure. The consciousness of the economic

Subject or Subject-investor, whose structure is different, remains at a distance from the unreal object.

The financial object-images which we have presented, unitary blocks or more complex chains, have a specific spatio-temporal structure: each financial proposal, representation or expectation creates its own time and space, in fact literally carries it along with it, once taken from the section cut out of the dense duration, i.e. the complete intertemporal summary of specific durations, in the same way one bores into the ground. This particular spatio-temporality provides the object-image with its independence but that does not mean a constant inertia or immobility. The mental object-image of finance and the Stock Market is not a frozen, dead image. An autonomous generality is provided suddenly but the consciousness will maintain a relationship of high or low tension with the object-image by driving the memory recall or lapse. It is these impetuses which make the image appear and disappear and, within the object-image, particular sequences or slices of duration appear and disappear, the whole of which contributes to the discontinuous and erratic nature of the object-image itself and to the link of tension between the subject-consciousness and the object-image which remains at a distance.

Saturated with anti-matter, the mental financial, economic or market object-image is a strange form of anti-world through which, paradoxically, the world appears and ultimately exists with regard to an economic Subject.

§ 149.   The object-image which is produced by the consciousness of a *homo economicus*, the Subject-investor or mere Subject is filled with that which is absent (which is literally not there, whether in terms of geographical remoteness, distance in time or any other form of absence expressed by reference to a space-time reference frame whose two dimensions foster negativity, nothingness), with what is inexistent (not yet, maybe, never, from probable to probabilised, such as a scenario of an increase in sales, in growth, in prices, a true illusion, that which will never be real but will live from time to time within unreality). Filled with anti-matter or anti-world, in the sense used above, the space-time reference frame of finance and the Stock Market, which is psychological in form, cannot mix with real objects. In order to target the existing (present) reality and also that which does not exist ("future" illusory project) – a targeting which will place the two dimensions on the same level of unreality -, the consciousness of the economic and financial Subject will for this purpose travel through the past, since the targeting, which makes the existing, absent or non-existent reality unreal, mobilises the past by making an intertemporal summary (in fact thousands of summaries) of sections of duration, which we have called individual durations. The act of consciousness which gives rise to the object-image is an act which both constitutes the object by transferring knowledge to it, knowledge of intertemporal summary, of duration and memory; and, more probably, by stimulating the block of the past which is already cut out and which constitutes the finance-object, such stimulation coming inter alia from memory recalls and lapses which are specific to the dynamics of the space-time reference frame of finance; in any event, by driving to some extent the dynamics of the spatio-temporal reference frame, once the object-images are created, by stimulating and distorting the dimensions of time and space.

All the processes and acts of appropriation, representation and expectation of the real world for economic and financial purposes, all such processes target real, existing, absent or inexistent items by means of knowledge constituted beforehand by the inter-temporal summary of durations, and therefore by means of psychological (mental) contents. The matter of this mental image, which backs all the economic-financial thinking and projects, is necessarily already constituted as a target for the consciousness, a matter which has been shown to be "knowledge" cut out of the dense duration accumulated in space-time. The consciousness will create the object-image from this matter, which will, in order to exist in unreality for the image-making consciousness, have to acquire the substance or structure of anti-matter.

The image-making consciousness of the economic and financial Subject contains the psychological contents of the target, including the dynamics of memory recall and lapse. However, these contents, located at the (transcendental) level of the Subject's consciousness, and which represent, expect and appropriate, cannot contain or incorporate the appreciable characteristics and qualities of the item, whether temporal or spatial, and such characteristics and qualities can only be represented and not possessed. The item which is represented and targeted remains external and alone, since the transcendental position of the consciousness cannot be assimilated to any exteriority. Here can be seen the possible illusion of inherence referred to by Sartre.

§ 150.   Economic and financial (market) matters are structured like domains of imagination. There is a fundamental analogy between memory and imagination. One remembers and forgets in the same way one expects or imagines. These are the essential assumptions of our work.

The financial, market or economic object-image constituted by the targeting of the consciousness contains nothing other than that which we have placed in it, i.e. the summarised intertemporal knowledge which we have called a block of duration – which is itself segmented *ad infinitum* into individual durations –, as one whole, which is the financial object-image, a unique, summarised whole. The fact that one only finds within the financial image what one has placed in it is certainly a sign that the essential structure of the financial object-image is inadequate – the same is true of all images, of any image – but it would be accurate if one were only to see a fixed and frozen object, since if it can only contain what we have placed in it, this matter experiences a life driven by memory recall and lapse. When it is stated that one can only find what one has *placed* there, this relates to an initial *placing* of a complete memory by the Subject who will, later, forget or remember.

The proposals, representations and appropriations which inhabit economics and finance are essentially structured by intentions which express the targeting relationship between the economic or financial Subject and a world of existing reality or of absent or inexistent reality. All that is stated in analyses of finance and of the financial markets in particular, translates an intention which creates an unreal object, namely the object-image, a mental form resulting from knowledge (duration), which is worked and sculpted by memory recall and lapse. Each intention presupposes a certain depth of knowledge accumulated by the consciousness of the Subject-investor or Subject – the *homo economicus*. The Subject will, within the relationship with the world, which is formed in the economic act, mobilise or lead to some extent and will include a whole body of knowledge, all sorts of layers of learning, an inheritance of conscious or unconscious duration, whether or not forgotten, whether in whole or in part but which, at any given time, will constitute the space-time matter for the operation of the financial and market reference frame. It is not readily established that each Subject investor, that each individual *homo economicus* possesses, as its spatio-temporal reference frame, all the infinite fields of knowledge, facts and events embraced by human history. Although, in theory, it can be assumed that each individual Subject individually includes a field of duration and knowledge, which is that of human history, each still has to place an individual filter of a specific history and journey from its slice of human life in the world as it is. In a similar vein, the question is raised whether, in the relations between the conscious Subject and the world, which constitutes the fundamental structure of economics, finance or the Stock Market, there exists a conscious section and unconscious section within the space-time reference frame, which we have described, since the Subject only represents as an object-image that which it actually knows in some way or another, which it has perhaps forgotten or repressed, in order to use the terminology of unconsciousness. Memory recall and lapse are therefore the structuring axes of the mental space-time reference frame, which should be intersected with the conscious and unconscious dimensions. The strictly individual time of the knowledge accumulated by the said Subject should be expanded to include all implied human knowledge (duration).

§ 151.   Let us return to the structure of the image of financial "objects" which circulate in economic and financial thinking, in financial practices and markets. Our assumption (theory) is that economic and financial matters – finance and the financial markets – are structured like domains of imagination and inhabited by object-images produced by the consciousness of the Subject actor (investor, consumer, etc.). It is the financial market as an essential, contemporary form which is the place of circulation, trade, confrontation, creation and destruction of object-images, going so far as to assume itself, in a certain manner, the form of a collective consciousness by incorporating, extending or dispersing the production of images from billions of individual unitary consciousnesses. It is to the same extent as economics and finance are traversed by negativity, i.e. the projection towards that which does not yet exist (the project, the action), the calculating and imagining expectation, that the object-image constitutes the fundamental form of such methods of relating to the worlds represented by these two disciplines, since the object-image is nothingness. This is where the intimate relationship with time is situated, in the gap of negativity which structures the act of consciousness (and action), since the projection towards what does not yet exist is an action towards what will come to pass (future) within a total, general summary constituted by the image-producing act of consciousness, which goes strictly hand in hand with the action. Economics and finance are traversed by absence and nothingness: that which does not yet exist or is not, will not perhaps be, that which is promised (promise, trust, credit), foreseen, projected, expected, agreed for the future (the contract), invested, all these structuring dimensions of the action. Since economics and finance are based on the idea that the Subject forms of the world and of the transformation which it can make it experience or undergo, since there is accordingly a degree of hindsight or distance on the part of the consciousness which forms such an idea, the object-image emerges from this creative act of the consciousness. There is at the very least a symmetry and often an identity between the creative act of the consciousness which produces the object-image and what is called "action" at the heart of economics and finance.

The financial markets in their contemporary form are therefore devices for dreaming, imagining, creating (and destroying), a physical form and the location of a total (and general) collective consciousness. In this place of object-images which have a price, there is a certain relationship with time, that of the consciousness, and space, that of the consciousness as well, and therefore a space-time reference frame, within which the temporality of unreal objects targeted by the consciousness is itself unreal, in the sense that it cannot relate to the temporality of clocks as we know it but, on the contrary, a time-matter which may contract and/or dilate, extend, accelerate, slow down, reverse or jump steps at will, while always remaining the same; a time-matter fostered by duration and stimulated by memory recall and lapse, a layer of knowledge which always precedes the constitution of the image, a pre-existing layer specific to each consciousness and its past but which will experience some sort of change in the process of creation of the image (cut out of the layer of duration; discontinuities and ruptures in memory recalls and lapses). Within the structure of the financial object-image, this mental production of the consciousness, there therefore exists a spectrum of determinants – specifically those determinants which we are aware of, which is finished (static, when a financial or economic image is provided) and unstable (dynamic, when the object-image experiences internal transformations or external shocks, in the same way as free electrons may collide with each other). Within this structure of the image, there are discontinuities, which result from the very special relationship between the financial image and its object, within a space-time reference frame which is specific to a mental universe of economics and finance structured by the conscious and active Subject. The image of the object targeted by the consciousness of the Subject investor, consumer (…) is not the real object, either because the real object exists but is kept at a distance by the act of consciousness, or because this real object is committed to a transformation (which will come to pass and which is therefore absent), or finally because the object is inexistent and will remain so. In any event, there is a structure of unreality in the sense of negativity, which conceals within itself either the definitive inexistence (the illusion) of a real object (however the unreal object will, itself, exist) or the departure of a real object or its transforming projection (however the mere capture by the act of consciousness is already a form of transformation).

§ 152.   The image of the real object refers to, is fostered by a duration, by knowledge, by a time-matter of duration, memory recall and lapse (e.g. the economic or financial results of ten years ago or a turbine project from thirty years ago, at the other end of the world...) which means that the real object, which is in turn situated within a "normal" space-time reference frame (which is linear, that of clocks with regard to temporality, that of linear movements with regard to space), is targeted by the consciousness of the Subject investor, consumer (...) through a specific prism, within a different space-time marked by the special features discussed above (temporal and spatial discontinuities; speeds which depend upon memory recall and lapse). Within this mental reference frame of the economic and financial imagination, the object of the image is defined within time and space in a different manner from the real object targeted by the act of consciousness. In particular, one moves more or less quickly within the space of the financial image depending upon whether one remembers or forgets to a greater or lesser degree.

The primary object of the financial matter, which is the financial image, results from the targeting of a real object within today's clock time and within space, as it appears to me today. This targeting is effected by mobilising a whole layer of duration and memory, linked to the real object, whether directly or indirectly, a mobilisation which will transform/transport the real targeted object into a different space-time reference frame. The real object, once targeted, becomes something else. This is true of a simultaneous targeting (I visualise today what the markets for some or other company are today). This is even truer for a future targeting, provided that I am trying to visualise what the said real object will become (I visualise today what the markets for such company will be). The real targeted object will undergo a transformation within the projection, a projection which goes beyond it (a negativity which makes the object "absent" from itself, part of nothingness) which will mobilise a whole layer of duration and memory which will in turn, like a dynamic concretion, foster and drive the future object. This future object is a transformation of the real object which seems reasonable, especially since the future object bears within it a mark of its origin and of the past. This future object (what the markets for such a company will be) is "inexistent" in the sense that it does not yet exist but already contains a certain intensity of truth. This "inexistence" is therefore relative to some extent, i.e. relative to a mark of origin, memory and duration. However, it can also relate to an absolute inexistence, in the sense that the object transformed by the targeting does not contain any direct or indirect connection with a real object which exists today and which can therefore be the subject of some form of transforming continuity. The same is true of the attempt to imagine what might happen to such a company in fifty years when extreme, climate, geopolitical or socio-economic risks have materialised. This inexistence is not yet absolute, since a link persists with the real object and it is not an illusion. The extreme imaginative projections (what will a company become in a hundred years?) may become closer to such inexistences, where the financial object-image is a black hole of negativity and almost an illusion.

§ 153.   These object-images which circulate and are traded on the financial markets therefore contain various, variable degrees of time-matter connecting them by means of duration and memory to real objects of the present day and the past, with variable densities of duration and memory, a variable negativity (which should be seen as anti-matter, almost as a black hole which hollows out the object-image from the inside) and which is all the greater, the stronger the "inexistence" of the projected object. The differences in density and their variability have some link to the determination of value and prices. Finance (and more generally economics) should be seen as a world of representations (in relation to a consciousness, a Subject), and therefore as unitary object-images, true primary elements of a system which we have called a "reference frame" of a specific space-time, which undergo transformations as we have just seen, which can also constitute chains, groupings and consolidations, chains of value and, at the same time, chains which form language.

The spatio-temporal reference frame for economics and finance is inhabited by primary elements, which are all unitary object-images produced by an infinite multitude of individual consciousnesses. Each primary element is characterised by a density of duration and memory (which contains the link between time-matter and value) and by a density of negativity or anti-matter (which contains the intensity of projection towards that which does not yet exist, which is not, which will never be, this space of what is possible and impossible, which is subject to gradations and segmentations). Such primary elements are in absolute and relative movement. Absolute, i.e. as compared to themselves and stimulated by the conscious Subject (memory recalls and lapses), within an internal set of dynamics of the discontinuous modification of the layers of duration and knowledge. Relative, i.e. of some as compared to others, once again stimulated by the conscious Subject, when the primary elements collide, consolidate into a chain, merge into each other and are, as a result, transformed. A transformation results from such relative movements, in addition to the internal movements which are specific to the primary elements, the whole of which forms the dynamics of the financial, and specifically the market, space-time reference frame. These mental physics of the primary object-images, that of the consciousness of the Subject investor, the consumer or, in general, of the *homo economicus*, are the basis for the dynamics and the language of economics and finance in the modern age.

§ 154.   Any unreal object-image brings with it a specific space-time reference frame, its own time and space, in proportion to the spatio-temporal references of the image-making consciousness which produced it. One of the important accepted facts of our work is the unavoidably specific or special nature of object-images, which attain a form of independence and inhabit the mental market universe: the anti-matter or anti-world, which forms the essential structure of market dynamics and finance. It will also be remembered that the constitution of the financial, market or economic object-image (pre)supposes a certain knowledge, that the image-making consciousness of the Subject investor (financial or economic player) is responsible for learning, since the consciousness which will produce the financial object-image can only visualise as an image – this image or images which inhabit the space-time reference frame and which foster the market dynamics – that which it already knows and/or remembers after having perhaps first forgotten. By being responsible for learning and knowledge, the image-making consciousness is only carrying out its task of accumulating and producing *duration*, which is the raw, primary time-matter driven, informed or distorted by memory recall and lapse, in a process which is literally that of market dynamics (it was demonstrated in *Théorie* that this process lay at the heart of economic dynamics); this layer of duration, which has been compressed and squashed, will be transferred to the financial/market object-image and will constitute its substance and structure, a summary of multiple times, of various temporal sequences, an intertemporal summary of various, individual durations. This compression of duration is not fixed and will not remain passive, since the impetus from the Subject's consciousness, represented by the memory recalls and lapses, will be responsible for dilating, re-compressing, informing and distorting, or will produce other images from which the spatio-temporal DNA has mutated. Contrary to agreed opinion, nothing prevents an internal form of life of the image from being placed within a spatio-temporal reference frame of duration which is driven, like electricity disseminated in a basin, by the phenomena of memory recall and lapse. Equally, nothing prevents one assuming, in addition to the primary, pure units represented by the images within the financial and market space-time reference frame, the existence of more or less complex chains of market object-images, which form a structure and language which mutate, develop or disappear or the existence of complex financial images which form one with an aggregation or chaining (there would accordingly be a category of fundamental, primary object-images, certain of which would perhaps have a given, stable spatio-temporal DNA and a category of complex images of groups of primary images); in any event, discussion on this spatio-temporal market reference frame, made up of simple elements and more complex elements, remains open. Finally, learning, knowledge and therefore duration, which contribute to the constitution of the market or financial object-image, undergo a modification, initially during the memory of an intertemporal section of individual durations, and then within the dynamic life of this structure, which is granted as a legacy, within the DNA, to the nucleus of the financial image. This is because the mobilisation and modification of duration within those space-times, which are specific to the mental universes structured by the image-making consciousness of the Subject investor (*homo economicus*), remain at the heart of market, financial and economic dynamics.

Rueil-Malmaison, Mauritius

January-July 2009 (Part II)

Wengen, Udaipuhr, Rueil-Malmaison, Sainte-Anne, Guadeloupe

December 2007-August 2008 (Part I)

We are greatful to Mrs Melanie Lanoe (Part II) and Mr MacDonald (Part I) for the traduction.

PART 1 was initially published in France, *Théorie globale de l'intérêt, du cycle et de la mémoire* (Economica, 2009).

PART 2 was initially published in France, *La dynamique boursière – Les fondements* (Economica, 2009).

TABLE OF CONTENTS

Achevé d'imprimer en septembre 2010
dans les ateliers de Normandie Roto Impression s.a.s.
à Lonrai (Orne)
N° d'impression : 103340
Dépôt légal : octobre 2010